JIM CRAMER'S
STAY MAD
FOR LIFE

GET RICH, STAY RICH
(MAKE YOUR KIDS EVEN RICHER)

JAMES J. CRAMER
WITH CLIFF MASON

Simon & Schuster
New York London Toronto Sydney

This publication contains the opinions and ideas of its author. It is sold with the understanding that neither the author nor the publisher is engaged in rendering legal, tax, investment, insurance, financial, accounting, or other professional advice or services. If the reader requires such advice or services, a competent professional should be consulted. Relevant laws vary from state to state. The strategies outlined in this book may not be suitable for every individual, and are not guaranteed or warranted to produce any particular results.

No warranty is made with respect to the accuracy or completeness of the information contained herein, and both the author and the publisher specifically disclaim any responsibility for any liability, loss, or risk, personal or otherwise, which is incurred as a consequence, directly or indirectly, of the use and application of any of the contents of this book.

Simon & Schuster
1230 Avenue of the Americas
New York, NY 10020

Copyright © 2007 by J.J. Cramer & Co.

All rights reserved,
including the right to reproduce
this book or portions thereof in any form whatsoever.
For information address Simon & Schuster Subsidiary Rights Department,
1230 Avenue of the Americas, New York, NY 10020

First Simon & Schuster hardcover edition December 2007

SIMON & SCHUSTER and colophon are registered trademarks of Simon & Schuster, Inc.

For information about special discounts for bulk purchases,
please contact Simon & Schuster Special Sales at
1-800-456-6798 or business@simonandschuster.com

Manufactured in the United States of America

3   5   7   9   10   8   6   4

Library of Congress Cataloging-in-Publication Data

Cramer, Jim.
Jim Cramer's stay mad for life : get rich, stay rich
(make your kids even richer) / James J. Cramer with Cliff Mason.
p.   cm.
Includes index.
1. Finance, Personal—United States.   2. Investments—United States.
3. Stocks—United States.   4. Financial security—United States.   I. Mason, Cliff.
II. Title.   III. Title: Stay mad for life : get rich, stay rich (make your kids even richer).
HG179.C68985 2007
332.60973—dc22   2007037838
ISBN-13: 978-1-4165-5885-9
ISBN-10:   1-4165-5885-3

For Ken Cramer,
our wonderful father and grandfather, respectively,
whose good parenting and financial savvy are doubtless
the reasons for our success.

CONTENTS

no empirical evidence of life beyond earth. Many hands go into making a book like this, and at Simon & Schuster those hands belong to Johanna Li, Phil Metcalf, Judith Hoover, Rebecca Davis, Leah Wasielewski, and of course the amazing Aileen Boyle, the go-to person whenever you want to spread book-gospel. And, while I'm praising Simon & Schuster, may I pose a question? What are those other authors doing working at those other publishing houses when they could be working with the absolute best?

I wouldn't have written this book, or any other for that matter, without all of the great folks at CNBC who have helped make *Mad Money* the most enjoyable part of my life, and perhaps the most enjoyable thing I've ever done. It shouldn't come as a shock to anyone that having your own national television program is a lot of fun—I haven't thrown a keyboard in anger for years because of this show! But it's the people I work with who make it so worthwhile.

I owe a great debt to everyone at CNBC who helps to make *Mad Money* great every single day of the week. First, Mark Hoffman, the CEO of CNBC, who gave us unprecedented backing to do a new and different kind of financial show, an interactive one *with you*, and then gave us the resources to promote and protect the franchise in a spectacular way. He gets the job done like no other and deserves total credit for the fabulous and fabulously successful *Mad Money College Tour*. Jonathan Wald, the senior VP of business news, who has been a fabulously creative influence for us and is the best TV newsman in the business. We're unbelievably lucky at CNBC to have someone of Wald's caliber urging us on every day and then praising us when we get it right.

On a day-to-day basis my life is made so much better by Regina Gilgan, who as executive producer of the show has done an absolutely terrific job, as have Rich Flynn, Chris Schwarz, Kat Ricker, George Manessis, Ben Rippey, Joanna Chow, Candy Cheng, Jackie Palombo, Jackie Fabozzi, Keith Greenwood, Bryan Russo, Laura Koski, Ed Hart-

ACKNOWLEDGMENTS

First and foremost, I have to thank all of the regular people who came up to me, called, or emailed to ask for help on more than just stocks. I wish I had a nickel for every person who hails me as I walk down Wall Street every day and says, "Jimmy, how about a good mutual fund?" or, "Jimmy, why don't you talk about 401(k)s?" Well, I've done it! Without them, without the well-wishers and the enthusiastic fans of my work, this book never would have come to be. Second, I need to thank the vast majority of personal finance writers out there who, though their hearts are in the right place, just haven't done the job, leaving the door open for me to write something from the perspective of someone who made his living managing money, not writing books about other people who have made money.

As always, behind this book and everything else I produce are legions of people who work hard to make it all possible and make me look great, but don't get anything like the publicity I do. In terms of the actual production of this book at Simon & Schuster, I continue to have the great pleasure of working with Bob Bender, whom I consider the greatest financial editor in the world, and David Rosenthal, the publisher and the man who got me to start writing books in the first place. He's the best on the planet, and I would go further, but I have ley, Kyle Remaly, Henry Fraga, Kareem Bynes, and Sean Riley. I would be just another 53-year-old bald dad talking to himself in an odd way if these people didn't work their magic and turn it into a TV show every night. Special thanks to Kevin Goldman, the head of CNBC PR, who's done more to spread the gospel of *Mad Money* than anyone else, along with Jenn Dauble, who's also been terrific when it comes to getting the word out. Beyond *Mad Money*, thanks to Erin Burnett for being such a great teammate and letting me rant on *Stop Trading* every day.

And a special thanks to Jeff Zucker, the head honcho at NBC Universal, who believed in *Mad Money* from the moment he saw it and has stayed a believer the whole way. He's so good he doesn't even seem like a suit, the highest compliment I can pay an executive! I intend to play for the Z-man for the rest of my career. He inspires loyalty in a business that allegedly has no loyalty.

At TheStreet.com, my thanks go to Tom Clarke, the still-amazing CEO, along with Dave Morrow, the editor in chief, and Bill McCandless, our new head of multimedia. Each of them has continued to make our business a real success. Without their hard work, I'm sure I would've had a nervous breakdown years ago. Bill Gruver, a member of TheStreet.com's board, in addition to being a professor at Bucknell and my own teacher at Goldman Sachs, deserves my undying gratitude. I cannot express enough thanks to Debbie Slater for practically running my life, and running it well, for so many years. Also at TheStreet.com I must thank my spectacular editor and copy editor on this book, Gretchen Lembach, and my brain trust: Dave Peltier, Jonathan Edwards, Michael Comeau, Frank Curzio, Larsen Kusick, Sanket Patel, and Patrick Schultz; without these guys I wouldn't look half as smart as I do.

For my two agents, both the best in their businesses, I have nothing but love, thanks, and praise. Suzanne Gluck is incomparable as a literary agent, and Henry Reisch is phenomenal at getting things done and getting me what I need, not to mention providing the more-than-occasional dose of inspiration. Plus, they're both great shoulders to cry on if ever the need arises. It should be William Morris, Gluck, and Reisch, but hey, I don't make the rules.

I owe another debt of gratitude, beyond the retainer, to Bruce Birenboim, my Paul Weiss attorney, who has saved my hide more times than I care to remember. I know that I would be writing this book while sipping bad Scotch on a cheap linoleum floor if it weren't for Bruce. Shakespeare was wrong about that "kill all the lawyers" nonsense; clearly he'd never met Birenboim, or maybe he had but from the wrong side of the courtroom.

Words cannot express my gratitude to Betsy and Gene Hackman, who taught me pretty much everything there is to know about life in general, let alone acting. Tremendous thanks as well go to Michael Chiklis, the majority leader of Cramerica, and the star of the show that I wish I was both acting in and writing. May *The Shield* rest in peace, and live long in reruns.

To Lisa Detwiler, who put up with an immense amount of angst about this book and everything else for that matter and smiled and cheered and encouraged endlessly and selflessly. Saints do exist, maybe even übersaints.

There are three people specifically whose work helped directly in the writing of *Stay Mad For Life*. Nick Nocera, our researcher and intern, was invaluable, and we never would have finished on time without his hard work and assistance. Nick, it was a pleasure having you on the team. Thanks also for the constant support to the lovely Jenny Graff, whose expertise in tax law helped enormously with every part of the book where taxes are discussed or even mentioned. And CNBC's own Luke Bauer also deserves great thanks for inspiring more than one crucial idea in *Stay Mad*.

I owe my sister, Nan, and my brother-in-law, Todd Mason, more than I can say. My sister is the one person who has always been there for me and stood by me, and her husband, still the smartest man alive, has given me so much personal and professional help that you might call him the man behind the man. They also deserve thanks for leasing me the use of their son, Cliff, and trusting me not to damage him beyond all repair. Cliff waived his Thirteenth Amendment rights when he turned 13 and he's never going to be emancipated if I have my way. Who said nepotism wasn't a good thing?

And thanks as well and as always to my two daughters, Cece and Emma, who make life worth living, and must never, ever know that I wrote this book when they were sleeping, because they are always worried that I work too hard.

JIM CRAMER'S
STAY MAD
FOR LIFE

Most people don't think about it, but there's a difference between making a lot of money and building lasting wealth. When it comes to money we think that striking it rich is the ultimate goal. I know because I used to feel that way. In reality, getting rich isn't the financial finish line. It's the first lap of a much longer race. I'm talking about ensuring long-term prosperity for you and your family: not just getting rich, but *staying* rich. That's what each and every one of us truly wants to achieve with our money, and I don't care who you are, who your parents are, where you live, or what you do for a living: you can do it if you let me help you. I don't care if you don't have two cents to your name or if you owe thousands of dollars in credit card debt. I am confident I can get you there. You may think of yourself as someone who's awful with money; you could be a person who's tried and failed to get anywhere with every single financial plan you've ever been handed, like so many failed faddish diets. Whether you're 16 or 60, sending your kids to college or sending yourself to college, I'm writing this book to tell you everything you will ever need to know and everything you must do to create and maintain the kind of wealth that lasts a lifetime. I want you to get there and stay there.

A lot of people who try to sell you advice about your money are doing it to make money themselves. They don't care whether you succeed or fail with their advice because they're just looking to sell books or earn fees. I made more money than anyone ever needs working at my old hedge fund, and if I wanted more, I'd start another one. I am confident that I could raise a billion dollars to manage tomorrow, but frankly, I'd rather help you. That means more to me than working for people who are already rich. Perhaps it's because I'm a good guy, or because I just want to look like a good guy, or maybe I do it because I love positive attention. Maybe it's because after years of making money for myself, it just feels right. At the end of the day, the "why" isn't important, as long as you're satisfied that I'm writing this book in good faith to help you. What's important is the "what." I spent fourteen years running a hedge fund, which means that the only higher purpose my job had was to make incredibly rich people even richer. I used to joke that my job was to move people higher on the Forbes 400 richest people list—not a higher calling.

I've now spent the past seven years since I retired from the fund writing books and columns for TheStreet.com and *New York* magazine and hosting a radio show and two television shows: first *Kudlow & Cramer*, then *Mad Money*. The venues have changed, but my goal was always the same: to share my experience and expertise with regular people to help them become rich. In this book, I'm aiming even higher than that: I'm teaching you how to make money and use it to ensure enduring prosperity and permanent financial security over the course of your entire life. The disciplines and the knowledge you need to build a firm foundation for your wealth and maintain it for the rest of your life are not the same as the ones you would need to make yourself rich by investing in stocks, the subject of my previous two books. If you're looking for long-term financial security, I would hope you'd set your sights higher. For long-term extravagant wealth, you need to know how to take advantage of tax-favored vehicles like 401(k) plans and IRAs; you need to know when you should buy bonds rather than stocks, not to mention the kinds of bonds you should choose; you need to know how to save for college; how to guarantee you have a smooth retirement; how to save; how to borrow; when you should buy a house; when you should be taking risks; when you should be avoiding risks; what you must teach your children about money; which mutual funds you should put your money in; and which stocks will look good for the long haul, the next twenty-five years. These are the subjects people beg me to address, and I am ready and willing to do so. I have the answers for *all* of the financial questions you, your parents, and your kids have about getting rich and staying rich. Don't be intimidated—I'll explain everything in layman's terms, not in the Wall Street gibberish the professionals use to scare you into relying on them instead of using your own judgment.

But what about my judgment? You want to know where my advice comes from, and I don't blame you. Most of what I know about making money I learned in my years on Wall Street, first as a broker at Goldman Sachs, advising the wealthiest of the wealthy about all these lifetime issues, and then as the manager of my own hedge fund, Cramer, Berkowitz & Company. I've had a long love affair with stocks, but stocks are only one of many tools, albeit the most important one, that we're going to use to create lasting prosperity for you and your family. I know better than most people the difference between having money and not having it, or having it and having a whole lot of it. I'm a self-made multimillionaire, and I'm going to share with you the lifelong disciplines that made me rich and have kept me that way.

As I said, I made my own money. I've also been poor. In fact, I wasn't just poor; I was homeless and destitute. In 1978 I spent six months living in the backseat of my Ford Fairmont while I worked as a homicide reporter for the Los Angeles *Herald Examiner*, unable to afford even rent money. By 1979 I had moved up in the world: I was living in the most spacious corner of my big sister's studio apartment in New York City. I was the last person in the world anyone was ever going to ask for financial advice, but even then I was diligent and self-disciplined about money. I may have skimped on the auto insurance and skipped on the rent, but I still put $50 a month into the best mutual fund I could find, Fidelity's Magellan Fund. I have always been fascinated with mutual funds and managers, and I am going to tell you all about which ones you need and which ones you should avoid. I know what it's like to need money and not have it, and ever since those early days I have lived in desperate fear of poverty. Living out of my car with barely enough money to get by convinced me that I had to become rich, that no amount of money was too much, and that I would have to do it with more than just my meager paycheck. I would have to parlay that paycheck into something much bigger, using whatever financial resources I could get my hands on. I spent twenty years single-mindedly pursuing greater and greater sums of money until well past the point where more money made a bit of difference. I know it's possible for anyone to get rich and stay rich because I did it myself and I'm no different from any of you.

Like most things in life, getting rich and staying that way take a lot of hard work, a lot of knowledge, and a little bit of good advice. There are many ways to get your hands on a whole lot of money, though few of them can be called easy. You can invest in the right stocks, get a high-paying job, start your own business, or inherit the money, to name just a few. But there's only one way to make sure your newfound wealth leads to long-term prosperity: you have to use your money to make more money, and you need to do it the right way. It's hard work, and it takes diligence, but in this book I've already done a lot of the work for you. No, I don't have six easy steps to financial security, nor do I have three magic habits that will make you a millionaire, and I can't tell you the financial secrets of the superrich because as far as I know, they're just as feckless with money as ordinary people. People who promise that they can make you truckloads of cash and help you keep it as long as you follow their simple five-point program aren't telling you the whole story. Easy steps turn out to be not so easy, and advice that seemed great in theory turns out to be next to useless in practice. I suspect that many of these people have never

made a dime *except in book sales*! I read a ton of these personal finance guides because every time someone writes a new one, which
seems like every five minutes, the publisher comes to me to pen the
introduction and give it my seal of approval. Many of these books are
well-written, some of them by terrific people, but they generally don't
tell you what you need to know. I swear, more books have been written about creating and keeping wealth than any one person could
read in a lifetime, but I have yet to find a single one that actually tells
you, in detail, what you must do during every stage of your life to
develop enduring wealth and ensure that you never have to worry
about your money again. So I decided to fix that problem by writing
this one.

For most people, there are few things that are more confusing and
frustrating than trying to manage their finances. I can't tell you how
many people I've spoken to who agonize over trying to pick the right
mutual fund and end up giving up, their money still in a checking
account, because the decision was too hard and reliable information
was too scarce. If you're looking for a financial plan, it's easy to get a
broad outline, but very hard to find anyone who will give you specific,
detailed advice. But that's exactly what I'm going to do. Others are
more than willing to show you the forest: save money, pay off your
credit card debt, contribute to your 401(k), start an IRA. But no one
will identify the trees, where the money is actually grown. How should
you manage your IRA? What, specifically, should you own in your
retirement and discretionary accounts? Which of the most popular
mutual funds available in your 401(k) plan is the best place to put
your money? I'll even recommend the best mutual funds, using all
the data available as I write this book.

Too many books about money go wrong because they try to offer
timeless advice. There's no such thing as great timeless advice. The
really useful financial information is time-sensitive. I don't know if
the people who try to write timeless advice do it to create financial
planning books for the ages or to avoid exposing themselves to risk.

Nobody will ever get pilloried for telling you that the best long-term investment is a low-cost index fund, like the Vanguard 500, which is the classic cheap Standard & Poor's 500 index fund. Never mind that unless we're talking about John Bogle, the man who invented the index fund, no one dispensing this advice is adding even an ounce of value to the conventional wisdom. Timeless advice is the lazy man's way out, and though I've been called almost every unflattering word in the dictionary, I've never been called lazy. Instead of regurgitating eternal principles, I've rolled up my sleeves, *Mad Money*–style, and found the best places to put your money *right now*.

When I select the best actively managed funds, I am choosing the best mutual funds that you should invest in *today*. It would be nothing short of miraculous if every single mutual fund I highlight in this book beat the market over the next few years, but I have total conviction that most of these funds will be winners. I would rather stick my neck out by giving you specific, timely advice than play it safe with timeless but vague suggestions. I'll tell you how I go about ranking funds too, but the point isn't just for you to use my methods, it's for you to try to make money in the mutual funds I recommend. I was a manager who beat almost every other manager. I know what to look for that others don't. I grade them the way a professor grades kids in college, except I grade them hard. As I say at the beginning of every *Mad Money* show, I am not about making friends, I am about making you money, and you must know that when I recommend a fund, it's not to please anyone but you. Unlike so many others, I have no skin in the game. I don't get rebates, referrals, kickbacks, percentages, commissions. Nothing. Just the satisfaction of knowing that I am using my twenty-five years of successful money management to help you become wealthy.

Sure, I've got plenty of things to say that will still be true a hundred years from now, when these mutual funds likely will no longer even exist. I'll explain everything you might need to know about creating wealth, from the day you're born until the day you decide you have enough dough. That means you'll read some things in this book that you've read before. I'm going to tell you to save money, to invest in your company's 401(k) if it has one, to start an IRA, and all the other boring but good advice. The difference between this book and all the other books that have been written about personal finance is that I don't stop there. I don't think it's helpful to tell people to start an IRA without telling them how to manage it and giving them some specific ideas about what to buy for it—nuts and bolts that will make you more money than the other guys because that's what I was put on earth to do.

If you're looking to build your wealth over the long term, to ensure prosperity for yourself and your family, then stick with me and I'll teach you how to get rich, stay rich, and stay mad for life!

1

GETTING STARTED

Let me get this right out in the open so you know exactly where I'm coming from: I believe that anyone can achieve financial security as long as they work hard, save, and manage their money wisely. All of us have the opportunity to become fabulously wealthy. You just have to know what to do and *how to do it,* which is something most advisors neglect to discuss. That's where we hit a snag, or at least where those of us in the United States hit a snag. America may be a nation of limitless opportunity, but it's also a nation that doesn't teach its citizens how to harness those opportunities. The vast majority of our children are financially illiterate when they graduate from high school, and no better educated about money after going through college. I'm not talking about anything complicated here; I'm saying that most of us have never been taught the difference between a stock and a bond. That's a real problem if you're trying to create a retirement fund, let alone lasting wealth for your family. But once you know what to do, and just as important, why you're doing it, building self-sustaining wealth is not particularly difficult, nor does it require more than a modest amount of willpower. Everyone knows that saving is supremely important, that it comes first, that without it you can't invest; and if you can't invest, your odds of getting rich fall through the floor. If you save merely 5 percent to 10 percent of your annual income every year from the time you start working until your retirement, and you invest that money wisely, or just not foolishly, you won't have to worry about money for most of your adult life. There's a good chance that your savings will turn into a sizable sum that keeps growing because of compound interest, snowballing until it becomes not just wealth but a source of wealth.

Here's an important point to consider, even if it is a cliché: it takes money to make money. Truer words were never spoken. It's why the rich always seem to get richer, and why it feels like everyone else manages only to tread water. Your paycheck is not enough; you're not going to earn your fortune, not in the traditional sense. Even for the lucky few who do earn enough to become rich simply by collecting their pay stubs, the possibility of long-term wealth, the type that lasts, is impossible without putting some money to work on the side. Why? As long as you rely on your job alone for income, you're not really building prosperity. *You have to save.* If you don't save some of your income in order to invest it, all bets are off. You can't count on getting rich or even retiring without savings. But it's important to view money saved as more than money in the bank. It's money that you can use to generate wealth. Someone who earns millions of dollars a year and spends it all will be just as broke come retirement as everyone else who didn't set money aside, no matter how low their salary. If you're well-paid, that means you have more money to put to work, and if you're smart you'll use it. But most people don't have a great salary or even the opportunity to someday be paid a great deal of money. You need something on the side; you need to make some part of your money start working for you. How do you do that? Generally speaking—we'll get into the specifics later—you invest your money in stocks, bonds, real estate, or any other asset that tends to increase in value over time. And you take advantage of every possible tax-favored plan that's available to you, like a 401(k) retirement plan or an individual retirement account (IRA), and you take every tax deduction and exemption you're eligible for to maximize the amount of money you have working for you.

This is the key to establishing lasting prosperity: save your money and invest it in the right assets at the right times. There's nothing original about this view, nothing new, but I have many different and, yes, *better* twists on the old rules that make them understandable and downright enjoyable to apply. I could take a different position, one that might be even more compelling, but it would also be wrong, and wrong loses people money. It would be uninteresting to tell you that compound interest is a great ally, perhaps the greatest, of the individual investor looking to establish long-term prosperity, but it's true. If you haven't been introduced to the concept of compound interest, it's a testament to the idea that little things here and there eventually add up to something substantial.

Here's how compound interest works: you deposit money in a bank at a 4 percent rate, and every year the interest compounds, meaning you receive your interest payment from the bank, and the bank starts paying interest on what had been its interest payment in addition to the interest it pays on your deposit. Of course, compounding works for you in many more situations than that. For example, from January 1970 to December 2006, the average compounded rate of return (including reinvestment of dividends) for the Standard & Poor's 500 was 11.5 percent. The S&P 500 is the most representative index of large-cap, American companies, encompassing all the large publicly traded companies in the country, and is frequently used as a stand-in for the market when judging the performance of mutual funds or investors. It's the benchmark all professional investors measure themselves against. If we assume that for thirty-five years, an investor compounded at only 10 percent annually, behind the S&P 500, we're looking at someone who made a great deal of money. If you were to begin with merely $2,000, and every year add an additional $2,000, you would have $652,458.48 at the end of thirty-five years. Back in the 1970s, $2,000 was a lot of money, but $652,458.48 is nothing to look down on today, especially on a $72,000 investment. If you went the extra mile and invested $4,000 at the beginning and added another $4,000 every year, you would have $1,304,916.97 after thirty-five years. At that point, you could retire, put your $1,304,916.97 in U.S. Treasury bonds that yield roughly 5 percent annually, and earn close to the median salary among Americans over the age of 44: $66,995. All of that because you used your money to make money, and that was with a conservative rate of return that lagged the S&P 500. If you had simply bought an S&P 500 mutual fund, a fund with very low fees that buys all the stocks in the index and holds them, you would have done even better. And these kinds of funds are easy to find; every mutual fund family has them. This scenario is a bit unrealistic, because as most people get older, they shift their investments away from stocks, which would return about 10 percent annually, and toward bonds, which would have produced a lower but more consistent rate of return. I am a believer that such a switch shouldn't happen until much later in life than most of the financial planners and so-called wise men out there suggest, but I'll take that up later in this book. The point is that with time on your side as a long-term investor, it's not all that difficult to really profit wildly. And I want you in on those profits big-time.

Later, I'll go into more detail about the appropriate distribution of your capital among stocks, bonds, real estate, and other potential investments. Don't worry: it sounds scary, but I have traded them all, invented a lot of them, and can tell you—in actual English, not Wall Street gibberish—what they mean and how to use them to make you even richer than you thought you could be. Capital, by the way, is just another way of describing the money you invest; the word actually can refer to any form of wealth that is used to produce more wealth. For everyone who already knows what capital is, please, bear with me. I'm not being patronizing; I just want to make sure that no one is left behind because they don't happen to know the meaning of a word. I want to help people at every level of skill and education to sustain and increase their wealth.

The strategy I'm going to teach you is a combination of "capital preservation," which is an investment strategy with which you try to avoid losses above all else, and "capital appreciation," where your first priority is to increase the value of your assets. Everyone should always have both preservation and appreciation in mind, but at any given time, one will be more important than the other. It's very important that you pursue capital preservation when times are tough for the stock market, because taking the risk necessary for capital growth will most likely result in capital shrinkage. In a bad market, it's easier for ordinary investors to lose money than make it, so your goal should be to avoid taking losses. That way, when the market improves and you make capital appreciation your number one priority, you have more capital to work with, and thus will make more money. I really worry that most people who manage their own money don't do this. I constantly hear people say that preservation of capital is their top priority all the time, or appreciation of capital is always more important. That's wrong. You might have a bias one way or the other, but there are times when caring more about preservation will mean missing out on big gains, and other times when a strategy focused on appreciation will tend to cause big losses.

That said, when you're taking a long-term view, the much more boring capital preservation is almost always more important than the exciting capital appreciation, even though most texts focus on the appreciation goal. There are several reasons for this. First, much of the money you will invest should be earmarked for certain necessary expenses: your retirement, or a home, or, if you choose to foot the bill, college tuition for your children. It would be disastrous if you were to lose a large chunk of your retirement savings because you bought riskier assets, like lower-quality stocks that don't pay good dividends. Even the good stocks can be considered too risky for some. And remember, if your portfolio declines in value by 50 percent, you will need to gain 100 percent to get back to where you started. Sometimes you just cannot afford to take losses. That's why I always talk and write about two different portfolios: one for retirement that is biased toward capital preservation, and one that I call discretionary and that has a bias toward capital appreciation. In the past, I've mostly dealt with growing your discretionary portfolio, but in this book I'll spend more time discussing retirement.

Devoting your retirement portfolio to capital preservation means taking on less risk and pursuing substantially smaller returns. It can be frustrating to own a bunch of U.S. Treasury bonds that yield only 5 percent annually. To give you some idea of just how frustrating, the consumer price index in the United States rose by 3.2 percent in 2006. The CPI is one of our key measures of inflation, which is the rate at which general price levels increase. In 2006, if you held a bond yielding 5 percent, and you adjusted your return for inflation, you gained only 1.8 percent. This ultraconservative path may seem like an agonizingly slow way to make money, but it's also an incredibly safe way to make sure your capital at least keeps pace with inflation. Again, you do not want and cannot afford to lose your retirement savings. People who disregard this warning get into serious trouble.

On my old radio show, *Real Money Radio*, I had a weekly segment when viewers would call in and I would try to fix, or maybe the appropriate term is "resurrect," their 401(k) plans. A 401(k) plan is an employer-backed retirement savings account that lets employees who contribute defer paying the income tax on their contributions and the earnings generated by those contributions until they withdraw that money after retiring. People would ask me what to do with their 401(k) plans after their assets had been savaged because they had invested in stocks that were too risky or, all too often, because they had poured all of their 401(k) money into the stock of their employer's company. My point here is not to get into a discussion of diversification, but to shine a light on some of the deficiencies in the conventional approach to long-term wealth building. You can tell people that their retirement funds should be invested more conservatively than nonretirement funds, with an eye toward capital preservation rather than capital appreciation. You can tell them that, but they might not listen if they've become frustrated with low returns and crave more risk. Though the conventional wisdom is correct, it doesn't address the real issue, which is that when we make bad financial decisions, it's not always out of ignorance. It's my job to give people who make mistakes despite knowing better a new way to look at their finances, a framework that encourages them to make the decisions they know are right.

If you follow the principles and advice laid out in this book, you should be able to use your money to create substantially more money, and you'll have dramatically increased your odds of becoming rich. What, precisely, do I mean when I say "rich"? Because the cost of living varies so much from place to place, it's not useful to come up with a sum of money and say everyone who has more than that amount is rich. Plus, people with children or other dependents will require quite a bit more money to have the same level of material luxuries as someone who is childless and single. In my view, a person is rich if he or she can stop working and still afford both to cover any child-related expenses like college tuition and to support the level of spending that the person in question is accustomed to for the rest of his or her life—and then some, just to make sure. Really rich people can live off the interest of their nest egg. That's a tall order, but I will try to get you there. So, though different people will require different amounts of money to be rich, the meaning of the term is essentially the same for everyone. No matter what you're after—retirement, college tuition for your children, a home, or just a big pile of money—I know how to help. I would love it if I could teach every single person who reads this book how to become rich.

Unfortunately, not everyone can get rich even by my relative standard. You can make all the right decisions, all the right moves, and all the right investments but still fail to become even modestly rich. That's not to say that it's all luck, but it's true that luck matters. In many ways, as I said in the conclusion of *Confessions of a Street Addict*, my first book, it is better to be lucky than good. On some level, trying to create prosperity for yourself and your family is still subject to chance. You can improve your odds dramatically or sabotage them, depending on your approach to money and your actions, but there is still a totally random, unfair element in the process of getting rich that may someday thwart even the best-laid plans.

If I can't guarantee that taking my advice will make you rich, you probably want to know what else I'm bringing to the table. Everyone wants certainties beyond the knowledge, disciplines, practices, and habits that increase their likelihood of becoming extraordinarily rich. Everyone worries about money, rich and poor alike, and we worry because of uncertainty. You picked up this book and now you want to know that if you follow my suggestions, you're not going to end up destitute. The earlier you start building your wealth, which means first gathering money and then using it to create more money through various investments and tax-favored savings plans, the easier it will be for you to get what you want. But even if you don't start actively planning your prosperity until your 50s or 60s, there are many things you can do to ensure financial security for the rest of your life. Getting rich, whether you stay that way or not, is terrific, but it's a secondary goal. What most of us really want is to be able to stop worrying about money, to stop living in fear of impending financial disaster and start living in comfort. Anyone can build enough wealth to sustain a relatively carefree lifestyle. You might not be able to retire early, but you won't need to fear ending up in the poorhouse. Building wealth is generally either presented as appallingly simple, even easy, or as an endeavor so complex that you should give up or get a professional advisor. The truth is that although each of the steps toward building lasting wealth can appear easy to take, there are a whole host of factors that most people who write about long-term financial planning do not discuss at all. That, I believe, is why people fail. You don't have to be talented or even intelligent; you just need the right combination of knowledge and discipline, along with the right perspective. When this stuff seems complicated and difficult, it's because many financial professionals have it in their best interest to keep regular people uneducated about money; that way, you still need an advisor. Anyone who has ever watched *Mad Money* knows I genuinely believe that the industry that spawned me is not helpful, because it if were, it would teach you to do it all on your own and not need the help of the so-called professionals. They want you addicted; I want to break the addiction. Once I lay out the right perspective, everything complex and odd should fit into a larger pattern and be easy for you to understand.

There's really no excuse for not taking all the necessary steps to modest prosperity, once you know what they are. I'm here to teach you those steps. I know you probably feel you're getting squeezed financially, but everyone feels that way. Heck, I lived in my car at one point in my life—talk about squeeze. But if you play your economic cards right, which I'm about to teach you to do, you'll eventually stop feeling squeezed, and if you preserve your wealth, the feeling will never come back. You'll have the potential to become truly rich, and no matter what, you can rest easy in the knowledge that you'll be building self-sustaining wealth, the kind that lasts for generations.

People always say money can't buy happiness, but I've never found that argument compelling. Money can buy peace of mind; it can take care of you and your loved ones, and to a certain extent, money means freedom. If you take a long enough view and do the work, you'll be able to set yourself up for a lifetime of prosperity, at the very least!

The First Step Is the Same for Everyone

It really doesn't matter what your goals are. If you want more money, the first step is always the same: you need to save. For many people, even the most assiduous of savers, hearing that is like being reminded you've got a checkup with your dentist, or even a root canal. I know. There's no topic more boring on its face than saving money. It's worse than boring; the way most people write or talk about saving, any kind of advice on the subject is totally useless. Everyone knows they're supposed to save. It's always the first piece of financial advice anyone ever hears. Here I come, beating you over the head with something you've already been told close to a million times. Saving is smart, and you should do as much of it as possible. All the boring old reasons that your parents probably gave you to save, even if they themselves were big spenders, are completely true. They're also completely irrelevant.

I don't want to harp on this theme, because too many people are excessively shrill about it, but most people in America have a problem with saving money. We all know it's "the right thing to do." We all know it's necessary if we want to do anything, from buying a home to retiring. Saving is what you're supposed to do. Why even discuss it, right? Well, the problem is that even though we all know we should save, that doesn't mean all of us actually do it. I've never really had this problem personally. In fact, I was still saving money back when I was living out of the rear seat of my Ford Fairmont. That's not because I was enlightened or good with money or even responsible; tell me how someone responsible winds up living in his car. I saved back then because I was brainwashed. I thought of saving before paying insurance, although I did get the windfall of not having to plunk down cash for a homeowner's policy! I don't mean "brainwashing" necessarily in a bad way. Being brainwashed about saving money turned out great for me, and as it happened, I did all the right things, but only eventually for the right reasons. I put away that $1,000 a year that I mentioned earlier, and the results from compounding from 1977 were spectacular. I invested with the legendary mutual fund manager Peter Lynch, whose books I still reread when I feel I have lost my way or when I have a cold streak picking stocks for my charitable trust, the only investment I am allowed to have, given my show's power to influence stocks. Although I've never had much trouble saving money, I've seen plenty of friends and family members go through tremendous difficulties because they cannot save money. The fact is, people who don't save are the majority. I don't think you can go two or three days without seeing some article bemoaning the fact that irresponsible people are piling up enormous amounts of credit card debt or just not saving any money. We have trouble saving. Even those of us who are diligent about it could generally do better.

The usual diagnosis when someone has trouble saving money is a bad case of irresponsibility. America has a negative savings rate right now, meaning that collectively we spend more than we earn. Everyone's eager to explain this fact as the result of some moral or cultural failing, compounded by the ease of obtaining cheap credit through credit card companies that demand high interest. Notice I didn't use the term "Shylock"; I've grown more statesmanlike since my first book! The rap on Americans? That we're too decadent, we're too taken in by consumer culture, we all spend too much on flashy items to keep up with our neighbors, or we're too easily influenced by advertisements. I don't buy it. Not for a Wall Street second.

We have a problem saving money for one reason, and it's got nothing to do with character: we think about saving money the wrong way. If you can't save money, or can't save as much as you hope to, or even if you save but find the whole exercise boring, you're not approaching things the right way. That's not your fault. We don't teach financial literacy—though with the work I am doing at TheStreet .com University, an educational section of TheStreet.com, the website I founded, I am sure trying to get you there, no matter who you are or how little you have. It's financial literacy, being facile with the basics that I know cold, that gives us a pretty old-fashioned idea of what the process of saving actually entails.

A lot of people are under the false impression that saving money is about self-denial and self-restraint. We think that the goal of saving, the act of saving, is to put your money in a lockbox and leave it to gather dust and interest for the next thirty years. There's nothing wrong with putting some of your money in a savings account. If you want to save by opening up a money market bank account and letting compound interest do the heavy lifting for you, I'm all for it. (A money market account is an account that is as good as cash but typically offers you slightly more interest than a bank savings account. Don't sneer at its potential, though, to add up to a lot more savings over time than money left in a lower-paying bank account, which many less savvy people insist on doing.) My point is that saving is not about giving up on choices, which is what most of us assume when we forgo buying something in order to save money. It's about opening new avenues to wealth. If you consider saving just another dull hardship, you need to be reeducated. So let's start from the ground up.

When you save money, you're giving yourself the one tool you need to actively pursue your dreams. Think of saving as equipping yourself for the lifelong march to prosperity. You don't save to deny yourself options in the present in order to increase them in the future, even though on the surface that sounds pretty logical and true. You save in order to take an energetic hand in building your own wealth, not so that you can put your money aside to pick up interest every year and compound over a couple of decades, at which point you finally pull out your money, untouched for all this time, and pay for retirement. Anyone who thinks that way is going to have a really difficult time saving.

We tend to think of saving money as a passive process. It doesn't have to be that way. For anyone who truly wants to build long-term wealth, saving is all about activity. So you cannot think of money saved as something static. The cash you put aside every month is going to see more action than every last penny you spend. Our goal is to make our money work for us, but we should never make the mistake of believing that our money will work for nothing. You're going to have to put in some effort managing your money. But that very fact makes it easier, not harder, to save. Why should something that takes effort—saving in order to actively manage your money—be more attractive than something effortless, such as saving in order to deposit your money in a money market or savings account and forgetting about it for years?

There's one part of the conventional take on saving money that I absolutely agree with: the best reason to save is that doing so opens up new possibilities. When most people say something like that, they mean new possibilities ten or twenty years down the line. Not me. I know that when you save money you create opportunities for yourself right now, opportunities to take control of your financial future and start building more wealth. Saving is the foundation and the cornerstone of working your way to wealth, but if you approach it as a passive process, you're going to end up waiting much longer for your riches. That's if you don't break down and start spending every penny you earn because you just can't take the responsible self-sacrifice anymore.

Saving is the basis on which every other aspect of building lasting wealth rests. You cannot invest if you have no savings. That seals the deal for me, and it should seal the deal for you too, because investing, even if not in stocks, is critical to your ability to accomplish any of your long-term financial goals. It is essential for your retirement, but that's a long way off for some of you, and you shouldn't have to defer your gratification from saving and investing for decades. If you save and invest, you will be taking control of a large part of your future, and the younger you start, the better. You will be able to do things that you couldn't have done before for the sole reason that you can afford to. I'm not saying that everyone who uses his or her money to make even more money should then spend it all on a good time. But if you don't reward yourself for your wins, it's possible you'll give up on saving, and thus give up on everything you might want to do with money.

Sure, there are other reasons to save. It's good to have something put away for emergencies, it's good not to be buried under a mountain of credit card debt, and it's good to have some financial flexibility. But the problem with these reasons is that they value saving money as its own goal. Saving makes everything else possible, so don't think of it as an end in itself. It's the first step in a long process of wealth-building, a process we've only just begun.

2

HOW TO STOP YOURSELF FROM BECOMING POOR

You want to get rich. Well, before you can do that you have to make sure you're not becoming poor instead. Saving is important: it's the first step that builds the capital you'll need to invest. But saving means nothing if your habits are leading you closer and closer to poverty. You don't need yet another harangue about the value and necessity of personal responsibility, so forget all of that. Remember, I've been poor, though I didn't start out poor. Many people are born into poverty and have to struggle every inch of the way out of it; they have it much worse than I did, no question. My point is merely that I'm someone who got poor, and though I'd never say I did it to myself—the jerk who broke into my home and stole everything was solely responsible—if I'd been a little bit more careful, maybe he wouldn't have been able to grab my checks, making it impossible for me to pay the rent. Obviously, there are some things that can't be avoided, though if you've locked your doors and gotten an alarm system, burglary may not be one of them. But there are plenty of small things within our control that, when added together, can mean the difference between wealth and poverty. It's the little stuff on a day-to-day basis that really breaks most people. Every time you make a decision about money, you're probably not thinking about what it will mean twenty years down the line. That's just insane, right? Most of the time you buy something, anything, why would you even think about what that purchase will mean in six months? Well actually, there are a lot of good reasons to do so.

When people talk about budgeting, controlling spending—all of those responsible personal finance habits—it's usually to encourage you to save money. You know why I want you to save: so you can build capital. That's not why I want you to budget. It's not why I want you to get yourself out of credit card debt. Forget saving for the moment. Think *fear*. Spending less money will mean that you save more, but saving is about getting rich. Decreasing the amount of cash you liberate from the chains of your wallet is about averting poverty. Saving and not spending are similar, but they're not quite the same. You can be growing your capital at a fabulous rate; let's say you're up 24 percent every year with the money you've invested. That's the same return I generated back at my hedge fund, and it was considered top-notch performance. You could have that same performance, but as long as you're hemorrhaging money in other parts of your life, it's not going to matter one bit. It's not uncommon to run into people who are great at growing their capital but not so great at keeping it when they go shopping. That's why this book is about getting rich and staying rich.

When you think of some slick Wall Street money manager bringing in millions every year, a master of the universe type—not like any of my friends on the Street, who are all great, down-to-earth guys— do you picture a person who doesn't like to spend money? Do you think the incredibly rich are cheap guys? Of course not: they love to flaunt their wealth. This is one of the great differences between those who merely get rich and those who stay rich.

I cannot stress enough how important it is to differentiate between saving and not spending. Yes, when you balance your checkbook, they both amount to the same thing, but when it comes to the behaviors that should drive both of them, there's a world of difference. If you're the kind of person who always has trouble making ends meet and never seems to know where all that money you made disappeared to, it's time for you to embrace fear. No one should have to live in terror of going broke, but a certain amount of fear is healthy. Many people forget that because the modern world is so terrific. In America today, the poor are more likely to suffer from obesity than starvation. Think about that. At any other time in history this would've been impossible. We no longer have to struggle to survive, and in a way that makes us complacent.

You don't want to have to live without the things you truly need, and while it's not likely you'll ever be truly impoverished, if you're not careful, you might end up having to forgo medical care or your heating bill for a month, and nobody should have to be in that position. So let me tell you how to avoid becoming poor.

You absolutely must create a budget for yearly, monthly, and even daily expenses. But you can't create that budget in the vacuum of just one year; it has to be in the context of your entire life. You can be totally responsible and more than able to make ends meet, but as long as you're planning to stay afloat only for the short term, thinking that the rest of your life will take care of itself, you could still be in trouble.

You must have health insurance. That's not optional, and I don't care if your employer doesn't provide it for you. Medical expenses are the number one cause of bankruptcy. The only thing worse than being sick is being sick and broke.

Next, *you cannot carry a balance on your credit card.* Most personal finance books declare a crusade, a jihad even, against credit card companies and the unspeakable villains who run them. If you've got a problem with credit card debt, they tell you, cut 'em up, and please-oh-please, protect your children! You'd think credit cards were stealing the souls of college kids everywhere, from the way many people talk about all the tantalizing but truly terrible credit card offers that college students are deluged with on an almost daily basis. I tend to believe that most people are pretty responsible with their money. The problem is, we don't teach people what true responsibility means. If you don't take a long-term view or understand much about compounding, or interest rates in general, then I can see how using a credit card to pay for things you can't afford might look pretty attractive. About half the people with credit cards pay only the monthly minimum balance, which every professional around agrees is one of the worst, albeit single most common, mistakes people make with their money. Some of you know this already, but many of you might not, and because this is a book for everyone, not just those who already have a sophisticated understanding of money, I'll do my part in the crusade against consumer debt. But I won't go overboard.

In our culture, debt gets a bad rap. No one wants to be in debt, and all too often we take it as a sign of personal weakness when we have to borrow money, a point that was first made brilliantly and boringly in Max Weber's *The Protestant Ethic and the Spirit of Capitalism*. Maybe you read it in college. It's a real snooze-fest with more than a tinge of racism, which is about what you would expect from a social science tome written about a century ago. The truth is, not all debt is terrible. Is a mortgage a bad thing? Is a loan to start a small business a bad thing? A loan to pay for college? Of course not, but we know that credit card debt is pretty darn awful. The difference between helpful debt and unhelpful debt is the interest rate you're paying. But even that doesn't tell us everything we need to know.

Obviously, the debt with the highest interest rate is the most unhelpful kind of debt. But how do we draw the line between what's okay and what isn't? I'm going to tell you how a money manager would approach this problem. What's that got to do with you? Managing money for a living and trying to balance your personal finances might not seem all that similar, but the fact is that some principles of finance are universal. This is one of them. Many hedge funds borrow a tremendous amount of money to make their investments, and much of the time that borrowing can lead to some extraordinary success. As long as you're borrowing at a rate lower than the return you're generating, your debt is helpful. It's that simple, for a hedge fund or a homemaker.

One problem faced by both the guys running big money in hedge funds and regular people is that interest rates don't sit still. If the rate at which you're borrowing money increases, that can cause huge losses for a money manager, just as it can entirely mess up your household finances. If you owe your credit card company money, it can jack up your interest rate at any time for any reason. This blindsides people, but it's right there in the cardholder agreement. This is one reason you don't want to maintain a balance on your credit card. You always want to pay off your credit card bill in full. I know, I know, you've heard this all before. I don't care. I can't have you getting rich on the one hand, generating a terrific return from your investments, and at the same time letting your credit card bill suck you dry at a much higher rate than you're making on your investments.

With the exception of organized crime, no one charges higher interest rates than credit card companies. (Actually, I'm not entirely sure that's true, as the mob isn't very forthcoming about its lending practices. Then again, if you've tried to read the terms and conditions of a cardholder agreement, you might think that credit card companies could be a bit more forthcoming too.) Make no mistake, very few people can earn a better return in the stock market, or anywhere else, than the interest a credit company can charge you. A 20 percent annual percentage rate (APR) isn't outside the norm. (The APR is the annual rate of interest you're going to owe, including fees, if you don't pay your monthly balance.) Sometimes the average interest rate people are paying on their credit card balance can be even higher than that. As a professional money manager, my hedge fund compounded at 24 percent a year for our investors, and we were considered a great outfit. It's possible that you can beat that return as an individual investor, but even if you do, as long as you've got a balance on your credit card, the card issuer may be sucking you dry at about the same rate.

I don't actually want to give these guys a hard time. Anyone who remembers what it was like before credit cards existed knows why. You had to get to the bank before it closed on Friday if you needed any spending money for the weekend and didn't want to be the person holding up the line at the grocery store by writing a check. It's also true that credit card companies lend to people who in the past never could have gotten a loan. Yes, they charge a higher interest rate, but that's just how this game works. Lending money to people who might not be able to pay you back is a pretty risky proposition, so it's no wonder these guys charge such high rates.

But there's absolutely no reason why you should be filling their coffers with your money—that's a speedy way to get poor. I'm sure there's a temptation every time your credit card bill arrives to pay the minimum. Month to month, it doesn't feel like you're paying that much more by maintaining a balance, but trust me, over time it adds up. And it's surprising, almost, how many pitfalls there are when you're dealing with a credit card company. When you look at a card-holder agreement, what you sign to get the card, there's a lot of fine print for a reason. They'll give you an up-front rate, and it might look pretty attractive, but often that's just a teaser rate, a low rate that lasts for the first few months or the first year before they spring a much higher rate on you that's spelled out only in the fine print. What's going on here hurts millions of people, but sometimes I have to stand back for a second, slacked-jawed in awe, and just appreciate the brilliance of what credit card lenders are doing. They make it incredibly tempting to rack up a huge balance in the first year you're using the card with the low teaser rate, and then the trap springs, the rate increases, and you're paying them a lot more money on the balance you accrued when the rate was low. These guys are smart, smarter than I am, no question, and even if you're brilliant, it's a safe assumption that your credit card company knows more about its business than you do. It will find a million and one ways to stick it to you. So don't put yourself in a position where it can. (Incidentally, when interest rates are declining or stabilize at a low level, companies that issue credit cards are terrific investments because of the high rate of interest they charge.)

When discussing how to prevent you from becoming poor, I want to deal with credit cards first because so many people have so much trouble with credit card debt. It eats away at your potential capital at such a fierce rate that we absolutely have to take it off the table. If savings are the foundation you need to build in order to create long-term wealth, then credit card debt is like damp ground sucking the foundation down into the earth and eventually destroying your prosperity. I haven't had to struggle to make ends meet in the era of crushing credit card debt, but every single day I speak to people who have. This stuff is ruining their lives, and they want to know why I never address this issue on my television show or in my writing. They were right, I was wrong, and now I'm here to help. If you have an unpaid balance on your credit card, paying it off should be a high priority. Should it be the highest priority? It should be second only to health insurance, which I'll discuss later. Saving may be the first step toward getting rich, but if you have savings and credit card debt, you have to take the money you have saved and invested and use it to pay off your credit card debt. Your credit cards will devour your capital faster than you can grow it. What if that's not enough? If you can pay off some but not all of your credit card debt, start with the debt that has the highest interest rate. After that, you've got some options.

The first option is usually called snowballing. If you've got more than one credit card, you can always transfer your balance from one card to another. So when you don't have enough money to pay off all of your cards at once, look over your cards and find the one with the lowest interest rate. Then find the card with the highest rate. Transfer as much of the balance as you can from the highest-rate card to the lowest one. Then pay off the lowest-rate card as fast as you possibly can, while paying at least the minimum balance for all of your other cards—more if you can afford it. Every time you pay off part of the balance on the lowest-rate card, max it out again by transferring another part of your balance from the highest-rate card. Once you've finished paying off the debt on your card with the highest rate, move on to the card with the next-highest-rate and do the same thing again, transferring its balance to your lowest-rate card and paying it off as quickly as you can.

You can do a variation on this same snowballing strategy by getting a new credit card. That's right: one solution to credit card debt is more credit cards! Most card issuers will offer you low teaser rates to transfer an unpaid balance from your old card or cards to a new one that they're issuing. It's usually not a bad idea to take the offer. Do some research—there's plenty of information available from card issuers on the Internet. Find the card with the lowest rate that you can transfer your balance to. But be careful. These rates are called teasers for a reason. Be sure you're not transferring your balance to a card that will end up charging you just as much or more than you're currently paying in interest after the teaser rate ends. It's tempting to believe you could keep doing this, taking advantage of the teaser rate until it ends and then switching your balance to a new card with another teaser, over and over again, but as I said, these companies are smart. You might be able to do this a couple times, but after that they'll take one look at your credit history and know exactly what you're doing. Then they will stop giving you those teaser rates.

Another option is borrowing more money. If you have a 401(k) plan, own a home, or have what's called a permanent or cash value life insurance policy (most people should not get this kind of life insurance—they should get term life insurance—but we'll discuss that later), you can borrow against any of them at fairly low rates to pay off your credit card debt. All of these are called "secured loans." A secured loan is a loan that's backed by some form of collateral: the money in your 401(k), the value of your house, or the savings in a permanent life insurance policy. Lenders will charge you a low rate because they know that if you can't pay them back, they'll be able to seize these assets. Your credit card debt, on the other hand, is an unsecured loan. If you can't pay back the credit card company, it doesn't have a claim on any particular assets you have. You might not even have any assets. That makes lending you money a riskier proposition, and it's one of the reasons the rates credit card companies charge are so darned high.

If you own a home or, as is usually the case, you have a mortgage, and over the years have built up some equity in your home, then you'll want to take out a home equity loan to pay off your credit card debt before borrowing against anything else. You'll get a much better interest rate than you're getting from your credit card company, and usually the interest you pay on a home equity loan is tax deductible, just like the interest on a mortgage. Combined, that makes for a substantial reduction in your monthly interest payments. If you have permanent life insurance, for which you pay very high premiums but accrue savings that will be paid out in addition to insurance—and again, I must insist this is something you almost definitely should *not* have— you can borrow against the cash value in your policy. Here you're actually borrowing your own money that's locked away inside the life insurance policy. That means you'll get to borrow at rates that are substantially lower than commercial interest rates. The lower the rate, the better the loan. That said, if you die without paying back all of the loan, they'll deduct what's left plus interest from the benefits that should be going to your loved ones. Because permanent life insurance policies make sense only for people who have dependents with serious disabilities that prevent them from working, this might be a big reason for you to avoid borrowing against the policy.

If you don't own a home or have permanent life insurance, then you'll want to borrow against your 401(k) plan, if you have one. You can't always do this, but the vast majority of 401(k) plans have a feature that lets you borrow against as much as half of the assets in your 401(k) account, up to $50,000. If you've got more than $50,000 in credit card debt, you've got some credit line. There are both upsides and downsides to this approach. The upside is that the rate shouldn't be more than 2 percentage points above the prime rate; that's the best rate that banks give to customers with the very best credit. But better than that, the interest you pay on this loan goes right back into your 401(k) plan. Yes, you're paying interest to yourself. So what's the downside? You don't pay taxes on your 401(k) contributions, but you do get taxed when you eventually withdraw money from your 401(k). The interest you pay on a loan from your 401(k) you will pay with after-tax money, so essentially you'll be taxed on it twice—when you pay the loan and again when you withdraw money from your 401(k). But that's not the worst part. You have to repay the loan within five years, and if you get fired or leave your job, you have to pay back the entire balance of your loan immediately. If you can't afford to do that, whatever you haven't paid back will be treated as a disbursement from your 401(k), which means you'll be taxed on it that year as part of your income. That's not the end. Any time you take money out of your 401(k) before you turn 59½, with a few exceptions for hardship, which includes buying your first home, that money is subject to a 10 percent excise tax, a penalty for withdrawing money from your retirement account before you are of age to retire. Still, if you think you've got some job security, this could be a great way to wipe out your credit card debt.

There are two more ways you can repay credit card debt: bankruptcy and the threat of bankruptcy. I'm only going to mention bankruptcy in this chapter, because unless you were on the verge of it when you picked up this book, I don't intend for you to get anywhere near bankruptcy. But if your finances are in terrible shape and you're loaded down with credit card debt, you can always talk to the credit card company. They really don't want you to go bankrupt, because then it's significantly harder for them to get your money. You'd be surprised how much clout you can actually have with a big, faceless credit card company. I know that sometimes it can seem as if you have no control over this part of your life, as if the people lending you money are the only ones who can dictate terms, but that's not true. This situation is a variation on what the great British economist John Maynard Keynes said: "If you owe your bank a hundred pounds you have a problem. If you owe them a million pounds, they have a problem." If you owe your credit card company money and you can't repay it, then you both have a problem, and it's possible to try to negotiate and come up with a mutually beneficial solution. They would much rather lower your rate than have you go bankrupt and clear all of your debts. If you call your credit card company, explain that you're in a dire financial situation, and say the word "bankruptcy," believe me, they'll listen to you. Credit card companies are either owned by other public companies or are individually traded, like Capital One. All that Wall Street cares about when it comes to credit card companies, or any other financial business, is whether they're going to get paid back for their loans. When people file for bankruptcy and stiff the credit card companies, that's bad for their earnings. Any increase in bankruptcy filings will kill a credit card company's stock, but people who are in trouble don't know that. If you have a lot of credit card debt, you have an advantage. No credit card issuer wants its stock to go down, just as you don't want any of the stocks you own to go down. Use this to your advantage when you negotiate with your credit card company.

Remember, we're doing all this because credit card debt is the enemy of financial security. It's not just a threat to your wealth, it's a threat to your solvency. You can't get rich or stay rich if you have a lot of high-interest debt eating away at your finances like an economic cancer. Yes, the comparison makes sense. Just like cancer, credit card debt can metastasize, hurting your credit score (something I'll discuss in more depth when I tell you about home ownership), making it difficult, if not impossible or prohibitively expensive, to borrow money for a house or a car. And just like cancer, once you get rid of your credit card debt, there's a high probability that it won't stay in remission. As long as you're used to piling up large balances on your credit cards, it's going to be hard to quit cold turkey. Even a healthy fear of destitution might not be enough to break the habit. And remember, the whole point is not to go broke.

The usual solution the professionals offer is that you have to build a budget. I agree, but if that were enough, people wouldn't have so much credit card debt, would they? Fear isn't enough, either. I've said it before: I'm not one of those curmudgeons who thinks that we've all got a problem with personal responsibility and controlling our spending, but we do have a problem with how we think about money, especially spending it. It's not that our spending is out of control, although for some it is. It's not that we're addicted to buying the nicest and newest expensive products that we absolutely must have. No, our problem with spending can be summed up in one sentence: "I deserve to treat myself."

When it comes to money, as Clint Eastwood said to Gene Hackman in *Unforgiven* (the best western since the '70s and perhaps the best of all time), "Deserve's got nothin' to do with it." I believe that it's more than okay to spend money on nonessential stuff; it's entirely necessary. If you don't spend money on the things you enjoy, what's the point in having money? But there's a huge difference between "I deserve it" and "I can afford it." We have to take "deserve" off the table. What do I mean by that? You work hard, you save money, and then you see something you want. If you're going to stay solvent, you have to ask yourself: can I afford to buy this? What you cannot afford is to think that good financial behavior should be rewarded by the kind of outrageous discretionary spending that gets people into credit card debt. You should treat yourself, but within limits—the limits of what you can afford.

How do you determine what you can afford? You make a budget—but it has to be the right kind of budget. Merely planning how to make ends meet with some savings left over every month probably won't get you there. This is my basic issue with how most people write about and handle budgets; it's always too short-term. You should budget to avoid becoming poor, and your time frame should be your whole life. That's because you're not going to lose everything you own this month, and even if your finances are in bad shape, you probably won't see destitution coming even a year away. That's why when you budget, you should budget for a lifetime.

How does that differ from the standard approach? Let me give you an example. There was a great article by Brett Arends on TheStreet .com, where I work and where I'm the largest shareholder, that came out right after the iPhone was released. It was called "The True Cost of an iPhone? Try $17,670." Arends was making the point that if you took the $600 you spent on an iPhone, plus the cost of the required two-year service contract with AT&T, and instead invested it in your 401(k), it should be worth about $17,670 when you retire and start withdrawing money from your retirement account. The same holds true for any other expenditure; Arends was just using the iPhone as an example. Now, I don't believe for one second that you should always give up spending money on things you enjoy in the present in order to have more money in the future, but if you want to stay out of the poorhouse, and especially if you want to get rich, you have to think like this. Buying something with a credit card and not paying off your full balance for months or years makes everything you buy much more expensive and seriously undermines your ability to stay solvent or generate long-term wealth.

I know that thinking thirty-five years into the future every time you buy a bar of soap doesn't make any sense. But when you put together a monthly budget for your household, long-term considerations are important. You have to ask yourself where you're going to be in ten years, or twenty years, and you cannot let hope get the better of you. Many people, especially young people, assume that in the future they'll earn much more money from their job than they do in the present. That may happen, it may not, but planning your future based on that assumption will more often than not result in your getting hurt. Remember, your paycheck isn't enough. Counting on a bigger one is not a strategy.

The first rule of budgeting, and just about everyone will agree with this, is that you have to make a budget. Even if you don't hold to your budget stringently, laying one out gives you a sense of what you can and can't afford. It will show you where you can spend less and save more. Making a basic budget is easy, as long as you're honest with yourself. Look through your expenses for the past month and the past year to cobble together an idea of what you'll have to spend on the necessities and what you've been spending on discretionary stuff. This will tell you what you need going forward and what you can do without. It will tell you what to change, but you have to know how to look at a budget before you can figure these things out. I'll explain.

Budgeting for the long term is about both trying to become rich and trying not to become poor, but at the end of the day these two goals differ only in their motivation, not their outcome. Getting rich is about greed, staying out of poverty is about fear, but each should encourage you to save money. How much of your paycheck should you save? How much should you spend on a place to live? On transportation? Food? These questions are, to some extent, pretty open-ended. How rich do you want to be? How secure do you want to be? Those are the two most important questions when planning a budget. The more wealth you want to build, or the more financial security you want to ensure, the less you have to spend. It really is that simple. You know that savings are about building the capital you need to invest and thus become wealthy. Saving does increase your financial security, but from the perspective of fear, a good perspective that keeps you healthy and out of the poorhouse. Spending less money on certain things is about averting disasters.

So how do you go about putting together a solid long-term budget? There are six steps to smart budgeting for life:

Step 1. Learn from the past. You need to put together a comprehensive record of your past income and spending.

Step 2. Judge your past. Look at your records to determine how much less money you could have spent.

Step 3. Create your short-term budget. Using your records as a guideline, put together a reasonable budget for the next three months and the next year. You don't have to live a totally Spartan lifestyle to maximize your savings, but if you can be happy doing that, then there's no reason not to.

Step 4. Create your long-term budget. Turn your short-term monthly and yearly budgets into long-term budgets by planning your future expenses. For example, if you think you'll buy a house in five years, include that in your budget and figure out a way to pay for it.

Step 5. Hold yourself accountable every month. At the end of every month compare your actual spending with the budget you planned and figure out where you're beating the plan and where you've fallen short. After the basic step of simply putting together a budget, this may be the single most important thing you can do to plan for long-term wealth. By examining how your actual spending differs from your projected spending, you can nip any serious problems in the bud and learn how to correct your mistakes before they start making your life difficult.

Step 6. If you fail, take drastic measures. This is only for people who have trouble sticking to a plan. If you really find you cannot meet your goals no matter what you do, you need to take drastic action. For example, many people try to automate as much of their spending and saving as possible. You can automate most of your recurring bill payments, either through your bank or by calling or accessing the website of whomever you need to pay, whether your cable company or the bank that owns your mortgage debt. You can also automate payments into a retirement savings account like a 401(k) or an IRA, and once you've contributed money to those accounts it's prohibitively expensive to take it out. I recommend this course only for people who have no success holding themselves to a budget. I believe that saving, and the investing that comes with it, should be an active process, not an automated one, and I think that most people are smart enough to take care of this stuff on their own. Automation should be a last resort, not an integral part of everyone's budget.

Let's get more granular. There's a lot of great budgeting software on the Web, but you can add up your past budgets and create future ones with a legal pad and a pen. You don't have to do this my way, but it's important to standardize your budgets. Divide your record of past income and expenses and your future budgets into four columns. The first column is for your investments, the second column is for your income, the third is for your necessary expenses, and the fourth is for your unnecessary or discretionary expenses. Most people focus on their income and their expenses when they create a budget, but because your investments are how you're going to get rich and how you're going to take care of yourself, I consider them the most important thing to keep track of. The larger purpose of building a budget is downside protection—keeping you out of the poorhouse—but your investments will do that too.

Step 1. Learn from the past. You should start by putting together a record of your past spending, income, and investments. I would go back at least a year to look at the big picture, and three months for a more detailed look at how you've spent your money. When you look at the whole year, you don't have to keep track of everything. Go through your bank statements, tax forms, or pay stubs to add up your income for the past twelve months. Write down how much money you started with and how much you currently have. We're looking only at liquid assets, so don't include money you've contributed to a retirement account or any other form of investment that you can't cash out of at no cost with a quick trip to the bank. This should give you a picture of your income and your spending over the past year. To determine your necessary spending, take the amount of money you spend on rent, food, utilities, medical care, your children, and transportation in a month, multiply by twelve, and write that number in the necessary expenses column. For your discretionary expenses, subtract your necessary expenses from your total spending, and that's the number. Next, if you have any investments, write down their value at the beginning of the year and at the end of the year in the investments column. Then write down the total amount of money you contributed to your investments over the year: anything that you diverted from your income to purchase stocks, invest in a retirement fund, or buy a home, to name just a few potential investments. Subtract the value of your new contributions from the total value of your investments at the end of the twelve-month period you're looking at, and then subtract the starting value of your investments from that number. The amount you end up with is your investment gain or loss for the year. Having filled out all the columns, you're looking at a record of your income, investments, and spending for the past year.

We're mostly going to look at your monthly records, but you want to put an annual record together because it can raise some important red flags. If your spending is greater than your income over the past year, you've got a problem. If you're dipping into your investments to make discretionary purchases and you're not retired, that's a problem. If you're losing money on your investments or you're not contributing to them at all, you need to change that too. That said, the real work goes on at the monthly level.

The rules are a little different when you put together a monthly record of your income, investments, and spending. For this you need to write down everything. Go through your bank statements and your credit card bills and list every single expenditure for the past month. In your necessary spending include only housing, utilities, debt payments, and children's expenses. I know you need to eat, but put everything else in the discretionary spending column. You'll see why we do this in a minute. Handle your investments and your income just as you did when putting together your annual budget. I know all of this recordkeeping is incredibly tedious, but the biggest mistake people make when they start budgeting is trying to put a budget together from scratch. You don't live in a vacuum, so you can't just declare that you're going to spend X amount and save Y amount every month and expect it to work. You already have habits and you need to use the past as a reference point for putting together a workable budget for the future.

Step 2. Judge your past. This is where you figure out how much less money you can realistically spend. We do that by creating an ideal budget. Go online and shop around to determine the least amount of money you can spend on the basics without making yourself miserable. The odds are, whatever this number is, it's less than what you put in the discretionary spending column of your records, where, if you remember, we included all kinds of necessary purchases. It's true that food and shampoo are necessary, but what you're spending on them might not be. You shouldn't have to live like a pauper, but by creating an ideal budget you can get a good sense of how much more money you could have turned into capital in the past month. The main reason to put this information together is to figure out where you're spending more than necessary. Break it down by categories too, and then compare your ideal budget to your actual expenses over the past month and the past three months. The difference between the real expense report and the ideal expense report is the maximum amount of money you could have turned into capital in the past and can potentially turn into capital in the future.

Don't stop there. Remember, we're creating a long-term budget. You'll want to annualize the difference between your real expenses and your ideal ones. I bet it adds up to something substantial. Then use a compound interest calculator to figure out how much capital you spent rather than invested over five years, ten years, and thirty years, compounding at 5 percent and then 10 percent. This is what I mean by budgeting for a lifetime. Figure out what your extra spending actually means in terms of future wealth. I'm not suggesting that you eliminate all of your extra expenses, because that would make you miserable. But you should understand their true long-term cost and shift as much of that spending to capital as you can.

Step 3. Create your short-term budget. Use your expense records to create a budget for the future. Take out all the onetime income and the onetime expenses from your records, but only if you can honestly say that you really won't be buying the same things all over again. If you're already saving more than 20 percent of your consistent after-tax income, then you're in great shape. You still need to create a budget, but you don't necessarily need to change your behavior. You're not in danger of becoming poor anytime soon. For everyone who's already turning more than a fifth of their income into capital every month, there's no reason not to keep going.

It's important to keep your goals reasonable when you put together a budget, but reasonable can mean anything. I think it's unreasonable to believe that you can invest 20 percent of your income next month if you have been investing none of it. I think if you're spending money like crazy, it's unreasonable to expect that you'll take a vow of poverty. Once you set an unreasonable goal and fail to meet it, the odds are good that you'll give up. That's why people who think they're doing all the right things often end up going broke anyway.

In general, when you plan a budget you want to create as much capital as you possibly can. Capital will make wealth; capital will keep you from going poor. The more of your income you turn into capital, the better your chances of becoming really rich. That's it. The only place you're going to find more money to invest when you're building a budget is in your discretionary spending. So, broadly speaking, your goal is to create and adhere to a plan that has you saving less and investing more, but that doesn't differ too radically from how you've been using your money in the past—unless you really believe you can hold yourself to the new plan, and most people can't.

There's really no magic percentage of your income that should go to the nonnecessities when you put your budget together. A lot of this depends on your income and on how badly you want to build wealth or stay out of the poorhouse. That said, you don't want to go insane. And you're not building wealth just so that you can retire comfortably; you want to buy things. My rules of thumb here: you have to be able to go out to dinner or go to the movies at least a couple times a month; if you have a hobby you're really passionate about, or just want a big TV set, then you have to figure out how you're going to pay for it over the long term before you buy it. If you make $46,000, which was the median household income in the United States in 2006 (if you took all the households in America and lined them up from the household making the least amount of money to the household making the most amount of money, the median household would be the one that's right in the middle of that line), then you need to decide if you can afford to buy something with your annual income alone, or if you will have to use some of the money generated by your capital to pay for it. You also have to look at the cost of that product over all the years you're going to use it, and you need to take a good hard look at what you're giving up in the future to pay for what you're buying in the present.

As for building capital, if your goal is financial security, a home, and retirement, then depending on your income, you can probably achieve that by saving 10 percent of your income, even if you make only $40,000 a year your entire life. You can absolutely achieve it if you save and invest 20 percent of your income, especially if you start early. And remember, the more you save early, the less you'll have to save as you get older, because with time and compound interest on your side, big savings in your 20s and 30s matter a lot more than big savings in your 40s and 50s. Isn't fate cruel? In your 20s, when you're young and want to be reckless and irresponsible, that's when budgeting money to save and invest is most crucial and most valuable. Youth really is wasted on the young! Of course, I believe that we need a little bit of recklessness and irresponsibility now and again, but only as much as we can afford. Luckily for the young, they can also take much bigger risks with their money by speculating on stocks, something I'll discuss later, and something that's a whole lot of fun.

I know there are many people, especially the young, who just cannot afford to save money. If you're barely making ends meet, then it's possible that you belong to this club. We want to build wealth, but before we can do that we have to keep you from becoming poor. That means you need health and disability insurance before you start to save and invest your money. You need a place to sleep at night. You need to eat. If, after the essentials, you have nothing left for savings, there are a few things you can do. If you're young and working at an entry-level job where it's likely you'll be promoted and paid more in the future, you don't need to worry. If your job doesn't offer you many opportunities to make more money, then you need to find a new one. There has to be room in your budget for savings.

Step 4. Create your long-term budget. You do this by turning your short-term budget into a long-term budget. A real budget is a plan for the future. It should take into account more than just your day-to-day, month-to-month, or even year-to-year expenses. Buying a home, having children, sending them to college, retiring—all this costs money, and if you don't budget for it, you either won't get it or you'll break the bank trying. Figure out what you'll need to reach your goals, estimate how much capital you'll need now to be able to buy what you're shooting for, and create a time line to see how long it will take you to get what you want. Keep your assumptions conservative: plan as though you won't get a raise and your capital won't give you stellar returns. The best way to be realistic about a budget is to be a constant pessimist, at least as far as financial planning is concerned. If you're relying on 20 percent returns from your capital in order to buy a house in five years, you probably won't get there. If your investments do that, well, congratulations, but if they don't and you have planned for a lesser rate of return, you won't be disappointed or in danger of going broke.

Step 5. Hold yourself accountable every month. It's not enough to create a budget and cross your fingers. Unless you keep detailed records of where your money actually goes and then compare your actual spending to the budget you planned, all of this is meaningless. It's hard to live successfully on a budget, and many people will find that they fail month after month. If you measure your actual spending against what you projected, most of you will find that you spent more than you planned. That's all right as long as you're improving. At the end of every month you should go over in detail where you spent more than you expected. In the future, you'll know where you need to watch yourself. Even if you find yourself living within your budget or beating it, you should keep holding yourself accountable.

Step 6. If you fail, take drastic measures. For some of you, no matter what you do, you can't seem to live within a budget. You need to automate. I really don't favor this method, but here's how it works. You can set up automatic payments tied to your paycheck schedule.

You don't want to set up automatic payments to something like a savings account, where you can easily withdraw money. You want to send your capital to a retirement account, where you'll have a lot of trouble trying to access it. Why? Once you've decided that you cannot trust yourself with your own money, you need to make sure you do not have the opportunity to spend it. I don't think many people actually belong in this category, and the idea of automating your savings or automating your bill payments goes against my core beliefs about money, but I know some of you out there have no other options. If you do automate your bill payments and your savings, you'll need to cut up your credit cards too. Otherwise you'll build up massive amounts of credit card debt, and no matter how well your investments do, you'll never be able to establish any kind of foundation for real wealth.

Beyond your budget, it's important to try to save money on housing, but within reason. It's not worth living a totally Spartan existence, and you shouldn't live somewhere you hate. But when it comes to things like rent or mortgage payments, where you can expect to pay the same amount of money every month for as long as you stay in the same place, keep in mind that if something terrible happens, you don't want to be committed to making large recurring payments every month.

When I started my hedge fund, I didn't buy a palace on the Upper East Side of Manhattan. I lived in a nice but hardly ostentatious one-and-a-half-bedroom apartment in Brooklyn Heights. It wasn't a bad neighborhood, nor was it a bad apartment, but it cost much less than I could afford if I was earmarking a third of my income for a home. I knew that I had to plan for the worst; I'd been homeless before. I understood that my hedge fund could go belly-up, so I didn't overspend on housing. I had a healthy amount of fear, which is exactly what I recommend for you. (I was able to sock away much more money because of my decision to save on property and not care that people might judge me as not being wealthy.)

My approach to building a budget isn't revolutionary or particularly original. Just like everyone else, I think it's important to keep track of where your money goes, to cut down on discretionary spending, and to invest as much as you possibly can. Boring, but true. What's really essential, and what most people don't do, is connect their short-term, month-to-month budget with their long-term goals. Figure out how much you need to invest to get what you want, and make sure you invest enough money each month to be able to buy what you want when you expect to want it. It's much easier to be disciplined about your spending when you can tie it to a concrete objective in that not-too-distant future. Of course, there are some things you absolutely must purchase. Spend what you have to in order to eat healthily, but that doesn't mean going out every night; it means paying for the fruits and veggies. Trust me: being unhealthy will cost you when it comes to health and life insurance premiums. It's also a liability on its own; you don't want to get sick and not be able to work. At my hedge fund, there was no such thing as a sick day. Even one or two sick days a year can be bad for your career.

There are two more items that must be in your budget, and you should purchase them even before you save, because they are the greatest bulwarks against poverty: health insurance and disability insurance. The goal of this chapter is to make sure you don't become poor, and there's no better way to do that than by protecting yourself from downside risk. You need to make sure that you'll still be able to get by even if you get sick or seriously injured. Most people get this insurance through their employer, or they might be in a family with someone whose employer offers a health plan. Let's talk about health insurance first. I think this is more important than disability insurance, but that's a tough call. Generally speaking, with a health plan you get through work your employer will cover some of the bill, but you'll still pay premiums that can add up to anywhere from about $500 per year for a less-comprehensive plan for someone who's single, to $2,000 or $3,000 for someone with a family. Some people don't elect to take their employer-sponsored health plan. If you're one of them, the first thing you need to do when you go to work tomorrow is talk to your human resources department and sign up for it. Believe me, it's worth it. I know how important health care is because when I got mononucleosis while I was living in my car, I had no insurance. I had to go to a farmworkers' clinic forty miles away from where I usually lived—or parked, as it happened. I ended up with hepatitis and a jaundiced liver, all because I had no health insurance. You don't want to end up in the same position. If my sister hadn't taken me in after that fiasco, I don't know what I would've done.

Medical expenses are the number one cause of bankruptcy. You don't want to get wiped out by enormous medical bills, especially if your employer is willing to foot most of the bill. Not everybody gets coverage at work. About 15 percent of Americans have no health insurance. Some of them are covered by Medicaid, but many are not. I don't care how expensive it is, and boy, will it be expensive. (This is a great reason, by the way, to lose weight and quit smoking, as this will substantially lower your premiums—not to mention the money saved on cigarettes and, of course, lung cancer, emphysema, and heart disease.) You might be in perfect health. That doesn't matter. When people say things like "Invest in yourself," they're usually talking about getting an education, going to college or graduate school, things like that. But I mean *get health insurance.* So many people are blindsided by a health problem and their lives fall apart financially because of it. If you get sick, you do not want the added burden of having no money. So please, do yourself a favor and get health insurance coverage.

Disability insurance is also essential. Like health insurance, you should be able to get it at a discount through your employer, but make sure you know what you're getting. There are different types of disability insurance, and you don't want to become disabled and find out that you're not getting nearly the amount of money you thought you would. Most policies will cover you for up to 60 percent of your income, meaning that if you become disabled and can no longer work, every month you'll receive 60 percent of what you would have made working, usually up to some dollar amount that serves as a cap. When you shop around for a disability insurance policy or look at the policy you can get through your employer, pay attention to the kind of coverage they're offering.

It's tempting to look for the least expensive policy. You might think you're getting a deal, but you're not. The least expensive policies are the worst policies, and if you get the wrong kind of disability insurance, it's possible that even if you become terribly disabled, your insurance company could give you nothing. With disability insurance, you get what you pay for. So what kind of policy do you want? There are three types of long-term disability insurance: own-occupation disability insurance, income replacement insurance, and any occupation coverage. Own-occupation disability insurance is the most expensive and the most desirable kind of policy. With this type of insurance, you'll get disability payments if you're injured and can no longer do the job you had while you were paying for coverage. Unlike other types of disability insurance, you keep getting paid even if you go back to work in another field. Some of you might be unable to afford own-occupation insurance; in that case, you'll have to get another policy. That said, good disability insurance is more important than investing, and unless you're fairly young and just entering the workforce, you should be able to afford an own-occupation policy. Unfortunately, most employers won't offer this kind of policy. I don't care. Getting disability insurance through your employer is cheaper and easier than getting it yourself, but if you can get only income replacement insurance or gainful occupation coverage at your job, go and get an outside policy. Why? Depending on the extent of your disability, it's likely that you'll want to keep working, but income replacement insurance is exactly what it sounds like, and that makes going back to work difficult. If you start working or earning income from, say, your investments, and you have this type of insurance, then your insurance company, which is insuring your lost income, will pay you less money.

If you earn enough, they can stop paying you entirely. Usually, income replacement insurance is less expensive than own-occupation disability insurance, but it's not substantially less expensive, and sometimes it actually costs more. It's never the more desirable policy.

Finally, you might be offered any occupation coverage. Under no circumstances should you buy this variety of disability insurance. It's the least expensive way to get coverage, but if you do become disabled, you'll wish you'd gotten a different plan. The problem with gainful occupation, or any occupation, coverage is that it pretty much lets the insurance company determine whether or not you're disabled. With any occupation coverage, you're not considered disabled if you can perform *any* occupation. This is almost as bad as having no coverage whatsoever.

There are a few more things to keep in mind when you buy a long-term disability policy. First, you've probably seen the terms "non-cancelable" and "guaranteed renewable." A non-cancelable policy lets you pay a fixed premium throughout the entire term of your insurance coverage. With a guaranteed renewable policy your premiums can go up over time. It's not hard to see that a non-cancelable policy is the way to go. Second, especially with a non-cancelable policy, the younger you are when you get disability insurance, the lower your premiums will be. Third, these plans all have waiting periods between when you become disabled and when you start getting payments from your insurer. The waiting period can be anywhere from two or three months to half a year to an entire year or even two years. The longer the waiting period, the lower your premiums will be. I suggest that you get a policy with a waiting period of no more than six months unless you have a great safety net or a lot of money invested. The fourth and final point about long-term disability insurance: your policy will usually stop paying out benefits when you turn 65, but some policies will give you only five years of coverage. I strongly recommend getting a policy that covers you until retirement.

What about short-term disability insurance? I consider it useful but not necessary, unless you have very little in the way of savings and no family to help take care of you. The usual short-term disability policy covers you for three to six months, although some can go as long as two years. If you're doing your best to build wealth and stay out of poverty, you should have enough money to last six months without working. If you don't, buy a policy. Short-term disability insurance is much less complicated, and you're far less likely to get cheated out of your benefits by insurance companies that profit from denying people's claims.

Pay off your credit card debt, create an honest, reasonable long-term budget, and make sure to get health and long-term disability insurance. Do these three things, and even if you don't invest to become wealthy, you certainly won't end up in poverty. I want to help you get rich and stay rich for the rest of your life, but I can't do that if you're setting yourself up to get poor and stay poor.

Now that we've dealt with everything that's holding you back, let's talk about how we can push you forward.

3

PLANNING FOR RETIREMENT

You've established a stable foundation and built up some capital. How should you put it to work? What should your priorities be when investing for long-term prosperity? You start with the future because *the future is cheap.* If you pay for your future expenses now, meaning if you invest a small part of your income today for the purpose of covering your costs twenty or thirty years down the road, your future costs of living, hopefully in luxury, will effectively be much lower. You won't actually pay lower prices, of course, but by investing a little money today, you're taking care of really big expenses in the years to come. The longer you keep your capital in a position where it can compound at a reasonable rate, the more you'll have when you start relying on that invested capital for income. If that sounds too much like financial gibberish, let me put it this way: when you save and invest a little bit of money now, it will be a lot of money by the time you retire, as long as you're a marginally competent investor. That's worse than being an adequate investor, and everyone can be adequate. You've heard this all before, but I'd rather be repetitive and right than original and dead wrong. Where I come from you don't get points for being wrong in a really clever, counterintuitive way; you just lose. I want you to be a winner, so I'm asking you to look at the other side of the equation that makes things in the future so inexpensive. The future isn't actually cheap; if anything, inflation should cause future prices to be much higher than the price you pay right now for similar goods and services. The future is cheap only if you decide to start paying for it today. If you're still in your 20s and you start investing as little as 5 percent of your annual salary in the right kind of account right now, you should be able to produce all the money you'll need when you retire. I know many of you are much older than that, and I know plenty of people my own age who haven't started saving for retirement. If that sounds like you, don't waste another minute. You need to put aside everything you can and more to get ready for retirement. If you're over 40 and you haven't started planning and investing for retirement, it won't be nearly as easy for you to build a hefty retirement fund. That doesn't make it impossible to retire comfortably—trust me, it's far from impossible—but it does mean you'll have to work harder and save more to make up for lost time.

Yep, retirement. You in the younger crowd, I know you abhor that word. You hate to think that just as you've finished school and started to work, your first priority becomes saving and investing for retirement. But don't think of it as your first priority because it's your responsibility to take care of yourself forty years down the line. Think of it as getting a really great price on something that, like it or not (most people do like retirement), you'll have to pay for eventually. When you put together a budget for your household, the necessities come first, right? Rent, food, water, heat, and everything you need to live, or to have a modern standard of living as opposed to a medieval one—you budget and pay for those things before the discretionary stuff, right? Well, investing for retirement, at any age, is like going to the grocery store and finding that all the food you have to buy in order to feed your family is on sale for 10 percent of its actual price. You're going to have to retire, just as you need food, and you might as well take the sale that's offered instead of trying to squeeze by later, when the future becomes the present and starts getting expensive.

Many of you, the ones who want to get rich first and foremost, might be turned off by my talking about something as boring and necessary as retirement. I understand where you're coming from, but you need to know that without a big retirement fund, you'll never come close to getting rich. (Actually, "retirement fund" is a misnomer, implying that you pull money out of it from time to time to support yourself. From now on, let's call it "retirement capital," because you can use it to generate more money even after you retire.) The same tools and the same rules apply to building retirement money as apply to building any other kind of wealth. Your investments in retirement accounts and your investments in discretionary accounts will both take advantage of the fact that the future is cheap. The only real difference between the two kinds of accounts, aside from what you might put in them, is that retirement accounts get tax benefits and, in the case of some 401(k) plans, matching employer contributions. Not only is the future cheap when you take care of the costs up front, but when you contribute to an IRA or a 401(k) plan to pay for a piece of that future, you get the equivalent of a discount or a rebate. (If you work for the government, you might have a 457 plan, and if you're a teacher or nonprofit employee, you'll likely have a 403(b). These are equivalent to 401(k) plans in all the ways that count.) The money you invest in a traditional IRA or a 401(k) isn't taxed when you earn it; it's what is called "tax deferred," meaning that you pay no taxes on contributions to your 401(k) or IRA and you pay no taxes on capital gains in either account until you start withdrawing money for retirement. Then it's taxed as ordinary income in the year you withdraw it. The "rebate" is more of a "buy one, get one free" special in many 401(k) plans, where your employer will match your own contributions to your 401(k) up to a certain point. When the company you work for matches your contributions, it's as though the company is paying you to take advantage of the fact that the future is cheap, which just makes the discount that much bigger. If you have a 401(k) plan, it's provided and administered by your employer, although companies outsource the actual administration the vast majority of the time.

In the previous chapter, I talked about dividing your income into three separate and distinct streams: a spending stream, a retirement stream, and a discretionary investing stream. Believe me, retirement deserves its own stream, but it doesn't have to be a third of your income, or anything like a third of your income, because—that's right—the future is cheap! When we talk about retirement today, we might well mean twenty or thirty years of rest and relaxation. Considering how new drugs and medical technology are extending our life span, you could spend a third of your life or more in retirement. If you choose to take advantage of the permanent fire sale on the future by investing in your retirement today, you're making it exponentially easier for yourself down the road. You really should not expect to keep working after you hit 70, and even 70 is pushing it for some people. We're talking about decades of your life when even if you can work, it's going to become a lot more physically taxing. We all age; that's just a fact of life. Keep in mind, you're listening to a guy who had to retire from the hedge fund game at the spry young age of 46 because the stress was almost sure to cause me multiple heart attacks and undeniably caused me absolute misery. In other words, I wanted to walk out, not be carried out in a box.

You might be wondering why I'm wasting your time with the same brand of vanilla conventional wisdom you could pick up in any book off the personal finance shelf at your local library. I've got two reasons. First, funding your retirement is so important that I'm happy to repeat myself and everyone else who writes about money, drilling the point home. Investing for retirement so you can live out your golden years in wealth and comfort is just that important. It's so important that investing for retirement needs to be your first priority after you've taken care of everything that could send you hurtling down into poverty. Second, my take on how you should actually go about investing for retirement, using the standard tax-favored retirement accounts, goes beyond the standard, soporific advice you'll hear from anyone who claims to be a financial expert. Most of these folks assume that their readers (how do I put this delicately?) are functionally brain-dead. They act as if IRA and 401(k) investing is a walk in the park, the kind of easy steps you can take to building long-term wealth that hardly even need to be explained beyond the basics. Or, worse, they skate: they don't think it matters, in part because they have never run money professionally or even made a lot of money. Which is why, not to brag or anything, I'm different. This is where I part ways with the conventional wisdom crowd. True, you can take advantage of these plans and make a killing without too much effort, but I am constantly amazed at how often people underestimate just how easy it is to mess up and wipe out all of their retirement capital. You have to understand that there are opportunities aplenty for anyone to ruin a perfectly good chance at the easy life, and unless you know how to avoid these pitfalls, you'll drop right in, taking your retirement capital down with you. I can teach you how to make the best of your 401(k) and IRA investments, how to achieve capital appreciation over the long term with this money, but that's not my most valuable advice. Remember, when we invest for the long haul, capital preservation tends to be more important than capital appreciation, and when we're talking retirement, capital preservation becomes even more significant. You've got great opportunities to make profits, but there are plenty of legal ways the financial services industry can cheat you out of those gains. It's particularly painful when I see so many fees these days that are charged for services that I used to provide for free as a broker, or as a favor to my hedge fund clients. But it's not just the industry that cheats you. I've seen plenty of people cheat themselves, especially when it comes to building up funds for retirement. Don't worry too much, just be cautious. I'll walk you through every step on your way to a prosperous retirement, and I'll make sure you don't get burned by the usual mistakes that so-called experts often forget to warn you about, or even try to talk you into!

In the old days, our parents and grandparents could rely on pensions and Social Security to provide for them in their old age. They didn't need to worry about retirement. Nowadays, thanks to the magic of capitalism, through 401(k)s, IRAs, and perhaps someday in the not-so-distant future semiprivatized Social Security, most of us are no longer held hostage to the performance of defined benefit pension plans that pay out only so much money and therefore limit how much growth we can see from our retirement savings. Today we have the freedom to manage our own retirement plans. We've been given the precious ability to sink or swim based on our own investing prowess, financial knowledge, and self-discipline. Unfortunately, for a lot of people that means they're sunk. It's terrific that we have the opportunity to make much more money with a 401(k) plan than anyone ever could have expected from a pension, but few of us have the tools to make that opportunity a reality. I knock 401(k) plans, but in all honesty, having an employer-funded defined benefit pension plan is far, far worse.

I really feel for the guys who work for Tribune Co., the big newspaper company (think *Chicago Tribune, L.A. Times,* and *Newsday,* among others) that, as I write this book, is being taken private by Sam Zell. The poor employees at this company have an old-fashioned pension that's run by the company, which means that if Tribune goes bankrupt, the employees lose their pensions. When companies get taken private, they take on a lot of debt to finance the deal, because all the shareholders must be paid for their shares. The Tribune deal is being financed as an employee stock ownership plan, which basically means that if Tribune can't repay its debt, then the employees will end up paying for it out of their pensions. If we had a serious Labor Department in this country, no business would be allowed so blatantly to take advantage of its employees. As it is, I'm not even sure most of the employees at Tribune know that they're getting a raw deal. I'm sure many of them have been sold on the idea that they're being allowed to participate in and reap the rewards of a fabulous deal, the kind of deal that regular people would never get a piece of in normal circumstances. But in fact, the Tribune employees are being brazenly exploited, and at the same time their bosses are probably telling them how lucky they are to be in this position. I know I have an over-the-top, amoral persona on my TV show, and I've always maintained that good investors need to be able to put their money in companies that do bad things—although there's a line that cannot be crossed—but what's happening now at Tribune is the kind of thing that makes me sick.

How can regular people, who really have never been taught about investing, turn this around and actually provide for themselves, at least when they retire? Where are you going to learn everything they don't teach in school? There is good advice out there, but there's no good way to tell the difference between helpful and harmful suggestions unless you've already made yourself rich and no longer need someone else's input about money. For most of you, that means you've had nowhere to go to learn how to set yourself up for retirement the right way without also having to hear a lot of useless or, worse, damaging nonsense. I am writing this book to take care of that problem.

I have always felt that I should leave any kind of discussion about saving for retirement to those who toil in the personal finance industry. I figured they were the experts on the subject, and since I specialized in making enormous sums of money in the stock market, my knowledge wouldn't really apply to the personal finance universe. I erroneously believed that the world of building enough wealth for a comfortable retirement didn't really intersect with the world of running a hedge fund. Then I read the many personal finance books and columns about retirement and I realized that most of the writers who cover this ground knew only what the terms of these retirement plans were and left you to figure out how best to use them. That's nonsense! How to properly use your retirement plan is the most important topic of them all, way too important to leave to the people who administer the plans or the people who write about them all the time, even though these writers have no particular insight into investing. You've heard a lot of this before, but you've never heard it from someone who's actually made a lot of money investing, and I think that makes all the difference. I just can't imagine how people can dole out advice about managing a retirement fund properly unless they themselves have already made a fortune or two using the same fundamental disciplines. The fact is that nobody writing books that tell you how to save for retirement actually has any experience successfully turning money into more money. Few people who are already rich have any incentive to write a book full of personal finance guidance. I don't have a serious financial interest in writing this book, because after a point, making more money starts to become pretty meaningless. I have never understood why I'm so driven to help people, or as my critics would put it, to shoot my mouth off, but at least my advice comes from the perspective of someone who has gotten rich and stayed rich.

If you feel as if we're going backward by starting with your need for lasting wealth in your retirement, then you understand exactly what's going on here. Channeling money into the retirement stream of your investments is priority number one. Investing in your 401(k) and an IRA is more about *staying* rich than it is about *getting* rich. You don't hear of too many 401(k) millionaires, but I have seen plenty of them. Mostly they're the ones who started with 401(k)s when the government first allowed them. I don't blame you for thinking that the money you contribute to your 401(k) won't add up to something big. I can remember when I was working at Goldman Sachs and I wanted to lay the groundwork for my clients by setting up their 401(k)s, which at that point were still a novelty. I was told not to bother because the money wouldn't amount to anything. My boss at Goldman Sachs, who was a savvy guy, said that. Everyone else makes the same mistake. Of course, 401(k) money is now the single biggest pile of retirement funds out there, and it just gets bigger and bigger. I need you in on the action. You don't have to get rich first in order to start laying the groundwork for staying rich. Just the opposite is true, actually. If you don't take full advantage of these plans from the get-go, it's going to be much harder both to build your wealth and to keep it if you manage to amass a large nest egg. You want to take advantage of these tax-favored gifts from the government. As soon as you have a plan to hang on to your wealth long after you retire, a plan that should involve a 401(k) and an IRA, only then can you start taking chances with the discretionary side of your investments. I know this is a really tough thing for many people to do, and I'm sure a lot of you are now quite upset with me for making this judgment, but it's the right one. When I do my college tours for *Mad Money*, I never hear of people investing their money in an IRA. All the college kids are taking fliers, Wall Street gibberish for chasing hot stocks. Now, I know most of them don't have serious sources of income that they can devote to anything other than paying off student loans, but they should take whatever money they have to invest and put as much of it as they can stand toward retirement. You take fliers after you've nailed down your first retirement contributions. I'm telling you: retirement is the highest financial priority there is.

Some things you don't want to take big chances on, and your ability to retire with plenty of money to spare is definitely one of them. Take care of your long-term prospects, and only then should you start fretting about the short term or the medium term. Even though you need to pay this month's bills well before you retire, if you are smart you will prepare for the long run first. Why is that? Why should we turn the world upside down and come at everything backward? Why does the horde of personal finance authors tend to take the same approach?

It's not because you are building wealth for decades down the road, putting together enough retirement capital along with something to pass along to your children. It's not because it's the responsible thing to do. It's not because you don't want to come up short on cash when you start having a harder time supporting yourself. It's not even because living from Social Security check to Social Security check is a pretty tough and undesirable bit of financial trouble. I should add that depending on when you were born, there's no guarantee Social Security will even be there when you retire. I can say without a doubt that you'll either be collecting those Social Security checks later than you expected or they'll be smaller than you expected, because the economics of the program will force either an increase in the retirement age or a decrease in the size of payments. Every one of these things is true, but they're not why we're always told to put retirement first.

What's the real reason? Because it's easy to set up plenty of retirement capital, and the sooner you get started, the cheaper the future becomes. The simple truth is that thanks to the power of compound interest and the generosity of the federal government, setting yourself up for a flush retirement is one of the least difficult elements of long-term financial planning. Don't get me wrong: depending on your circumstances, building enough wealth for a comfortable and secure retirement can be anything but a cakewalk. And I don't want to belittle the daily struggle many retirees face just to make ends meet. Far from it; my goal is to help create long-term prosperity for people of all ages. But investing to support yourself in the future is one of the least difficult things to do here and now.

You know the steps already. If your employer offers a 401(k) retirement plan, then the best use of your capital, from a long-term perspective, is almost always to contribute to it. *Almost* always. I'll take you through all the ins and outs of 401(k) investing in a moment, but first we need to go through the rest of my plan. Ready? You should also start up an IRA, and actively invest in that as well. If you've only got the income to afford funding one or the other but not both, you should go with your 401(k) contributions first (except in a very few situations, which I'll describe). You should be saving as much as possible so that you can invest as much as possible, but you might not have the money to fund both accounts and still manage to make ends meet. If you're in that situation, you can still use your capital to ensure a cozy retirement, even without much income. After all, that's the whole point here. The entire premise of this book is that your salary won't be enough to create true, lasting wealth. That's why you ought to take as much of that salary as possible and turn it into the kind of money that makes more money: capital. That's the plan, minus all the caveats I'm about to share with you: contribute to your 401(k) plan if your employer provides one, and then contribute to your IRA after that. Sounds simple, but there's a right way to go about this kind of investing and countless wrong ways. Remember that the future is cheap as long as you pay for it in the present, and that's exactly what it means to invest using these two tax-favored plans.

I wish I could unequivocally tell you to fund your 401(k) plan at least so that you get the full matching contribution from your employer, fully fund your IRA, and leave it at that. I wish it were that easy, as easy as it's ordinarily made out to be by the industry of authors who extol the virtues of tax-favored retirement plans while at the same time rarely explaining in any useful way how you should actually take advantage of them. But fortunately for you, I'm a worrier, and I would be worried sick about the safety and security of your retirement dough if I didn't tell you about the downside. Let's start by looking at your 401(k) if you have one. This is going to be the first and best place for many of you to start investing.

If you're going to take my advice, you need to know that I'm being completely honest with you. So when it comes to 401(k) investing, I have to tell you that there are only two good things to say about a 401(k) plan, just two positives, but they're so good that they more than make up for all the faults of the average 401(k)—and there are a lot of faults. The first positive is that your contributions to a 401(k) plan are made with pretax income; the taxes on each contribution are deferred, along with the taxes on any earnings from your 401(k) investments, until you start withdrawing money from the account after you've retired, and then you'll pay ordinary income tax on any withdrawals. This tax benefit alone is enough to make even the worst 401(k) plan worth your time and money. I don't like to complain about taxes; in my own personal history, the way I've invested has meant incurring a lot of tax charges. I can live with that, but why put up with taxes when you don't have to? You can compound your money year after year without paying a dime of tax on your gains. But outside of a 401(k), your investment gains would be taxed when you realized them, when you sold something at a profit. Inside your 401(k) the government doesn't take its cut of your capital gains. That leaves you with more money to continue to invest in your 401(k) plan, and over time the tax advantages really add up. In fact, the tax advantages are evident and pretty helpful from the get-go.

Suppose you make $50,000 a year. Your marginal tax rate is going to be 25 percent with that level of income. Now let's say you follow my 10 percent rule of thumb, and invest $5,000 a year in your 401(k). All of a sudden, you're not paying any income tax on that $5,000. You would have had to pay the government $1,250 in income tax on that $5,000, but you get to *defer* that tax bill until after you've spent years or even decades putting that extra $1,250 to work. In thirty years that $1,250 will look more like $9,515.32, assuming you compound at a 7 percent annual rate, which is conservative for a stock portfolio but, given the high fees associated with 401(k) plans, seems like a reasonable assumption. If we look only at the earnings you would generate entirely from the tax savings of a single year, we're talking about an $8,265.32 profit. When you start taking money from your 401(k), you'll have to pay income tax on those withdrawals, but considering the tremendous profit you made merely by deferring the income tax management. If an asset management company runs your [40]1(k), the odds are good that your plan will let you choose from [man]y funds that belong to the company that's administering your [retir]ement plan, whether they're good or not. Many insurance com[pani]es have also gotten into this game. If you learn only one thing [from] this book, learn that insurance companies are not to be trusted. [It's] not unlikely that an insurance company is in charge of your [401](k), especially if you work for a small company or if you have a [403](b) plan, which is what teachers, professors, and nonprofit em[ploy]ees usually have. The insurance companies often package their [401](k) as an annuity and charge you much higher fees, as well as in[clu]de their own high-fee annuity offerings that no one should buy.

[Yo]u can always ask about the type of 401(k) plan a prospective em[plo]yer offers when you interview for a job, and you can compare your [po]tential employers based on the types of plans they offer, but it's not [lik]ely you'll have much luck finding a good 401(k). You might be able [to] find yourself the least bad plan. That said, it's absolutely essential [th]at you examine the 401(k) prospectus when you look over the com[pe]nsation any potential employer offers you. It doesn't take that much [in] fees to cost you tens or hundreds of thousands of dollars come re[ti]rement, so you need to assess this as you'd assess any other benefit. [O]nce you get a job, you can always try to agitate for a better 401(k). [Y]ou can go to human resources and push for better offerings or a bet[t]er plan administrator. There's no reason why everyone shouldn't do [t]his. Agitation from employees and from politicians has steadily made [4]01(k) plans better and better, and I believe that on average it will [c]ontinue to do so into the future. But for now, 401(k) plans are mostly [d]isappointing (and completely necessary, 100 percent mandatory un[l]ess you have very low income and aren't planning on staying with [y]our current employer for long), aside from the fact that 401(k) con[t]ributions are tax-deferred and your employer likely matches some part of your contribution.

Investing in your 401(k) is one of the smartest, best things you can

on a single $5,000 contribution to your 401(k), I doubt you'll be too bothered by the tax. Still, you'll have to keep track of inflation, of the overall increase in prices while you're earning those extra returns with tax-deferred dollars in a 401(k). If we assume that we have a 3 percent increase in prices every year, which is a little on the high end, then over thirty years, the general price level will have increased by 143 percent. What costs $1.00 today will cost $2.43 in thirty years if prices rise at 3 percent annually. That means that in thirty years your $8,265.32 will pay for what $3,401.43 would cover today. That's still a tidy gain compared to the big fat $0 you would have produced had you not invested in your 401(k).

Even though most 401(k) plans are organized terribly, with high fees and a poor selection of mutual funds, and even though most 401(k) plans are quite inflexible—in most cases, you can adjust the distribution of your assets among the investment options your 401(k) administrator offers only once a month, or once a quarter—the extra profits you would make from deferring your taxes alone would be enough reason to invest heavily in your 401(k) plan. In the vast majority of cases, there's another great reason to contribute to your 401(k): the employer match. Typically, for every dollar you contribute to your 401(k), your employer will match some part of that contribution up to a certain point. For example, your employer might match 50 percent of your contributions: the company puts in 50 cents for every dollar you put in, up to 10 percent of your income, so once you contribute 10 percent of your income to your 401(k) in any given year, the boss stops giving you free money. You should always take your employer for every last dollar it's willing to put into your 401(k).

There's one hitch here: most employers will gradually vest their contributions over time. In plain English, that means you become entitled to the employer match in full only if you stay with the company for some period of time. There are two ways your employer is likely to vest its contribution to your 401(k) over time. It might give you 20 percent per year, so that after five years working for the company, all company contributions will be fully yours, even if you leave. The other common way employers vest their contributions is harder on you: they'll vest 20 percent after three years, and add 20 percent every year until they finish at year 7. This is a drawback, especially in an age when people increasingly move from company to company looking for work. But not every company vests its contributions over time, and even if you leave after a year or two, getting 20 percent to 40 percent of your employer's contribution is still a lot better than getting nothing.

If you contribute enough to get the full employer match every year, you've taken a huge step toward building long-term wealth. Unfortunately, that wealth is locked up inside a 401(k) plan, and aside from the two points I just mentioned, there's nothing nice to say about most of these. What's so bad about a 401(k)? Let's start with the legitimate rules. This is a retirement account: end of story. If you contribute to your 401(k), there are very few circumstances in which you'll see that money again before you turn 59½. Those special circumstances are called hardship withdrawals, and they're difficult to get. First, your employer isn't required by law to permit hardship withdrawals, so if your employer doesn't include rules regarding hardship withdrawals in the Summary Plan Document for its workers' 401(k) plans, you're out of luck. If the company you work for does permit hardship withdrawals, you still have to pay a 10 percent penalty excise tax, in addition to the income tax you'd pay on any distribution from your 401(k). You can get a hardship withdrawal to buy a primary home, to prevent a lender from foreclosing on your home or evicting you, to cover the cost of college tuition for yourself or a dependent within the next twelve months, or to pay medical expenses that will not be reimbursed for you or your dependents. But before you can even take a hardship withdrawal, you'll have to prove to your employer that you genuinely need the money and cannot get it anywhere else. And again, this all depends on whether your em-

ployer even permits hardship withdrawals. You
money from your 401(k) before you turn 59½ in
stances, but they aren't circumstances you want
come totally disabled; if you go into debt for me
7.5 percent of your adjusted gross income; if yo
court order to hand over the money to a divorced
other dependent; if you are laid off in the same year
you lose your job and set up a regular, approximat
ment schedule for distributions from your 401(k) o
your life expectancy.

Forget trying to get your money out early; it's too
about the fees instead. In a typical 401(k) plan, you'll
anywhere from six to twenty different funds, or even n
allowed to invest in as part of your plan. Plus, you'll
chase stock in your employer if it's a publicly traded
before you even determine where to place your capital,
paying a fee based on the amount of money you're contr
people don't notice these administrative fees, because
ceive your monthly or quarterly account summaries, th
ply subtracted from your actual return before it's repor
fees are not included as separate items in your account s
possible that your employer takes care of these costs for
won't know unless you check, so ask your human resou
sonnel department for a quick breakdown of how you
administered and who's footing the bill. Just ask for the
spectus. These are truly hidden fees and you don't want
slip past you.

In my view, one of the worst aspects of a typical 401(k) i
selection of approved mutual funds. This is what you'd exp
how a 401(k) is set up. The offerings in your 401(k) h
chosen either by the company in charge of administering th
or by the human resources department at your company
though adept at hiring and firing people, usually isn't well tr

do to build lasting wealth for yourself and your family. But investing in a 401(k) badly is one of the worst possible things you can do to your chances of ever becoming rich, or even achieving modest prosperity. And the way the system is set up, it's very easy to do a bad job of running your 401(k). Letting workers manage their own retirement funds is great, but we forget that we live in a country that makes no effort to teach anyone practical financial lessons, and few companies that offer 401(k) plans try to teach their employees anything about investing for fear that they'll be sued if their employees lose money taking even the blandest advice. So how can you take advantage of this terrific—tax-blessed, as I sometimes call it—retirement plan without falling victim to the many perils of 401(k) investing? I've got you covered. Here are the five most common mistakes people make in their 401(k) plans that ruin their future, and how you can avoid them:

The Five Most Common 401(k) Mistakes

1. The most popular 401(k) investment is your employer's stock. Don't ever buy any.
2. The second-most popular 401(k) investment is different versions of the stable-value fund. Avoid these unless you're close to retirement.
3. Most 401(k) investors assume that the mix of funds offered in their 401(k) plan is representative of the mix of actual investments in the market and a good proxy for diversification. Don't be confused by your 401(k)'s offerings. Stick to my bedrock principles and you'll be fine.
4. When people leave their jobs, for whatever reason, most choose to cash out their 401(k) plan or leave their plan alone and pay higher fees to maintain the old 401(k) with their old employer. Both of these decisions are bad. When you leave your job, be sure to roll over your 401(k) into an IRA.

5. Increasingly, workers are falling victim to automatic enrollment in 401(k) plans, which come with a terrible set of default investments. Don't let this happen to you. Pay attention to where your money's going, and allocate your assets yourself.

1. Don't ever buy your employer's stock. This has been said many times before, and apparently to no effect, as people continue to invest more money in their employer's stock than in any other type of 401(k) investment. There are very few situations where you want to own stock in the company that writes your paychecks. Remember, diversification is the single most important principle of investing, and you need to put your income on the table when you look at your investments. Let's say you work at CVS Caremark, making $60,000 a year. Should you also own CVS stock? I think it's a great stock; in fact I recommend it later in this book as a great long-term investment. But no, you shouldn't own even a single share of CVS as long as you work there. Your fate is already tied to the performance of CVS even if you don't invest a penny in its stock. As the professionals would say, you're already levered to CVS. If something really terrible happens to the company and it needs to take drastic measures to cut costs, you're already in trouble just because you're on the payroll. Let's say you get laid off. In this case your income is already plunging from $60,000 to $0 a year. The last thing you need is to have your retirement funds tied up in CVS stock. If you were contributing $10,000 a year to your 401(k) and plowing all of it into CVS stock, then both your salary and your portfolio would take a hit. What happens to you if the same trouble that cost you your job also takes 50 percent off the value of the stock? All those $10,000 contributions will get sliced in half too.

A huge part of the reason we invest is that we need to augment our paycheck, which just doesn't provide enough money for all the finer things in life. If you get fired, you want to be able to rely on your investments, and you can't do that if you're invested in your employer's stock. Think of the sad hypothetical CVS employee in my example.

What if this guy is just a year away from retirement? All of a sudden, not only is he out $60,000 of income that he was expecting to earn in his last year on the job, but he's also just had his whole retirement fund cut in half. There's no way he can retire now.

This is beyond the realm of possibility for a massive, well-established company like CVS, right? Maybe it feels that way now. Think of those poor Enron employees. They're Exhibit A for why you absolutely cannot invest your 401(k) money in your employer's stock. They worked for a massive, well-established, well-run company, and the idea that its stock could get cut in half in a day must have seemed preposterous to them. But that is just what happened when the first news of the fraud broke, before we even knew the full extent of the malfeasance. I'm sure those who invested 401(k) funds in Enron's stock never thought it would go all the way to zero, which it did, thoroughly wiping out all of their retirement savings. You rely on your employer for your income; don't also rely on your employer to fund your retirement. As an investor, your job is to spread the risk around, not to concentrate it all in one place, which is exactly what you're doing when you buy shares of the company you work for with your 401(k) contributions.

I don't care for any of this "Know what you own, own what you know" nonsense either. Peter Lynch, the brilliant investor who originally said that, didn't mean that you should buy stock only in companies that you're personally familiar with, either because you work for them or because you use their products. He meant that you should be familiar with your stocks, and that therefore you should buy only what you can comprehend and have some level of experience with. The advice does not mean you should buy stock in whatever company you know best, which in most cases would be your employer's stock. As I've just explained, that's a recipe for disaster. Familiarity is no reason to invest in anything, especially not with crucial retirement capital. Familiarity might give you a useful perspective on whether a given company is worth owning, but by itself, it means nothing.

I'm sure some of you will say, "Cramer, what about those workers at Apple and Google who made fortunes because they were compensated in stock, stock that subsequently quintupled in value over a brief two-year period? Don't they disprove what you're saying about buying your employer's stock?" Not at all. We're looking at two totally different situations. Especially at big tech firms like Apple and Google, higher-ups are often paid largely in stock options (in this case, call options). A call option gives you the right, but not the obligation, to buy a stock at a certain price, called the strike price, within a certain period of time. When we're talking about executive compensation, these options are normally "struck" at the stock's closing price on the day they're issued, which is incidentally why so many executives got busted for backdating options—they were basically paying themselves with options and claiming that they were issued on days when the stock was particularly cheap. This has nothing in common with retirement investing, and even less in common with investing in a 401(k). The people who made fortunes from being paid in the stocks of particularly successful companies were taking enormous risks, and for every stock option millionaire, there are a dozen stock option failures, guys who were paid in options while working at failed start-up companies and who ended up with options worth nothing *and* no wages. People who are paid in options are pursuing a high-risk strategy, way too risky for the money you're going to use to retire. Many executives get paid with stock options because it's a great way to pay executives for performance. If their stocks go higher, they make fortunes; if the stocks tank, their options are worthless. But these executives usually are already making enormous six- to seven- to eight-figure base salaries, and I guarantee you they're not relying on stock options to fund a comfortable retirement. They're hoping that their stock options will allow them to throw lavish, decadent parties for themselves and their rich friends. You're probably not in that position.

I'll say this one more time: it doesn't matter how great your employer is as a company, or how great its stock is. Under no circumstances are you allowed to invest any part of the money in your 401(k) in your employer's stock. This is the single most common way people wipe out their retirement savings, and honestly, you know better than that. When people who worked at Enron or WorldCom made this mistake and then called in to my old radio show during the segment where I would tell workers what I'd do if my 401(k) was as devastated as theirs, at first I felt pity for them, because it's awful to lose your retirement savings. But then, almost always, I would harden my heart because these people committed the most basic, elementary investing mistake, one that is sure to hurt you over the long term. In the end, I still pitied these guys because they didn't know better. No one had ever told them what I'm telling you. But now you don't have that excuse, so sell your company stock. Some employers provide their matching 401(k) contribution in their own stock. If so, take the first opportunity you have to sell that stock and move your funds to a better investment—in this case, *any* other investment is better than owning shares of your employer, especially in your retirement account.

Honestly, I regard buying your company's stock in your 401(k) as the single most dangerous investment you could ever make. I would rather buy Treasurys, U.S. government bonds. These are the ultimate unambitious investments, with spectacularly low yields and even less risk than shares of my employer for my 401(k). That's how serious I am about this.

2. Avoid stable-value funds unless you're close to retirement. There are worse investments than stable-value funds, but there's no reason anyone should ever put a dime of their retirement savings into one, and there's certainly no reason why these things should be the second-most popular 401(k) investment. I'm sure people like them because of the name, but when you look at what they actually are, there's no reason to own a stable-value fund rather than a short-term to intermediate-term highly rated bond fund.

I can't believe that most people truly understand what a stable-value fund is, so my best guess is that 401(k) investors are attracted to the conservative sound of the name. When I say that capital preservation is more important than capital appreciation, I don't mean that you should invest in a fund that sounds like it can't lose you money. So what is a stable-value fund? These are funds that invest in money markets, highly rated short- and medium-term bonds, and insurance contracts. To make sure the value of your investment is "stable," these funds will buy what are called "wrapped bonds." Take an old high-quality bond, and then get an insurance company to give it a "wrapper," or "wrap contract," which is basically an insurance policy on your investment. These wrappers are, in my opinion, really bad deals. Here's how it works: a wrap contract has a set rate of return. If the stable-value fund is forced to sell a wrapped bond for a loss, the insurance company will pay it the difference between the insured price and what your fund actually got when it sold the wrapped bond. Maybe that seems like a good way to minimize your downside. If you think so, keep reading. Wrappers don't just minimize the downside, they also prevent the possibility of an upside. If your stable-value fund sells a wrapped bond, or anything else with a wrap contract, for a profit, it gives the profit to the insurance company too. These funds have truly stable values: they don't go down, but they also don't go up.

Typically, a stable-value fund will give you a slightly higher return than a money market fund (different from a money market account) and a lower return than a high-quality bond fund. That really breaks it for me. Why on earth would anyone invest in a complex fund that they probably don't understand when that fund has a lower yield than a straightforward, simple bond fund? Even if you're enthralled by the idea of wrappers, shouldn't the fact that on average you will make less money in a stable-value fund be enough to discourage you from contributing to it? It's not as though high-rated bonds are very risky. In fact, they're quite stable and reliable. As I said before, people invest in these funds because the name is comforting. You don't want your 401(k) to comfort you during the thirty to forty years you're contributing to it; you want it to comfort you in retirement, and it won't do a good job of that if you invested in lower-yielding funds, producing less money for your retirement, because it felt safe at the time.

In the old days, stable-value funds relied on guaranteed investment contracts, or GICs, and you can still find and invest in these too, but again I don't see any reason to. A GIC is a contract between an insurer and a retirement plan that guarantees investors a fixed rate of return. The GICs fell out of favor in the 1980s after several insurance companies used low-quality debt to finance the contracts that they'd sold to various retirement plans and then went bankrupt. If your insurance company goes bankrupt, it can't pay off that guaranteed contract.

The difference between the risk you take on putting your money in a high-quality short-term bond fund and the risk you take on investing in a stable-value fund is tremendously small, and in my opinion not consequential. A bond fund should have a higher yield and slightly lower fees. Plus, stable-value funds tend to charge high redemption fees, meaning they could take 1 percent or 2 percent of your investment when you take your money out. There's no world in which going with stable-value funds over bonds makes sense.

3. Don't be confused by your 401(k)'s offerings. Stick to my bedrock principles and you'll be fine. People view the options offered by their 401(k) plan as though they represent the rest of the markets. What do I mean? If your 401(k) offers you ten funds, let's say five stock funds and five bond funds, you're more likely to believe that a 50-50 split between stocks and bonds is the correct allocation of your capital. (This is the gist of what Jeffrey R. Brown, Nellie Liang, and Scott Weisbenner found when they surveyed investors for their 2007 article for the National Bureau of Economic Reserarch, "Individual Account Investment Options and Portfolio Choice: Behavioral Lessons from 401(k) Plans.") It's not. Don't mistake being diversified among the handful of funds your 401(k) allows you to invest in with being genuinely diversified among different sectors of the world economy. The only thing the list of funds your 401(k) offers tells you about is the list of funds your 401(k) offers. You might learn a thing or two about the quality of the people selecting the investment options for your 401(k) plan, but you won't learn squat about diversification.

4. When you leave your job, be sure to roll over your 401(k) into an IRA. This is extremely important. The average worker in the United States will switch jobs eleven times over the course of his or her working life. That statistic probably vastly overstates the number of times the average American will move from job to job by including things like the summer jobs you had as a kid, but you get the idea. Today's workforce isn't committed to staying at one company to build an entire career, and young people especially have very little problem moving from employer to employer.

There's nothing wrong with that, except that when many of us switch jobs, we really screw up our 401(k) plans. When you leave your job, you're given thirty days, mandated by law, to decide what to do with your 401(k) from that job. You have four options: you can cash out your 401(k) plan; you can leave it with your old employer; you can roll it over into the 401(k) at your next job, if you have one; or you can roll it over into an IRA, which I'll explain in more depth later in this chapter. Something like 45 percent of people who lose their job choose to cash out of their 401(k) plans. This is the worst possible thing you can do. First of all, when you cash out, you pay the taxes. The whole point of a 401(k) is that your investments can compound over time and you won't have to pay any taxes on gains until you withdraw the money and it's taxed like ordinary income. Well, you're withdrawing the money when you cash out. Your employer is required to withhold 20 percent of the money in your 401(k) to pay the taxes, and you also pay a 10 percent penalty for pulling your money out of a retirement account early. Again: this is a retirement account. *It's for retirement.* If you intend to pull out your money well before you retire, there's really very little reason for you to contribute.

If you don't have a lot of money, there are other options. You don't have to fund your 401(k) if you're barely making ends meet, but what you absolutely cannot do is invest in a 401(k) and then cash out the plan when you get fired, because that's just a waste of your money and your time.

If you lose your job, you will probably feel upset, helpless, and resentful. That's natural, and even healthy, but it's not conducive to making smart decisions about how to fund your retirement. I'd bet that many of the people who cash out their 401(k) plan after they lose their job do so because they think they'll need the money between jobs. That's rarely going to be true. You can apply for unemployment benefits from your state's department of labor and get half of your weekly wages, up to a cap that varies from state to state, for six months, although you'll have to wait a week before collecting the benefits. It's much better to go on the dole than break into your 401(k) and pay a huge penalty and all those taxes. Every penny that goes to Uncle Sam when you cash out is another penny that won't be compounding when you get a new job and decide it's time to start investing for the future again.

I'm sure some people are unclear about what their 401(k) options are after they lose their job. For some people, thirty days isn't a whole lot of time if you're struggling to find a new job and live within your reduced means. But if you don't make a decision, your former employer will cash you out, and that's one of the things that will absolutely ruin your ability to retire and make the whole exercise in 401(k) investing pointless.

So why do I think you should roll over your 401(k) into an IRA, rather than leaving it with your old employer or rolling it over into a new employer's 401(k)? If you leave your 401(k) with your old employer—and by the way, they don't have to let you do this—they are allowed to charge you higher fees. And it can be impossible to reallocate your assets, meaning your former employer basically freezes the account as it was when you got fired, and you can't rearrange your investments to your liking. Leaving your 401(k) with your old employer is like a more expensive, less-free version of your 401(k) before you got fired, and if you remember, I was none too thrilled about the lack of control and the high fees before. It's that much worse when you have less control and bigger fees.

What if you want to roll over your 401(k) into an IRA and not your new 401(k) because you believe an IRA is better than a 401(k) plan? Here is what you should know. An individual retirement account is quite similar to a 401(k) in that it's a tax-deferred account, meaning you contribute to it with pretax income and don't pay any taxes on gains until you cash out, at which point all your distributions are taxed as regular income. The difference is that you open an IRA with a bank or a broker or a mutual fund company, not through your employer, so there are no matching funds. It's better to contribute new money to a 401(k) plan than an IRA as long as you haven't maxed out the company match. But once your money's in one of these plans, you'd much rather have it in an IRA. Why? Well, there's the other difference: you actually get to run an IRA yourself. There's no choosing from different approved offerings as with a 401(k). You get to decide to invest almost any way you want once your money is in an IRA. I'll talk about these accounts in more depth later, but you can see why rolling over into an IRA is more appealing than putting that money in a new 401(k). Unfortunately, you can do this kind of rollover only once every twelve months.

There's a right way and a wrong way to do this as well. Call the bank or broker where you set up your IRA to get specific instructions from them, and then call your old 401(k) administrator and ask to have your 401(k) funds transferred directly into your new IRA. The IRS gives you sixty days to complete the process, but if you do it right you won't be pressed for time. How could you screw this up? Often, your 401(k) administrator will try to give you a check. Many people who don't understand the process take the check and try to fund their new IRA with it. Here's the problem: if your 401(k) administrator gives you a check, they have to withhold 20 percent of it for tax purposes, just as they do when you cash out. It gets worse. You'll have to make up that 20 percent withholding from your own money when starting up the IRA. Otherwise the IRS will decide that the 20 percent the old administrator withheld was actually a payment to you, and they'll then tax and penalize it accordingly. You can avoid this as long as you're careful and make sure the money goes straight from your old 401(k) to your new IRA.

5. Pay attention to where your money's going, and allocate your assets yourself. Most of the people who write about 401(k) plans assume that ordinary people are dolts who can't take care of themselves or make good decisions. I've read way too many columns blasting workers for failing to contribute, or contribute enough, to their 401(k). I have plenty of issues with how these plans are structured, but the complainers finally came up with a 401(k) solution that manages to be worse than the problem. The solution is called the Pension Protection Act of 2006, and one of its provisions makes it a great deal easier for companies to enroll you automatically in their 401(k) program. Every personal finance writer and his mother loves the idea of automatic enrollment. Not me. I can understand their thinking, though. Most people who are automatically enrolled in a 401(k) choose not to take themselves out of the plan, so the people researching this stuff concluded that the majority of workers don't care whether they're enrolled or not. And since investing in a 401(k) is supposed to be an easy, slam-dunk decision, automatically enrolling workers is the best thing a company can do. At least, that's how the advocates of automatic enrollment put it.

I have a wholesale distaste for anything involving your money that can be described as automatic. Everyone is capable of making sound financial decisions. When you take away the need to decide, people stop caring, and people who don't care about how their money is managed don't manage their money well. But entirely aside from that fundamental objection, automatic enrollment in 401(k) plans has far bigger problems. Everyone who advocates increasing automatic enrollment has his heart in the right place; these people just want to make sure you can retire comfortably. Unfortunately, their heads are not in the right place. What's wrong with automatic enrollment? Most of you are probably familiar with Murphy's Law: whatever can go wrong, will go wrong. If you've seen me on TV or read *Confessions of a Street Addict*, my memoir, you know that I'm an anxious guy. It's probably one of the reasons I was such a good money manager. If you're good at running money, you fret constantly about the downside, about what can go wrong and lose you money. Obsessing over what can go right will cloud your judgment, but obsessing over what can go wrong will make you cautious and concerned about everything you should be concerned about.

So let's take that logic and apply it to automatic enrollment in 401(k) plans. If your enrollment is automatic, you get hired and the company you work for invests some chunk of your salary in its 401(k) plan unless you check the box telling them not to. How do you think they're going to allocate your retirement capital? The great thing about the 401(k)—the reason these plans far surpass old-fashioned defined-benefit pension funds, which are becoming increasingly rare—is that with a 401(k) you control how your retirement funds are invested. Your future isn't in the hands of some pension fund manager you don't know, who in the old days often legally or illegally robbed you blind and could not care less about your retirement. It's in your hands. When your employer automatically diverts a part of your paycheck into a 401(k), you lose some of that control. You don't actually lose the ability to control where your 401(k) money gets invested—you can still decide where that money goes—but remember, the whole reason for automatic enrollment is that a lot of people don't pay attention to this stuff. Those people will get hurt.

Why? Because when your employer automatically enrolls you in its 401(k), it doesn't invest your money in the best possible mix of assets available through the plan. It doesn't find the lowest-cost index fund for stocks so that you have the right amount of equity exposure in your retirement account. No, it invests your 401(k) money in the worst possible way. That's why I believe automatic enrollment will really damage your retirement funds if you don't pay attention and know what you're doing. The two most popular default options for automatic 401(k) enrollment are company stock and what are known as target-date funds. You already know why company stock is the worst thing you can have in your 401(k). Plus, doesn't it seem a little fishy that your employer can automatically enroll you in a 401(k) plan whose default option is to invest your money in the company's own stock? Call me cynical, but that doesn't seem right. And then there are the target-date funds.

According to Vanguard, the fabulous investment management company that created the index fund, two-thirds of companies that automatically enroll their employees in 401(k) plans have target-date funds as their default investments. So if you're automatically enrolled and don't specify where you want your 401(k) money to go, the odds are good that it will end up in one of these funds. And that would be pretty bad for you. I'll go into much more detail about target-date funds, which are also called life-cycle funds, in the next chapter when I explain the ups and downs of every kind of investment, but these target-date funds warrant special attention in this chapter about funding your retirement because they've become such a popular and incredibly well-marketed type of fund. The idea behind target-date funds, or at least the way they're sold to regular investors, is that they're the only fund you'll ever need. It's clever, even insidious, but it just isn't true. Let's say you plan on retiring within five years of 2025. You could put your money in a 2025 target-date fund now, and the fund would automatically adjust its asset allocation as you get closer to retirement. Actually, the guiding principle of these funds is the same as the guiding principle of this book: to be the only product of its kind that is totally comprehensive and effective for your entire life. The difference is that this book *does* contain everything you need to know, but target-date funds aren't the only fund you ever need to invest in.

As you get closer to retirement, the conventional wisdom says you should keep less and less of your money in stocks and more and more of it in fixed-income investments, meaning bonds. I can't quibble with that advice in general, because bonds are much less risky than stocks, and as people get older they should shift their focus away from capital appreciation (remember that term: growing your money) and toward capital preservation (making sure you don't lose your money while staying ahead of inflation). A target-date fund will reallocate your assets for you as you get closer to retirement, so if you put your money in one of these, it will automatically sell stocks and beef up on bonds to keep up with the conventional wisdom. You allegedly benefit, according to the people who promote these funds, because you don't have to worry about making the switch yourself.

There's so much buzz surrounding target-date funds as the ideal investment for inexperienced, incompetent, and indifferent investors that I feel I have a responsibility to warn you away from them. At the end of 2002, there were only forty-five of these funds, but there were 209 by the end of 2006. They are on the march, and if they haven't invaded your 401(k) yet, the odds are good that they'll invade it soon. If you're auto-enrolled in your 401(k) there's a good chance your money will end up invested in one of them. You don't want that, and you need to correct it if it does happen to you.

The worst aspect of target-date funds is how they're advertised. The idea that a target-date fund is an easy, one-size-fits-all investment for people without much financial savvy, that it's the only fund you'll ever need, is deceptive and untrue. Packaged into this marketing ploy is the notion that if you put your money in a target-date fund, you won't need to do any homework. You won't need to think about your investments, you won't need to worry about them, and you won't need to actively manage them, because the target-date fund supposedly takes care of everything for you. Wrong, wrong, and wrong. Every investment requires homework, period. You need to do less research to own mutual funds or index funds than you do to own stocks, but you're being completely reckless and irresponsible if you leave your money with someone and don't spend at least one hour per week per investment—be it a stock or a fund—to check on the performance of your capital and decide whether you need to put it somewhere else. That's no less true if you invest in a target-date fund that allegedly obviates the need for paying attention to your retirement capital. You still need to do the homework, if only for the basic reason that not all target-date funds are built the same way. For example, if you're twenty years away from retirement and buy into the appropriate target-date fund, depending on who offers it, it could have anywhere from an 80-20 mix of stocks and bonds to a 50-50 mix of stocks and bonds. The whole point of these funds is that they're supposed to have the right mix of equities and fixed income, but there's a wide variety of mixes even for funds that are supposed to cater to people retiring at the same time. At the very least, if you want to invest in one of these funds, you have to figure out what the mix of stocks and bonds is and whether that's the right mix for you. Since they aren't all the same—far from it—you're going to have to first learn what the mix is, and then keep track of your target-date fund to make sure that it continues to give you the right mix as you get older. Does that sound like a hassle-free, homework-free investment to you? It doesn't sound like that to me, but the advocates of these funds seem to think otherwise. These target-date funds cause you to take your eye off the ball, and the companies that offer them make more money off of you. These one-size-fits-all solutions are good only for them, not for you. You're not the same size as the next guy or the guy after that. You are your size, and target-date funds don't address that. And worse, even if their funds fits you, it's still overpriced and made of low-quality material, to keep extending the metaphor.

Then there's the question of the mix. Though target-date funds vary wildly in terms of the mix of stocks and bonds they offer, it's rare to find one that offers the right mix. I'm not the only guy making this point, but it's right on the money: target-date funds are way, way too conservative. I have a more aggressive perspective on investing, even retirement investing, than most people in this business (I'll go into more detail on that in another chapter), so take the numerous other critics as a sign that the average asset mix in target-date funds, and not yours truly, is wrong. Basically, these funds own too many bonds. If you're aiming to retire in forty years—if you're 25 and plan to retire at 65—there's no reason for you to own bonds. At that age, you should be 100 percent in equities, meaning stocks, which time and again have proven to be the single best investment over any twenty-year stretch. Fixed-income securities are for older investors who are on the cusp of retirement and can't afford to take serious risks with their capital. But if you invest in a target-date fund that's tailored for those seeking to retire within five years of 2045, you're going to own many bonds— anywhere from 8 percent to 15 percent of your investments will be in bonds. That's no good.

In sum: target-date funds require as much maintenance home-work as any other type of fund, despite how they're pitched; they're way too conservative; and to top it all off, their fees are way too high. You might disagree with me on the first two points; I think you'd be wrong, but at the end of the day, we're talking opinions, not numbers. But the third point is irrefutable. The most recent data I've seen, from an article in *Pensions and Investments* by Susan Kelly on February 5, 2007, found that the expense ratio of the average target-date fund was 1.29 percent, but the expense ratio of the average fund offered in 401(k) plans is only .75 percent. That means if you put $1,000 into a target-date fund, they'll take $12.90 in fees a year, while that same $1,000 in the average 401(k) fund would charge you only $7.50 a year. It may not look like much, but over time, with compounding, those extra fees really devour your capital. Let's do the math. If you contrib-ute $5,000 a year every year to your 401(k) and you put it into the average fund offered by 401(k) plans, assuming the returns for this fund average 10 percent every year, after thirty years you would end up with $809,918.07 after paying .75 percent in annual fees. If, however, you contributed to the target-date fund, where fees eat up 1.29 percent of your investment every year, and we assume that before fees this fund produced the same 10 percent return as the 401(k), then you will have only $723,456.06 when you hit retirement. It's only slightly more than half a percentage point difference in fees, but over time it adds up to more than $86,000. You might not feel the little bite of the large fees every year when you have to pay them, but don't try to tell me they don't add up, because $86,000 is a lot of money.

So if you have been automatically enrolled in a 401(k) by your employer—something that will happen increasingly now that the Pension Protection Act of 2006 has kicked in—you still have to take control of your investment. If the 401(k) plan is invested in company stock and target-date funds, pull it out and reinvest that money in a superior fund so that you don't end up with your money in bad investments.

Now you know how to avoid the worst, and the most common, 401(k) mistakes that have already done so much damage to so many people. It's time to build up your retirement capital. Once you know what pitfalls to avoid, how can you get the most out of your 401(k)? I have four more rules that will help you become a successful 401(k) investor, not just someone who doesn't make the worst mistakes everyone else makes.

Four Ways to Exploit Your 401(k) Plan

1. Set up your 401(k) so that every month you contribute one-twelfth of what you expect to contribute during the entire year. Whenever the stock market falls dramatically, double your investment the next time you're allowed to contribute. With your typical 401(k) you don't have much control over when you invest or how much you invest. You can rebalance your assets or change the amount of money you're contributing every month with most plans, but only every three months at a sizable minority of plans. When you start your job and set up your 401(k), usually you'll designate a percentage of your income that you want the company to withhold and contribute to your 401(k). Because most 401(k)s operate on a monthly schedule, your contributions are split up among all twelve months, and every month you automatically add the same amount of money as you did the month before into the same mix of funds. I'll explain the thought behind this later in the book when I get into more detailed advice about investing, but the basic 401(k) rule is this: you should double down when the market (and when I say "the market" I'm talking about the S&P 500 or the Dow Jones Industrial Average) declines by 10 percent from the peak, the top, to what's called the trough, or the bottom. It may not actually be the bottom; you're just looking for a 10 percent decline. When you see that decline, you need to talk to your 401(k) administrator or whoever is charge of the plan for your company's human resources department and tell them that you want to double down the next time you can contribute.

Look at it like this: in a whole year you expect to make twelve contributions, each one the same size, month after month. What I've always done is make a double-size contribution after a 10 percent decline in the market in order to take advantage of the weakness by spending more money than I usually would on stocks that have become especially cheap. So if we experience a 10 percent decline—or a 10 percent correction, as they call it in industry gibberish—in June, then come the beginning of July you want to make sure you contribute not one-twelfth of your annual 401(k) contribution, but one-sixth of it. It's true that if you catch the decline in December you're not well poised to take advantage of it, but you can always contribute more money. Once you stop receiving the company match, however, there's really no good reason to invest in a 401(k) if you haven't yet contributed the maximum to your IRA.

2. Recognize that stocks are still king, and invest with the right mix of stocks and bonds, which means tilt heavily toward stocks. Even as you approach and enter retirement, your retirement fund should still have a healthy amount of stock exposure, about 30 percent to 40 percent. This is a pretty radical position; most of the people who give out retirement advice insist that in the years immediately preceding retirement, and certainly during retirement, you should completely or almost completely divest yourself of stocks. People who say you should have all of your retirement capital in fixed income by the time you retire simply refuse to acknowledge that for most people, relying 100 percent on bonds won't be sufficient. We're living longer than we used to thanks to modern medicine; that's terrific from every perspective except that of your retirement fund, which needs more money to support you for a longer period of time. The best way to do that is by continuing to invest in stocks—not risky stocks, but large-cap, conservative, dividend-paying stocks. Only with a sizable chunk of your portfolio in equities or equity funds as you approach and reach retirement can you be sure you'll have enough money to retire wealthy or even retire comfortably. Of course, if you have enough money in your retirement fund to support yourself for thirty years on bonds alone, then bonds alone it is. Most people won't have that much, and I believe it's better to play on the safe, responsible side by investing heavily in riskier securities with the upside you need, like stocks.

Your 401(k) portfolio does not need any bond exposure when you're in your 20s, and I think that anything over 10 percent to 20 percent bonds when you are in your 30s is downright irresponsible. To get the right mix of stocks and bonds in your retirement account, increase this range by 10 percent with each decade. So in your 40s, a good allocation would be 20 percent to 30 percent bonds; in your 50s, we're looking for 30 percent to 40 percent bonds; in your 60s, 40 percent to 50 percent bonds; and once you retire, no more than 60 percent to 70 percent bonds. This last is a bigger increase in bond allocation, but that's because you don't want to have to come out of retirement and start working again after taking big losses in stocks. I'm not just saying that you will make more money if you keep about one-third of your retirement fund in stocks after you stop working; I'm saying this is the responsible thing to do.

How can that be true? In what universe are stocks ever a more responsible investment than bonds? Here's how I like to look at it: if you retire at 60, which is early for most people, and thus also more desirable, you need to plan to support yourself for the next thirty years. It's true, you may not live to the age of 90, but remember, when we plan for the long term we always prepare for the worst, and in a perverse way, from a financial perspective "the worst" means living longer, because it's more costly. It certainly won't feel like the worst-case scenario if you're lucky enough to live to be 90 years old, but when you're saving for retirement at close to 60, you might feel it's the worst that can happen because you're so desperate to declare you've got enough money to retire, and every extra year you expect to live is more money you need to save.

Since I'm a conservative investor, I assume that everyone lives for thirty years after they retire, and my plan requires you to have wiggle room to be able to afford to live even longer. If you're planning to support yourself without working for three decades, putting all of your retirement fund into bonds when you retire probably won't take you far enough. Put two-thirds into bonds. Those two-thirds can pay for the first two decades of your retirement safely and securely. Then, to finance the third decade of retirement, because inflation should make your cost of living higher than it's ever been before, you'll want that last decade in stocks until you get a few years away from turning 80 or thereabouts. We leave this money in stocks longer simply because I want you to have more money. High-quality, dividend-paying stocks have been proven to be the best way to make money over any twenty-year stretch of time. Use bonds to pay for the first twenty years of retirement, but after that you can be almost certain that owning stocks will make you a lot more money without requiring you to take on that much more risk, because we're looking at a twenty-year period, and over lengthier periods of time the risk of owning stocks diminishes.

3. Invest in index funds or the lowest-cost mutual funds offered by your 401(k) plan. This is the conventional wisdom on Wall Street, but it's advice that most people fail to take. People always want to know which mutual fund will give them the best return, but it turns out that's a bad question. Even before you add up the fees, actively managed funds fail to beat the market 80 percent to 90 percent of the time. That means that at least in your 401(k), you're better off investing in an index fund with low costs that simply tries to mirror the performance of the entire market than in a mutual fund that tries to beat the market. I'll explain the difference between actively and passively managed funds in greater depth in the next chapter. For now, let's just say that an index fund has no head. It's designed to follow a certain stock index, and that's all it does. Aside from your annual fees, which should be substantially lower for an index fund than an actively managed fund, your index fund will simply track the performance of an important index like the S&P 500 or the Wilshire 5000 Total Market Index. An actively managed fund has professionals at the helm trying to beat these benchmark indexes. Some of them can do it consistently, and later I'll talk about the best of these consistent winners. But for the most part, it's fair to generalize and say that mutual funds seldom beat the market. Your 401(k) plan might offer a dozen different stock funds, but the odds of finding just one that can outperform a simple S&P 500 index fund two years in a row are slim. The odds of finding an actively managed stock fund that can beat an

S&P 500 index three years in a row are even slimmer. And that's not even taking into account the higher fees charged by actively managed funds.

You already know that a small difference in the fees that two different funds charge could add up to tens or even hundreds of thousands of dollars over thirty to forty years. It's always important to pay close attention to the fees that any type of fund charges you, but it's never more important than in your 401(k). Why? Because in a 401(k) plan, despite the fact that it's supposed to let you manage your own money, the truth is that you don't have very many choices. You'll be offered only so many funds to invest in, and though most 401(k) plans offer at least one stock index fund, some don't even do that.

In general, I advocate hunting down a mutual fund that can consistently beat the market, but there's little point in doing that for your 401(k), because you can invest only in the offerings they give you. You could successfully convince your plan administrator to allow you to invest in a really great mutual fund, but often you'll fail, no matter how persuasive you are and how many other employees agree with you. It's rarely worth the effort. You're not going to get to invest in the best funds in your 401(k), but that's fine. A 401(k) plan is for the tax savings and the company match, and you can afford to invest in a less-than-perfect fund as long as those two things are going for you. Just remember to exercise the little control you have over your 401(k) by investing in index funds, and, if you have no index options, by finding the actively managed funds with the lowest fees.

4. Never mind what the so-called experts say: don't contribute the maximum allowable amount of money to your 401(k) plan every year. You want to contribute the maximum amount of money that's eligible for your employer match, but that shouldn't come near the annual ceiling on tax-deferred 401(k) contributions. Starting in 2008, the maximum contribution is $16,000 a year. Contributing that much money to your 401(k) is just nuts. Anyone who's making enough money to comfortably contribute $16,000 a year to a 401(k) plan is what's called a highly compensated employee, or HCE (which also stands for "hateful cultured elite" and "hostile class enemy"). If you make more than $100,000, you're an HCE and there's a different kind of limit on the amount you can contribute. In any given company, the amount HCEs can contribute is limited by the average percentage contribution of normal employees at the company. If regular employees on average contribute 3 percent of their income, an HCE will be allowed to contribute only 5 percent. In any company, HCEs can always contribute 2 percentage points more than the average employee, but no more than that.

For those making less than $100,000, what about that limit? If you make $90,000 and decide to contribute the maximum $16,000 in 2008 to your 401(k), you'll be diverting 17.7 percent of your pretax income into the plan. Few people have enough control of their finances to actually pull that off. Remember, your retirement funds should make up only about half of your investments. It's the most important half, but you have to leave room for your discretionary investments too, just in case you want to use your capital to pay for anything before you reach retirement age.

You can't seriously consider maxing out your 401(k) contributions, because of the way the rules are set up. As soon as you exhaust the company match for the year, stop funding your 401(k). Why? Some of you might not like the idea of passing up the opportunity to save as much as you possibly can tax-free, but there's a good reason not to. The only thing about a 401(k) plan that's better than an individual retirement account is the employer match. As soon as the match runs out, your next step should be to fully fund your IRA. Your 401(k) plan probably has sky-high hidden fees, and it won't let you actually manage your money. The fact that your 401(k) gives you a crummy menu of possible investments makes it a really bad place to invest. An IRA gives you the same tax savings as a 401(k), but you're not limited to investing in the handful of offerings that your plan administrator has deemed worthwhile. With an IRA, you've got the whole market to choose from, and that makes a big difference. So contribute just enough money to your 401(k) to get the full company match, and not a penny more. Your next step is to max out your IRA. Starting in 2008, you'll have a $5,000 cap on the amount of money you can invest in an IRA every year.

What about after you max out your IRA? Should you come back and top off your 401(k) to save every last tax-free penny the government will let you? No, and this is really a cruel twist of fate. Because of the HCE rules, only people who make less than $100,000 are actually eligible to contribute the maximum amount of pretax earnings to their 401(k) plans. If you're making less than $100,000 before taxes, and you contribute $5,000 to your 401(k) every year to get the full company match along with another $5,000 to your IRA every year, why am I insisting that you not go back and take full advantage of your 401(k) plan's tax-deferred status? Because as important as your retirement portfolio is, you still need a nonretirement portfolio. Your 401(k) may let you save and invest without having to pay taxes for years and years, but you can't use that money until you turn 59½. It's important to create a really robust retirement fund, but it's also important to recognize when you've done everything you need to for retirement. Someone who's contributing $5,000 a year to an IRA and getting a full company match on another $5,000 a year in a 401(k) is effectively saving $15,000 a year before taxes, and if we're conservative and assume our investments compound only at a lowly 7 percent annually, in thirty years you're looking at $1,533,859.37. Even with that paltry return, $1.5 million is enough for you to retire comfortably. If you're making under $100,000 a year and investing $20,000 in both retirement accounts with pretax income, you're shortchanging your discretionary, nonretirement investments, and you don't want that. After all, you should be able to enjoy some of the rewards from investing before you turn 59½ and your 401(k) and IRA become accessible.

That's all you need to know about being a good 401(k) investor, but being good at running a 401(k) doesn't necessarily mean you're any good at investing for retirement. You still need to start an individual retirement account.

Look, I'm sure you've seen hundreds if not thousands of advertisements for IRAs and Roth IRAs at this point in your life, and the most you want from an IRA is to not have to hear about it endlessly during the next commercial break. But these things are too good to pass up. An IRA is another form of tax-deferred account that lets you compound over and over again without needing to set anything aside for taxes until you start withdrawing money. In that sense, it's just like a 401(k). But aside from the lack of any kind of matching funds, IRAs are superior to 401(k) plans in every other respect. With an IRA you can invest almost anywhere—choose from among thousands of stocks, thousands of funds—and you can do it without having to pay high administrative fees. The rules for taking money out of an IRA are similar to the rules for 401(k) disbursements. You can start taking the money out without penalty once you turn 59½, and you're required to start taking your money out once you turn 70½. If you want to take money out of an IRA before you hit retirement age, you'll get hit with a 10 percent penalty, just as with your 401(k) plan, unless you meet the hardship requirements, which are similar to 401(k) hardship requirements. You're allowed to withdraw without paying a penalty if you become permanently disabled; if you need to pay nonreimbursed medical expenses in excess of 7.5 percent of your income; if you've been out of a job for twelve weeks and need to pay health insurance premiums; if you need to pay for education costs; and you can withdraw $10,000 from your IRA without penalty for the purchase of your first home. Other than that, any time you want to pull your money out before you turn 59½, you'll have to pay income tax on your withdrawal and a 10 percent penalty. Just as with a 401(k), you really don't want to pull money out of your IRA before you retire and give up your ability to compound ever-larger amounts of money thanks to your tax savings.

Another big difference between a 401(k) plan and an IRA is that the limits on IRA contributions are lower. In 2007, you can put $4,000 in an IRA, and in 2008 the limit goes up to $5,000. Anyone over 50 gets to contribute an extra $1,000, which is a kind of catch-up provision. You should invest in an IRA as you would anywhere, only slightly more conservatively. We'll cover everything you need to know about your IRA investment options in the next two chapters.

Now what about the Roth IRA? This is an altogether different kind of retirement account. Contributions to a Roth IRA are made with after-tax income, so, unlike a regular 401(k) or an IRA, your contributions are not tax-deferred. The upside here is that you pay no taxes on your investment gains in a Roth IRA, so any earnings from the stock market with this type of account are totally untaxed as long as you follow the rules. Plus, the rules for taking money out of the account are much less stringent, largely because you've already paid taxes on your contributions. You're allowed to withdraw the full amount you've contributed to a Roth IRA at any time without paying any kind of penalty. After you turn 59½, as long as your Roth IRA has been open for five or more years, you can start withdrawing your investment earnings tax-free. Just as with a regular IRA or a 401(k), none of your transactions in the account can be taxed. For example, you won't pay dividend or capital gains taxes on the earnings from your Roth IRA investments. In addition, you can withdraw up to $10,000 of your investment earnings tax- and penalty-free to buy your first home. But you can have a Roth IRA only if you make less than $110,000 a year if you're single or $160,000 a year if you're married and file your taxes jointly.

In addition to Roth IRAs, you can now also get a Roth 401(k), although only if your employer gives you the option. A Roth 401(k) is what you'd expect: your contributions are made with after-tax income, but you won't pay any taxes on your gains as long as you don't withdraw the money early and have had the account set up for at least five years. You can even get an employer match for Roth 401(k) contributions, but the match will go into a traditional 401(k) plan, not the Roth 401(k), and the match will be determined by your pretax income, not the after-tax income you actually end up contributing to a Roth 401(k). There's one more rule: the contribution limits on 401(k) plans and IRAs include all of your accounts. So in 2008, if you have both a 401(k) plan and a Roth 401(k), you can contribute only $16,000 between the two. The same goes for IRAs: if you have an IRA and a Roth IRA in 2008, you're allowed to contribute only $5,000 between the two accounts.

So when do you want a regular IRA and when do you want a Roth IRA? This question isn't nearly as important with 401(k) plans because it's unlikely you'll be offered a Roth 401(k) option, and that is not nearly as enticing as a Roth IRA, because you can't easily withdraw your contributions. The rule of thumb when choosing between an IRA and a Roth IRA is that you want to contribute to a Roth when you're young and in a low tax bracket, as long as you expect to be in a higher tax bracket after you retire. You pay your low tax rate on your Roth contributions, and then don't pay any tax on disbursements as long as you wait until the year you turn 59½ to take them. Of course, once you're making $110,000 if you're single or $160,000 if you're married and file your taxes jointly, the government will take the Roth option away from you.

What about deciding between making an IRA contribution and a 401(k) contribution? As long as you still haven't used up your company match, you want to contribute to your 401(k) before putting a dime into an IRA. As soon as you've taken full advantage of the employer match, it's time to stop funding your 401(k) for the year and max out your IRA, because without the employer match, a 401(k) plan is a pretty crummy way to invest, even with the incredible tax savings. And an IRA gives you the freedom to manage your money well. In a 401(k), the high fees and poor fund offerings doom you to substandard returns. Once you've got the full match in your 401(k) and you've filled your IRA to the max for the year, you've got your retirement taken care of. Just keep up that routine for the next thirty or forty years.

I know these retirement accounts are pretty dull, but you can't start to make yourself wealthy in the present until you've done everything you can to make sure you're even wealthier in the future. I know it sounds backward, I know it's boring, I know you just want to invest in some great stocks that are going much higher, or if you don't have the time for stocks, one of the few mutual funds that consistently beats the S&P 500. But you need to understand that no matter what else you do, you need to pay for your retirement, and the cheapest, smartest time to start paying is as soon as possible. Now that you know that 401(k) plans and IRAs are worthwhile and how best to take advantage of them, it's time to get more detailed and look at what you'll actually be buying with these accounts and with your discretionary account, where you're allowed to have fun and aim to get rich tomorrow rather than by the time you turn 60.

4

INVESTING FOR A LIFETIME— AND WHAT YOU'RE INVESTING IN

We've gotten to the stage where you know how to live, spend, and save in order to set yourself up to start building the long-term wealth and security that you're really after. But if that's all you know, you won't get too far. Who cares about your fund or your IRA or that you know all the tricks to 401(k) investing if you're no good at investing, period? That's really what it all comes down to, and it's why I've spent so much time teaching people how to become better investors in my previous two books, my columns, and, of course, on my TV show. Knowing how to invest goes well beyond retirement. Being able to save and invest for retirement is enough only if you're happy to spend most of your life living from paycheck to paycheck and suddenly strike it rich when you reach retirement age and are allowed to start withdrawing from your 401(k) and your IRA.

I told you before that building a retirement fund is your top priority, but keep in mind that you also must build your nonretirement fund, what I call your discretionary portfolio. That is only slightly less important than your retirement money. For anyone who wants to build wealth to use in that big chunk of your life that happens before you turn 59½, you need to invest as much as you can in your discretionary portfolio without looting what should go to retirement funds. You don't just need to know how to do this when you're 25, 35, 45, or 55. You need to be growing your nonretirement capital for your entire working life—this book isn't called *Stay Mad for Life* for nothing. You should start sooner if your family and relatives loved to shower you with money as you grew up.

To create the best possible retirement fund and the best possible discretionary fund you need to know what you're investing in and what you *should* be investing in. It's my job to teach you both of these. I talk about how most people in this country don't know the difference between a stock and a bond. I'm usually exaggerating to make a point, and if you're familiar with some of my more flamboyant work, I'm sure you're used to it by now. Most people understand the difference between why people buy stocks (for capital appreciation) and why they buy bonds (for capital preservation), although I doubt many people would use those terms. That's not enough. In fact, it's a recipe for trouble. The more you know, the less money you're liable to lose. Knowledge is power only because knowledge leads to profit, and that increases your spending power. You have to know what a stock actually is and what a bond actually is, and here too I'll concede that many people know this. But can most people explain what makes a high-quality bond different from a junk bond in a little more detail than just what the names suggest? And while we're on bonds, what's the difference between a Treasury note, a Treasury bill, and a Treasury bond? You need to know that too.

I will teach you what you need to know in order to decide whether or not to invest in something, be it a security or a fund. I'll tell you who they're for, I'll tell you what you need to do to successfully invest in them, and I'll tell you something about how to evaluate them. I won't go into stocks in much depth here, because stocks are a big subject for at least an entire book, and I've already written two of them. But that's the thing—I am and have been such an ardent proponent of stocks that I've neglected going over almost everything else, all the nonstock investments, in the same kind of detail. Not everyone has the time, energy, and patience to make money with stocks, or at least to do it well. Not everyone should own stocks. In fact, and don't accuse me of hypocrisy for saying this, most people should not invest in individual stocks, because investing in stocks takes too much homework for people with full-time jobs, unless they have a tremendous inclination to do this homework. I have to admit, though—proudly—that if you can watch my show, you probably have time to practice stock-picking and do a good job at it.

In the past, I may have done more harm than good by encouraging people to invest in individual stocks. I don't feel guilty about it, because I have always hammered home the point that if you're going to invest in stocks, which can make you an incredible amount of money, you have to be willing to work really hard at it. I know that when I give that disclaimer, the immediate response of most people, as with any other disclaimer, is to ignore it. Who cares that I'm saying stocks take hard work and devotion when I'm also telling you my life story and you know that in less than a handful of years I made myself a millionaire using stocks? Warnings don't work when there's a compelling story. That is, I believe, why so many of these get-rich-quick books sell so well and work so poorly.

I'm not the first self-made millionaire to write a book telling you how to get rich. The difference between me and most of the other guys, the ones who've already made it, is that most of them sell their story, not their advice. I made my story a separate book, *Confessions of a Street Addict*, which I think sent a mixed message about being a great money manager. When I say these guys sell their stories, I mean that their books go something like this: "I made a fortune doing this thing—let me tell you all about it. And if I did it, so can you." If it's a book about real estate, more often than not it probably doesn't contain much good advice about investing in real estate. Instead, the book sells you a false promise, the promise that if the author got rich investing in real estate, you can too, as long as you follow in his or her footsteps.

I will not make that promise, and I certainly won't sell it to you. I did get rich investing in stocks, and some of you can do the same, but that's not a plan. It's not advice. And if I came out and said, "Hey, stocks worked for me; they'll be great for you too," that would be terrible advice. Stocks are great if you have a lot of time and you're really interested in investing. Most people don't have a lot of free time, and they rightly don't want to spend ten hours a week researching and learning about stocks. That's the majority. They can still get rich, they can still build long-term prosperity, but they don't need to know about stock trading to do it. They need to know how to invest well in a way that's much less time-consuming, and they must know how to change their approach to investing as they age. Statistically speaking, when I say "they," I probably mean you right now. I call changing your approach to investing as you get older "investing for a lifetime." Now I'll teach you not just investing for a lifetime, but also *what* to invest in for a lifetime.

Before I go through everything you might consider investing in, and at what time of life you should do it, I just want to remind you that as I explain each of these potential investments, I'll also be explaining what's right for your discretionary fund and what's right for your retirement fund. The rules are a little different for each, and you'll be a very unhappy retiree if you forget that. You can and should take more risks with your discretionary portfolio. That means investing more aggressively in riskier assets and caring just a little bit less about capital preservation most of the time and a little more about capital appreciation. Also, unlike your retirement fund, your discretionary fund doesn't get all those nice gifts from the government. The money in your retirement account, as you know, comes from your pretax income, and you don't get taxed on your gains for as long as you keep them inside the 401(k) or IRA (unless it's a Roth, and then you don't pay income tax when you withdraw money once you retire). Unfortunately, that's not the way it works inside a regular, old-fashioned nonretirement account that you have with a bank or a broker. You're investing your discretionary capital with after-tax income, and as you saw in the previous chapter, doing that, along with the tax on your capital gains, takes a big bite out of your ability to make massive investing gains. Investing your discretionary capital isn't like having one arm tied behind your back; it's just that retirement investing is like having an extra arm, thanks to the tax savings.

This is part of the reason you should take more risk with your nonretirement portfolio. You need it to make up for what the tax man takes away. Of course, the main reason is that you're using your discretionary money to pay for things like college tuition, a home, or maybe a new car. (Incidentally, buying a new car is considered the classic example of a bad investment, because as soon as it leaves the lot it loses half of its value. If you don't consider your car an investment—I consider mine a necessity because I live in the suburbs and need to drive to get anywhere—the fact that it's a poor investment shouldn't matter.) These things, while important, aren't as essential as paying for retirement. If you take a lot of risk in your discretionary portfolio and you lose the money you'd earmarked for the Lexus, it's not the end of the world if you have to drive a Kia, especially since Kias are pretty decent cars. But if you invest a lot of money in your IRA in a really risky stock or in stock options, which are very risky (and I'll explain what you need to know about them later in this chapter), and you lose that money, not being able to pay for a couple years of your retirement is a serious problem.

Although your retirement capital and your discretionary capital are different in many respects, there's one way in which you need to look at them the same. I'm talking about the level of asset allocation. I'm talking about diversification. I've already referred to diversification in this book, and I've gone over it extensively in my previous two books, in addition to hammering home the point every day on *Mad Money*, but it's important enough for me to remind you again. I'm sure you know that you need to be diversified, although some of you who are new to investing might not be entirely sure what that means. When I say you must be diversified, I mean that your investments shouldn't overlap. If we're talking about a portfolio with five stocks in it (five stocks is the minimum number required for a good nonprofessional portfolio and ten stocks is the maximum), no two stocks in that portfolio should occupy the same sector. They shouldn't be in the same business. So if you own Bank of America stock, you shouldn't also own Citigroup stock. And it's not just about competitors. If you have some General Motors, you shouldn't also own Goodyear tire, even though Goodyear makes more than just tires these days. The reason is that you don't want all of your eggs in one basket. If there's a huge downturn in the economy and people buy fewer cars, then two of the five stocks in your portfolio will go down, the two that depend on people buying cars to make money. Because 50 percent of a stock's movement depends on its sector, you can't afford to have more than 20 percent of your capital in any given sector.

When you're figuring out whether you are diversified, you have to look at your retirement fund and your discretionary fund together. This is very important. If you're not diversified when you look at both portfolios as one, you have to sell something in order to diversify. One last point on diversification: I'm about to explain stocks, bonds, and different types of funds. Don't think for a minute that you need to be diversified across different kinds of investments. It would be insane to invest 20 percent of your portfolio in stocks, another 20 percent in bonds, another 20 percent in mutual funds, and so on. This is *not* what diversification means.

As long as you keep all of this in mind while we go over your potential investments, you will be less likely to lose money, which is just a pessimistic way of saying you will be more likely to make a great deal of money over the long term.

Stocks and Bonds

What's the difference between stocks and bonds, and when do you want one or the other? A stock is figuratively a tiny piece of a company. When you buy a share of a business, you become a partial owner, with emphasis on the word "partial." Unless you're running a big activist hedge fund and you buy a big piece of the company—think 5 percent to 10 percent—you don't get to be involved in the decision-making process at the company. Activist hedge funds buy enormous pieces of companies and push management around until it does something to increase the value of its shares. All your ownership actually entitles you to is a seat at the company's annual meeting and maybe a cup of coffee and a bagel or Danish at the snack table. (At TheStreet.com's annual meeting we cut out the Danish because nobody comes anyway.) You don't buy stock so that you can tell a company what to do. You buy stock because you expect that stock to make you money by going higher or by paying you a dividend, preferably both. I know this firsthand. At my hedge fund I bought 4 percent of Dow Jones and went to the board meeting and spoke about closing a division, Telerate, before the company plowed $800 million into it. I said that the division was a total loser—it helped people trade bonds, a business Bloomberg had already won—and should be closed. Despite my multimillion-dollar stake, the chief executive officer dismissed me with a laugh. Of course, I got the last laugh because the division was closed soon after, a total waste, and later on the company was sold to Rupert Murdoch's News Corp. Murdoch was someone the company and its board of directors hated, but they could do nothing to avoid him because the company had squandered so much money in many failed attempts to grow that his offer to buy the company was the only real one on the table.

Bonds are a totally different story. Most people think of bonds as stable, conservative investments that give you a fixed amount of income. That's generally true, but that tells you nothing about what a bond is and very little about who should buy bonds. A bond is actually a kind of loan, expressed in complicated terminology to make things more difficult for regular people who want to invest in order to convince them that they need professional help. In reality, bonds aren't that complicated. When a company or a government wants to borrow money, it doesn't have to go to the bank and apply for a loan. Instead it can issue a bond. The company or government that creates and sells the bond is therefore called the "issuer." If they were regular people borrowing money, they'd be called the "borrower." See, not complicated. Whoever buys the bond becomes the bondholder, which is what we in the real world would call the "lender." Unlike regular loans, bonds don't pay interest. Instead, a bond issuer (borrower) will pay what it calls the coupon (the interest) to the bondholders (the lenders). Like a regular loan, at some point in the future the bond reaches its maturity date and the bond issuer has to pay the bondholder the principal, which is the amount of money the issuer originally borrowed. If you're looking for a good analogy, a bond is kind of like an interest-only loan, where you pay only the interest (the coupon) every year. If you got a thirty-year interest-only mortgage, at the bond's maturity at the end of thirty years you would have to give back all the money you had borrowed at the beginning of the loan. See, all of this is simple stuff. What's not so simple is keeping track of all the various kinds of bonds, which I'll explain later. Not only are bonds incredibly complicated when you stop talking about bonds and start talking about agency paper, convertibles, bills, notes, and munis, but it's also tedious trying to invest in them yourself.

So let's have some fun instead of lingering on bonds for too long. Suppose a company goes bankrupt. Would you rather be a shareholder in this company or a bondholder? Obviously, you'd rather not have anything to do with the company, but in this situation it's better to be a bondholder than a shareholder. When a company goes bankrupt, the creditors take over, and the bondholders are the creditors. It's possible that shareholders of a bankrupt company will lose their whole investment, because even though individual shareholders don't have any personal liability to the bondholders, they do own a piece of paper (or, as happens now, a virtual piece of paper because nobody gets actual stock certificates anymore) that represents part of a company with a lot of debts that can't be paid. Remember that the bondholders are in charge when a company goes bankrupt. Until then, they have no say in how a company is run.

But back to the subject at hand. Beyond knowing the difference between stocks and bonds, you really need to know how to use them, and more than that, *who* should use them. Let's start by talking about stocks. There are a lot of ways to own stocks. You can invest in individual stocks or you can invest in a mutual fund, a hedge fund, or an exchange-traded fund that owns stocks. Everyone should own stocks, except for wealthy retirees who can afford to support themselves comfortably past the age of 100. Everyone who wants to get rich and stay rich must own some stocks. But not everybody should own individual stocks. In fact, most of you might be better off getting your stock exposure somewhere else. Of course, some advisors think that picking your own stocks is a terrible idea.

The great thing about the tech boom at the end of the 1990s was that it encouraged so many people to get into the stock market. The worst thing about the tech boom at the end of the 1990s was that it encouraged so many people to get into the stock market without knowing the slightest thing about stocks, except that they never stop going higher. This dot-com-inspired boom created a huge class of people who understood the promise of stocks and gained firsthand experience of just how bad owning stocks could be in 2000, 2001, and 2002. Many of those brand-new, first-time investors from the 1990s really soured on stocks. I'm sure the plethora of accounting scandals—Enron, WorldCom, and HealthSouth come to mind—added insult to injury. Everyone felt burned by stocks when a rash of scandals gave the impression that while regular people were losing big, the market was a perpetual playground for the superrich and superunethical. Many people went from being excited about stocks to being disgusted with stocks. But the past few years have been good ones, and if you want to build lasting prosperity, owning stocks is a must.

I've seen a lot of people who really got burned by the dot-com bubble go through this transformation. They decided that since they lost money, no one else could make money either. These embittered souls go in one of two directions. They either stop trying to outperform the market by buying index funds, or they abandon the market for good. The latter group swear off stocks entirely because they're too risky, or the game is rigged, or the market's impossible to understand, or every stock that ever goes up is just part of another bubble that will eventually burst and cause tremendous heartbreak, so why bother at all? Many people have gone in that direction. No matter what their argument against owning stocks in general might be, their objection is always based on the same idea: I lost money in the market, and if *I* lost money, how could anyone else ever make money? You can tell this concept has won out in the fast scheme of things because of the huge decline in self-directed trading and investing and an amazingly large and ever-expanding bulge of money fund assets—sidelined cash that, as I write, stands at more than $4 trillion dollars. That's unconscionable, but it is the legacy of the burn-and-bust moment at the turn of the century. Then there's the index fund crowd that still believes in owning stocks, but not picking them. Their attitude is just another example of sour grapes (I hear Aesop was the Warren Buffett of his day). You can still read columns by people who think something like this: Only a tiny minority of mutual funds consistently beat the indexes, and if the pros can't do it, it's no wonder I screwed up, so you'll screw up too! These types know that stocks are winners, but don't believe anyone can consistently tell good stocks from bad, so they give up and smugly buy an index fund. Then they act like those of us who pick stocks are dopes for even trying. They can call us dopes all the way to the bank.

These are all people who leaped to get in near the top of the market in 1999 and 2000 and quickly got burned out of the market in 2000, 2001, and 2002. If you sign up for incredible, almost magic gains, which is exactly what most people thought they were signing up for back in 1999, and instead you get one heartbreaking loss after another, you'll probably feel like somebody gave you a false bill of goods. You'll feel cheated. You'll want to accuse the whole world, or everyone who was encouraging people to get in on the stock market action, of committing fraud. Of course, that is generalizing from a few years of intense personal experience. Sure, the market was down in 2000, 2001, and 2002, but it was up over 20 percent a year from 1995 through 1999, so if you take a long-term perspective, you can see that even though it was terrible to be a regular-guy investor from 2000 to 2002, that fact really doesn't say a lot about the performance of stocks, or your ability to pick winners.

I've always been a champion of owning stocks and managing your own portfolio. Although people claim that it's impossible to consistently outperform the market, making more money year after year than you would make if you simply invested in an S&P 500 index fund, I think that's baloney. I'm living proof that it's possible. We thrashed the S&P at my hedge fund, and if you'd been one of our clients, your investment would have compounded at 24 percent annually after fees, assuming you'd been with me the whole time. From 1987, when I started the fund, to 2001, when I retired, the S&P 500 gained an average of 16.1 percent per year. That's sustained, consistent outperformance. It's possible because it happened. The same people who tell you to just give up and buy an index fund, which I'll talk more about later in this chapter, will say that in any given year 80 percent to 90 percent of actively managed mutual funds underperform the S&P 500. Because these funds are run by professionals, how can you, an individual who invests on the side, possibly do better than the pros, who are paid fortunes and have years of experience? That's more garbage. If you do all the necessary homework, which I've explained in great detail in my two previous books, you can pick your own stocks and run your own money well enough to do better than the pros who run most mutual funds. I don't recommend that everyone do this, but don't let anyone tell you it isn't possible.

Of course, mutual funds can only rarely beat the benchmarks. A mutual fund, if it's good, will be managing a lot of money, and the more money you have under management, the harder it is to beat the market. First of all, once a mutual fund gets big enough, every time it buys or sells a stock it ends up moving the stock because the fund needs to buy an enormous amount of shares to make any difference in its portfolio. When you buy a ton of stock—I'm talking multimillion-dollar positions here—you dramatically increase the demand for that stock and prices go higher. Selling an enormous position increases the supply, and that drives down prices. So mutual funds are anything but nimble. You, on the other hand, won't cause a splash, at least as long as you use only limit orders and not market orders to buy.

When you tell your broker, electronic or human, to buy or sell a stock, you're placing a market order. You're also giving your broker a license to rip you off, for he now has permission to get you a bad price, and that's exactly what will happen almost every time. You need to understand that your broker isn't there to look out for your best interests. He's there to generate commissions. So whenever you buy or sell a stock, place a limit order—it's the easiest thing in the world and doesn't cost you a penny more. You just tell your broker the price you're willing to pay if you're buying, and the price you're willing to take if you're selling. It's that simple. If you don't place a limit order, expect to be confused and angry, because you're paying more than you expected, or selling for less. With a limit order, sometimes you won't be able to get your stock, but you'll never buy for more or sell for less than you wanted.

The other problem mutual funds have that individual investors don't is that when they have a really successful year, they'll get a lot of new people flooding them with money. So any fund that's really good will be hobbled unless it closes itself off to new investments, and the companies that run mutual funds hate that because they make their money by charging investors fees as a percentage of their invested assets. More assets means more profits for the mutual fund. Once a mutual fund gets really enormous, it becomes more and more like an index fund with high fees. This is what happened to Fidelity's Magellan fund, which Peter Lynch used to manage. Magellan was one of the few mutual funds that consistently beat the market by really large margins, but too many people invested too much money in it, and ever since then it's had trouble beating the market (although the latest manager has finally had some better-than-market performance). You are not a mutual fund and you should not aspire to be one with twenty or thirty stocks under your own management. There's no way you're going to end up investing billions of dollars (and if you do, that's a high-quality problem to have), but if you actively manage your own money, you can beat the market with a handful of stocks you pick and follow, and take gains when *you* think the time is right. Even hedge fund managers are constricted by assets. I think that if I were allowed to start a fund to actively manage only my own money, I'd do better than I had when I was running my hedge fund, because I wouldn't have to worry about producing short-term results, meaning daily results, to keep my clients happy.

If anything, an individual investor managing his or her own money has a leg up on the mutual funds. So don't let anyone tell you that you can't beat the market by picking your own stocks. That said, you shouldn't try to do this unless you are ready to put in the time and work necessary to win at stocks. My standing rule is that in order to do well, you absolutely must spend at least one hour a week doing homework on each stock you own, in addition to doing a lot of re-search before you buy. That research includes actually listening to the company's conference calls, reading its quarterly and annual reports, and familiarizing yourself with the market's current attitude toward the stock, which you can do by reading articles about it, looking at its recent performance, and looking at the performance of companies in the same business. I also believe that you have to tap Google fairly regularly to read any articles about the stock around the nation and the globe. This is a time-consuming process, but you can do all of this online. You shouldn't try to own more than ten stocks because any more than that and you practically have a second job keeping on top of them.

I need to be very clear about this, because even though I repeat these rules practically every night on my TV show, people still don't listen. So I'm going to give you a better explanation of them, with more of a "glass half-empty" perspective. If you try to manage your own money and invest in your own stocks, and you don't listen to the conference calls or you don't read the quarterly reports or you don't do every single piece of homework necessary, you will not do well. You won't beat the market, and you'll probably lose money. I can't make it any clearer than that. People really hate listening to the con-ference calls and reading the company's filings with the SEC, the an-nual 10-k filings and the quarterly 10-q filings because this is the most time-consuming part of your homework. It's also the most important part. You cannot cut corners. Be honest with yourself: if you don't have the time or the inclination to do this work, then I'm begging you, please don't try to invest in individual stocks. I'll tell you all about other investments that can still make you money, but owning stocks without homework just isn't on the table.

When investing for a lifetime, you need some kind of exposure to stocks for your entire life. If you don't have the time to manage your own stocks, there's no shame in going with a mutual fund or an index fund to get your stock exposure. No matter which way you go, stocks are key. High-quality, dividend-paying stocks are the single best investment over any twenty-year period, and that makes them an essential part of both your retirement portfolio and your discretionary portfolio. If you're under 30, there's not much reason for you to own anything but stocks across the board, whether we're talking about retirement or discretionary capital. The line on stocks is that they're more risky than bonds, but they also produce higher returns. That's true, but I don't think the risk should be overstated. Too many people are too conservative with their investments, believing that they're being prudent when in fact they're being quite reckless. Investing in stocks over a long period of time pays off, even if you do nothing more than put money in a simple S&P 500 index fund. That might be risky from year to year, but over the long term—and this book is all about the long term—it's a great decision. Consider this: if you invested everything in the market on the Friday before Black Monday, the big crash on October 19, 1987, you got in when the Dow Jones Industrial Average, which is often used as a proxy for the market, was at 2,500. You'd have felt like a fool a year later because you bought at the absolute worst time to buy. (Interestingly, if you had bought just the ten most active large-cap stocks that very worst day, you would be in the black a year later on most of them.) But let's take the long-term perspective, the right one. By the summer of 1997, the Dow had leapt more than 5,000 points. That's a lot of performance to miss. And by the summer of 2007, the Dow hit 14,000. In less than twenty years the market went up 460 percent, and that's if you got in at the worst possible moment. Believe me, you're not being prudent if you avoid stocks; you're passing up a truly incredible opportunity to make money, because you fear short-term losses. Don't let the potential for downside tomorrow stand in the way of enormous upside in the years ahead.

Although everyone should own stocks, not everyone should own the same number of stocks or the same kinds of stocks. In the previous chapter I gave you a guide to the mix of stocks and bonds you should have in your retirement portfolio as you get older. Here are those numbers again:

AGE	PERCENTAGE IN STOCKS	PERCENTAGE IN BONDS
Under 30	100	0
30–40	80–90	10–20
40–50	70–80	20–30
50–60	60–70	30–40
60–Retirement	50–60	40–50
Retirement	30–40	60–70

My advice is more aggressive than the conventional wisdom, which holds that you should pare down your exposure to stocks and build up your exposure to bonds faster, and that you should own no stocks when you retire. This is another case where the standard advice sounds and feels more responsible than it actually is. If you start with the idea that stocks are inherently more risky and less reliable, then you approach them as a necessary evil. They're not. People think they're being prudent if they cut out stocks, because stocks are risky, and who wants to rely on a risky asset to fund their retirement?

That whole perspective is wrong. Yes, stocks carry more risk than bonds. They also have much more upside. What's more risky: continuing to own stocks as you get older, or not having enough money to retire? For most people, not owning enough stocks means not making enough money. Yes, there's some risk, but as I've said before, if you're properly diversified—which you are in a good mutual fund or the right kind of index fund—over time the risk of owning stocks declines. On the other hand, the risk of not owning them stays the same.

It's true that as you grow older, capital preservation—making sure you don't lose money—is more important than capital appreciation. But that doesn't mean you can ignore capital appreciation. If you don't grow your capital, what's the point of having it? If you have $100,000, and you decide you're going to take it out of stocks and put everything into bonds, let me explain what you're sacrificing for a sense of stability. After ten years, if your bonds end up compounding at 5 percent (they can compound because you can reinvest the coupon payments into more bonds), you're looking at $162,889.46. If you kept all that money in stocks for the same ten years, and they compounded at 10 percent annually, which I'll remind you is worse than the S&P 500 has done on average per year over the past thirty years, you would have $259,374.25. You'd make $96,484.79 more in stocks. That's huge. That extra $96,484.79 could be the difference between being able to afford a home and being a renter. Of course, your bond returns are almost guaranteed, whereas with stocks you're taking a chance. That's why I agree that you need to decrease your stock exposure as you get older, and this goes for your discretionary portfolio as well as your retirement portfolio (for your discretionary funds, go with the higher-end percentage of stocks in the chart, so when you're in your 30s, your portfolio should be 90 percent stocks). But your capital needs an engine to grow, and that engine is stocks.

Of course, not all stocks are created equal. Again, I don't want to spend too much time focusing on stocks in this book because we've been there before, but there's some stuff that absolutely must be covered here. There are different kinds of stocks. You can classify them as growth and value stocks, but here I want to look at what I'll call speculative and high-quality stocks. These two types don't cover the entirety of the market, not by a long shot, but they're the stocks that are most sensitive to your age. Later on in the book, I have a great list of high-quality stocks that I believe will work for years to come, but of course, if the reasons I give for liking the stocks change, then those stocks will no longer be any good. That's why we do homework. You can define speculative stocks as the ones with the greatest amount of risk, and also the most upside potential. That's a true definition, but it's also a terrible one because it doesn't help you spot them. Usually a speculative stock will have several characteristics. First, its *price*, the actual dollar amount you pay for one share of the company, is under $10. Remember, no company deliberately sets out to price a stock this low. When a company issues a stock, the underwriter, who sets the price, rarely wants it to be below $19 for fear that it will look speculative. Second, speculative stocks are *small*, meaning their market capitalization (a way to measure the total value of the company, taking the price per share and multiplying it by the number of shares, giving you a picture of how the market values the company) is low, usually under $2 billion. Third, they are either not making a *profit* now or they may have been making a profit at one time and are no longer doing so. Fourth, when you buy a speculative stock, you should do so knowing there is some *catalyst* ahead, something—a bit of news, some company-shaking event—that could send the stock much higher or lower, depending on how it turns out. (The best example of this is a small biotech stock waiting for FDA approval on a new drug. If the drug is approved, the stock soars; if it's rejected, the stock tanks.) I believe that everyone who owns individual stocks should speculate, but with less and less money as they get older. Stocks are the only truly fun investments, and speculative stocks are by far the most enjoyable, which is why everyone wants to own them.

Speculative stocks are great for the really young, especially college students and recent graduates, who have decades to win back anything they lose while speculating. My rule of thumb has always been that no one should speculate with more than 20 percent of his or her discretionary portfolio. But that number changes with age. People in their early 20s can get away with putting as much as half of their discretionary funds into speculative stocks. (I think it's a bad idea to speculate in your retirement account, which shouldn't hold investments that are this risky.) But if you're in your 50s, as I am, you shouldn't speculate with any money you cannot afford to lose. And unless you're rich, you can't afford to lose any of your money. While it's critical to speculate in your youth, because the gains can be truly enormous, that window starts to close in your late 20s. You should speculate less as you get older, with no more than 20 percent of your nonretirement capital in speculative stocks in your 30s and early 40s, and then scale down the size of your speculative investments after that.

Then there are high-quality stocks. You should always own some high-quality stocks, no matter your age, but as you get older you might want to make them a larger and larger part of your portfolio. I consider a stock high-quality if it has a significant buyback (this is when companies use their money to buy up their own stock and take it off the market; a buyback reduces the number of shares, and since a company's earnings per share are the single most important thing to look at when valuing a stock, buybacks should make your shares more valuable); a moderate to large dividend (a dividend is money a company pays out every quarter to its shareholders) that has a history of increasing frequently; and a low price-to-earnings ratio relative to its growth (the P/E, or multiple, is the true price of a stock; it's simply the stock's price per share divided by its earnings per share). On my show I always use the example of Procter & Gamble. Here's a stock with a gigantic buyback that has among the best records of increasing its dividend every year in the S&P 500. It is as close to a "blue-chip" as is possible, though I always rebel at that term because it lulls you into a sense of security that is reckless when it comes to any piece of paper. (If P&G were to report a series of bad years, it could quickly lose its blue-chip status, and you would be advised to make changes.) If a stock has these three characteristics, it's a high-quality stock. That doesn't mean it's a stock for all seasons. You could have a high-quality automaker, but if the market for cars is bad, the stock will be bad too. General Motors, for example, has raised and cut its dividend so many times that it's been a virtual yo-yo when it comes to yield. However, high-quality stocks tend to have less risk without sacrificing the ability to go much higher. That's why I favor them, especially for older investors.

The buyback means that the company is buying, and that puts a cushion under the stock during bad days when the market's going down and few investors want to buy. Many companies have buybacks, but I don't consider a buyback good unless it's shrinking the float (all the shares that trade on the open market) by roughly 5 percent. I don't want you to think that a buyback creates such a level of security that you can ignore your holding. A company is allowed to buy back only a certain amount of stock as a percentage of the volume each day, and it can't buy stock at the closing bell because it will be accused of manipulating the stock's closing price. I find a buyback gives you a soft floor, and no more. Lots of times buybacks aren't active enough for my tastes. That's why I can't wait to see the quarterly report of a stock I own that has a buyback. I like to see how many shares it bought and at what price. If you have a stock that has a buyback, but that information is not enclosed in the quarterly report, that buyback is probably not active enough to put down anything but a floor full of holes.

The dividend creates what's called "yield support." If a $100 stock pays out an annual dividend of $2 per share, its dividend yield, which is simply the dividend payment divided by the price per share, is 2 percent. As a stock's price falls, its yield increases. So if that $100 stock fell to $80, its dividend yield would rise to 2.5 percent. And as the yield rises, the stock becomes more attractive to other investors, slowing and eventually halting its decline. I would like to see a yield of at least 2 percent on a high-quality stock, but a little lower than that is fine. High-quality stocks often don't seem to have a high yield, but again, we return to the example of Procter & Gamble, which has a yield that seems small—but that's because of the stock's price appreciation. Often a good yielder does better than the stock market, but when you add in the dividend and you reinvest the dividend, the record's much, much better than the market.

Finally, we want a stock with a low P/E. When I say low, I mean low relative to stocks with similar growth rates. The growth is just the increase in earnings from one year to the next, and it's of critical importance when you value a stock. So if a stock has a price-to-earnings multiple of 20 (a P/E of 20) and a growth rate of 15 percent, but other companies with that growth rate have multiples close to 25, you can say that your stock has a low P/E.

A stock with all three of these traits deserves to be called high quality, and makes for a safer, smarter investment as you get older. Remember, Wall Street is just an oddsmaker. When you have stocks with all three characteristics, I believe you are likely to beat the odds, meaning outperform the averages. Not a sure thing, but certainly something that helped me beat the market for years and years at a time.

Back to Bonds

Now let's go back to bonds. The big problem with everything but stocks is that they're no fun whatsoever. I like to make investing as fun as possible, but even I have to face the inevitably boring task of choosing and describing bonds. There are many different types of bonds, and I'll tell you about all of them. Bonds are tedious, but they're absolutely necessary for building long-term wealth. Let me give you the pecking order, from best to worst, and then explain what you should do with them.

Treasurys are at the top of the pile. These are issued by the full faith and credit of the U.S. government, making them, for all intents and purposes, risk-free. There are three different kinds of Treasurys. Treasury bills mature in a year or less, which makes them the least risky, or the most risk-free bonds you can buy. Instead of paying a coupon (remember, that's the interest), T-bills, as they are known on the Street, sell at a discount, so that a T-bill that costs you $98 will pay you $100 when it reaches maturity in six months. Treasury notes, or T-notes, mature in two to ten years, and they'll pay out their coupon every six months. Treasury bonds (T-bonds), or the long bond, as they are known, mature in ten to thirty years and also have coupon payments every six months. All of these Treasurys are sold by the government but also trade on the secondary market. When we speak of bonds, as in "The bond market did well today," we are speaking of the ten-year Treasury. Typically we are also speaking of the most current bond, the last one issued, which is called the "on the run" Treasury. If you were to buy a ten-year note, that is the one you would be buying.

After Treasurys there are *agency bonds*, which are issued by government-sponsored agencies like Freddie Mac, Fannie Mae, and Ginnie Mae. You probably won't come near this stuff except in a bond fund, but for the interest of thoroughness I'll explain them anyway. Fannie Mae and Freddie Mae are both publicly traded companies that were created by the federal government and still get huge benefits from being affiliated with the Feds, such as not having to pay state and local taxes and being allowed to borrow money at special low rates. Ginnie Mae is actually a part of the Department of Housing and Urban Development. There are other agency bonds, but these are by far the most common. They tend to generate better returns than Treasurys and are only slightly more risky because they have the implied insurance of the government entities themselves.

Then there are *corporate bonds*, which individual investors also probably won't be buying any time soon. These also come in different forms. When a corporation issues first mortgage bonds, those are secured against its property, usually real estate and also machinery, and if the company goes under, these bondholders get first dibs after the U.S. government gets its tax take. You will most likely end up whole if you own these bonds, because bond holders have a call on the assets remaining that are sold in bankruptcy. Next in the pecking order of corporate bonds you'll probably never own unless you're a pro are *unsecured bonds*, which can be senior or junior. The junior bondholders have subordinated debt, meaning that if the issuer can't pay, they have to wait until the senior bondholders are paid off before they get paid off. Companies will also issue *convertible bonds*, or converts, which have lower yields but allow you to convert your bond into a fixed number of shares in the company. These offer some upside, because if the stock goes up after the bond is issued, you can convert the bond into stock and make a quick profit. Similar to convertible bonds are *preferred stocks*, which you can think of as a kind of cross between a stock and a bond. Preferreds, as they're called, are basically special shares of stock that pay much higher dividends than common stock. These aren't bad investments, because they have great yields, and if the stock tanks, you can hold the preferred stock until its maturity date and get back the initial amount you invested. There are also *convertible preferreds* that let you convert your preferred shares into a fixed amount of common stock, so once again you get upside when you convert to the common stock (as long as it has gone up since the convertible preferred was issued). You have to watch for opportunities when companies issue these kinds of pieces of paper. For example, Ford Motor Company recently cut the common stock dividend and soon after that issued a convertible preferred with a nice yield, much better than the yield on Treasurys. Yet, judging by the people who call me on *Mad Money* and want me to opine on Ford, few know that this is a much better piece of paper than Ford common stock because it converts into Ford common at only a few dollars above where the stock was then trading.

Now I know this stuff bores you to sleep, but it's important to know what all of these bonds are just in case you end up in a situation where it really matters. What kind of situation? We had one in the summer of 2007. That was a good time to know about *structured bonds*, which are bonds that are created—packaged really—with the backing of assets; usually they're backed with mortgages or auto loans. The mortgage-backed bonds blew up, and that led to a credit crisis. Who would have thought that such a little, obscure thing would put hedge fund after hedge fund out of business? But they did. Many hedge funds thought these kinds of structured products, meaning bonds that are literally crafted of lots of mortgages from around the country, some prime and some subprime, backed by mortgage holders of dubious quality with dubious credit, were so secure that they borrowed billions of dollars from brokerages to buy these bonds and pocket the interest differential between the broker loans and the mortgage-backed paper. When the price of housing collapsed and the mortgage holders began walking away from their homes, this kind of paper proved to be worth a lot less than the hedge fund managers thought. When the investors in these hedge funds recognized the problem, they tried to withdraw their funds with these managers. That led to the managers trying to sell the structured product, which typically had no buyers and even no market entirely, so they had to virtually give away the bonds. After the managers had paid off the brokers who loaned them the money, there was often little or nothing left for the clients themselves. That's how the credit crunch spiraled and why the Federal Reserve had to get involved, if only so the borrowers underneath these securities could attempt to refinance their houses and stop defaulting. If at the very least you'd known about the existence of structured products, you would have been better prepared for the damage this problem did to the market. Always check to see if any manager you are with owns this kind of paper. Simply look at the prospectus or ask the customer service rep; they know what the paper is and they have to tell you whether the fund owns it. What is most outrageous about this stuff, by the way, is that the pricing was left to the manager, so the manager typically valued the bonds at the price they were purchased, not the dramatically reduced price that they really traded at. If you are with a hedge fund manager, ask for a valuation independent of the one the manager would give. If he or she won't give you one, take your money out now!

You probably know about *certificates of deposit*, or CDs, which banks issue. CDs are not bonds, but they are very similar from the perspective of a regular investor. It's really easy to get one from your bank, but they're typically not as good as Treasury bonds, and they can have heavy penalties if you take your money out early. That penalty is not worth the slightly higher yield over Treasurys. There are also *money market funds*, which are an agglomeration of short-term paper that allow you to get a cashlike return on your money. These are extremely popular because they are priced at a dollar and can be redeemed instantly. They are what we call "cash" when we speak of their asset class, something that has mystified many of my viewers when I use the term.

Finally, you've probably heard of *municipal bonds*, which are issued by state and local governments. The earnings from these bonds are tax-free, so their yields are also pretty low. Keep municipal bonds out of your 401(k) and IRA, because they are already tax-advantaged. In an IRA, municipal bonds are simply low-yielding bonds with nothing special going for them. Municipal bonds are great if you're already rich, because the rich are taxed at higher rates and thus get a better break on tax-free income. Short-term municipal bonds, or munis, are practically like cash, and the longer term ones can be structured by brokers. Because I'm rich—okay, I said it—and because I am not allowed to own individual stocks because of the obvious conflicts of owning stocks and hosting a stock show that moves stocks, I'm in the New Jersey Vanguard Admiral Fund (Vanguard's funds are the best) for short-term municipal bonds. I can actually write checks against that account, and your ultimate goal should be to join me in that no-brain-required, little-risk fund, where the returns are solid and you can access your money at your leisure. I like this fund in particular because it has extremely low fees, something that, again, matters all the time but particularly when you are dealing with bonds, because they don't make you much money and fees depress their limited returns.

That's really what it all comes down to with bonds. All this stuff is incredibly eye-glazing, and if you're still awake, I congratulate you because there's nothing more boring and tedious than bonds. You can buy them yourself; just set up an online brokerage account. Or if you want to save money, you can set up an online account with Treasury Direct to buy Treasurys directly from the government for a much lower brokerage fee. You can call or mail Treasury Direct too. It's not solely online, but that's become the best way to buy them: www .treasurydirect.gov.

But why, after reading all of this, would you ever want to buy bonds directly? The best way to get your bond exposure is to buy into a bond fund rather than investing in individual bonds, provided, again, that the fees are extremely low, meaning a small fraction of a single percentage point. Since you're buying bonds in order to buy stability as you get older, I recommend you go for a fund that buys Treasurys, because it's simply not worth the extra hassle and worry trying to pick up most of these higher-yielding but less secure bonds. Investing in stocks can and should be engaging, interesting, and fun. Investing in bonds is something that will always be necessary and boring. Outsource your bond-buying to a bond index fund and stop worrying about it.

Mutual Funds

For those of you who don't have the time or the desire to invest in individual stocks and don't want a bond fund, you've got a lot of options, but few are good. There are thousands of mutual funds out there. In fact, there are more mutual funds in the United States than there are stocks listed on the New York Stock Exchange and the NASDAQ put together. If this fact seems ridiculous to you, that's be-cause it is. We have a voracious appetite for people who claim they can make us money, or at the very least claim that they'll worry about the money for us. For every person who desperately wants to be a day trader, there are easily another dozen people who want to know the best mutual fund they can invest in. And that makes the mutual fund business a really terrific one. Throw in the fact that money we invest in our 401(k) plans has to flow into mutual funds almost by default, and the companies that run and sell mutual funds are making fortunes. (What are your options in a 401(k) plan? Remember, it's usually company stock or mutual funds, and you know you should never own company stock.)

I'll put all of my cards on the table. You know I'm a stock junkie, and you know that investing in individual stocks is the best way to go. But you've also been told repeatedly that if you can't or won't do every last piece of your stock homework, you'll end up making a big dent in your capital. This is a situation where the best is the enemy of the good, and I wouldn't be quoting Voltaire unless the phrase really summed up the situation. You want to invest in stocks to earn great returns, but since few people really want to listen to conference calls and read quarterly reports, what usually happens is that you end up owning a stock, not doing all of your homework, and then sooner or later you start getting confused and begin hemorrhaging money. And then after you lose a bundle investing in stocks without the right kind of education, without the right kind of homework, and without a clue as to what's going on, you decide that it's impossible to make money in the stock market. Instead of going through this excruciating process, why not honestly figure out whether or not you actually have the time and inclination to manage your own portfolio. For most people the answer is no, and that's fine. You won't take the best path to wealth, you'll take the good one.

Before I tell you what I'd do, let me tell you what's out there, because a lot of it is trash, and you need to know how to avoid it. When I said there were more mutual funds in this country than there are stocks on the NYSE and the NASDAQ put together, that was slightly misleading because the term "mutual fund" includes more than just the funds that invest in stocks. Typically a mutual fund will invest in stocks, bonds, and even cash if it's a money market fund. There are mutual funds that invest only in equities (stocks); there are funds that invest only in bonds. But since you know how many different types of bonds there are, you also know that's meaningless information. These days there are even mutual funds that invest only in other mutual funds, called "asset allocation funds," and I consider that highway robbery, pure and simple. One big downside to all mutual funds, and this is as true of actively managed funds as it is of ETFs (exchange-traded funds) or index funds, is that they all charge fees. The fees vary from fund to fund, and in fact there's an enormous amount of creativity in how they come up with ways to gouge you, but the one constant is that there are always fees. Fees don't just eat into your profits—that would be one thing—they eat into your assets. That's how mutual funds do it. When you invest in a mutual fund, you'll pay out some percentage, called the "expense ratio," of your assets, no matter what. It doesn't matter if the fund loses you money. You're still paying those fees.

I have absolutely no right whatsoever to complain about high mutual fund fees, but it's the one thing every fund has in common. Hedge funds, by contrast, are meant to make you money in good and bad times; they short common stocks in bad times to profit from the declines. Because of their ability to go both ways and the promise of a steady return no matter what the market does, the fee structure is much different and higher. At my hedge fund our fee structure was simple: we took 2 percent of your assets every year and claimed 20 percent of the profits. Those are much higher fees than you'll find from most mutual funds, but I was running a hedge fund and, not to brag, it was a great hedge fund. My clients compounded their investments at 24 percent annually *after fees*. Not many mutual funds can sustain that kind of performance for over a decade, as I did. But this is practically a moot point: there are regulations governing who is allowed to invest in hedge funds, so all you need to know now is that unless you're an accredited investor, you're legally prohibited, with some exceptions, from investing in a hedge fund. To become an accredited investor you need either a net worth of over $5 million or you need to have earned $200,000 or more last year, and $200,000 or more the year before, along with having a reasonable expectation of earning $200,000 again this year. If you've got the money, you want to find a hedge fund with a great manager. What defines a great manager and what defines a hedge fund worth investing in? (1) The manager has to have a great long-term record of beating the market *and* making money even if the market goes down. (2) The fund should make you money after all fees are taken out of the equation. (3) The manager should invest most of his or her money alongside you. (4) The manager will tell you what you are invested in and whether prices of the merchandise are all readily available online. (5) The manager respects that it is *your* money, not his or hers. Some people like to invest in hedge funds through what is known as "funds of funds," where people select the funds for you. My feeling is that hedge fund managers are like stocks: you have to pay attention to them and you should not trust anyone else to do so. Plus, the funds of funds I have seen can take up to 2 percent to do this placing and following of your monies. You can save money and do much better watching these funds yourself. I would like to focus more on hedge funds in this book, given my extensive knowledge of the industry, but since most people don't have the money—and hey, if you've got 5 million smackers already, you can afford to wait—I'd rather tell you about funds that most regular people can actually invest in.

You can invest in mutual funds, but again I have to stress that you need to be very picky when choosing a fund. And you have to understand that being a good mutual fund investor does not mean investing in a fund and letting your money sit there for decades. You have to find a good manager and keep track of him or her. Actively managed funds make or break themselves based on the quality of their managers. If you get into a fund because it has a good manager and the manager leaves, it's time for you to get out too. Despite the labeling, there is no such thing as a "team-managed" fund. There is always a captain, and if the captain leaves you should leave too.

I could have started with all the different ways mutual funds classify themselves based on the assets they invest in and how they invest, but I want to hit the one thing all funds have in common before I break them down into their categories. In terms of fees, a lot of mutual funds get you not just coming and going; they get you coming, staying, and then going. When you invest in a mutual fund, you're giving up a lot of control over your assets. That's fine, because you've recognized that you don't have the time or the inclination to manage your own money. But because you're giving up so much control, you need to exercise the best judgment possible with the elements of mutual fund investing that are within your control, and picking out funds with lower fees is totally within your control.

There are several different fees a fund might charge you, and you can see some of them when you look at the fund's expense ratio. That's the percentage of your assets that you owe the fund for keeping your assets with them for one year. These can vary from minuscule fees in ETFs and more traditional index funds, to enormous fees for actively managed mutual funds. A fund has administrative costs; it has management costs, especially if it's an actively managed fund; but it also has distribution and marketing costs, and you pay for these through 12b-1 fees. Nothing offends my sense of fair play more than these 12b-1 fees. Remember, as funds are given more assets to invest, their performance generally declines. Funds can use money from these fees to market themselves, and even more ridiculously, they can use the money to compensate brokers for directing their clients to the fund. How corrupt and awful is that? This is why I'm always saying you cannot trust your broker. The worst thing is that you could be paying up to 1 percent of what you put into the fund every year, and the fund can spend three-quarters of that money on marketing and distributing. You are paying your mutual fund to make itself larger and thus hurt its own performance: you're paying them, with these 12b-1 fees, to make you *less* money.

It's preposterous, I know, but size-wise those fees are far from the worst. Many mutual funds also have what are called "front-end loads" and "back-end loads." These are fees that can be enormous and are paid either when you invest in the fund (front loads) or pull your money out (back loads). This is money that goes to your broker or, less frequently, the mutual fund, and it could be as much as 5 percent of your investment, which is a mighty big bite. Not every fund has loads—in fact, most don't these days—which is why you want to steer clear of any "loaded funds," as they're called, unless they have some incredible genius fund manager with a record of consistent outperformance that's impressive enough to negate the big hit you're taking by paying a load. Also, most mutual funds are divided into three different classes: A, C, and institutional. The actual investments for each class are the same, because they're part of the same fund, but the fee structures are different. One might have no loads but a higher expense ratio; one might have a huge back-end load but a lower expense ratio. Institutional investors typically pay much lower fees, but they're forced to deposit much larger sums of money to get their special, low-fee status. Remember, never select a fund without analyzing its *after-fee* returns, because the before-fee returns might look huge, but after fees, the return could be below the market's performance. If you own this mutual fund through your company's 401(k) plan, maybe enough of your coworkers participate, or enough of the planner's other participant plans want to buy into this fund, so they can pool their resources and then pay much, much lower fees—this happens all the time with anything even vaguely pension-related. Most funds with high fees aren't worth it, but that's probably simply because most funds aren't worth it. You get the idea. You can afford to shop around, especially with the list of great mutual funds I'm giving you in a later chapter. All of these fees and the different tiers of funds should be wiped out or regulated much more aggressively by the federal government, but the mutual fund industry is very powerful and has stopped repeated attempts to do anything but force fine-print disclosures of these fees. You have to work hard to find the true numbers, because most of the fees are high to get brokers to steer you into the funds regardless of the performance. This is why the industry has such a bad name, but nobody's doing much about it to protect you, so you have to protect yourself.

Enough about fees. On the most important level, there are just two different types of mutual funds. They have been categorized in so many different ways by so many people and institutions that it's sometimes hard to keep track of them. What is a large value fund or a medium blend—isn't that something you get at Starbucks? I'd like a medium blend with a front load and some international flavor, please. Anyway, the distinction I'm talking about is between actively managed funds and passively managed, or index funds. In an index fund there's some set benchmark, maybe the S&P 500 or the Wilshire 5000 Total Market Index, but it could be any index, and the job of the fund is simply to match the index by owning all of the stocks in the index and weighting each stock the way the index does. The job of an index fund manager is simply to make sure the fund matches the index. These funds are universally cheaper than actively managed funds, and any index fund will consistently beat the vast majority of mutual funds, if only because the fees are so much lower. With very few exceptions, I'm a strong advocate of owning index funds. I think John Bogle, the man who created the first modern index fund and opened up indexing to nonprofessionals, is both a genius and, from what I saw when I brought him on my old TV show *Kudlow & Cramer*, a really good guy. Even if Bogle were a jerk, he'd still be right about index funds. If you really cannot or will not spare the time and energy to research your own stocks, index funds are a great way for you to get exposure to pretty much everything you need. As long as you own a solid, diversified index, like the S&P 500, you'll do almost as well as you would have done on your own. Perhaps you'll do even better in an index fund than you expected to do while managing your own money. Bogle is adamant that most actively managed funds can't beat index funds over the long term, because in the end they will look and act too much like index funds but charge higher fees. I remember being upset with him about this and confronting him directly: didn't I disprove his whole thesis by consistently outperforming the averages? Bogle stopped me cold by asking me one simple question: "Did you restrict the number of investors in your fund and the amount they could invest?" I said, "Certainly." He said, "There's your answer. If you opened up your fund to everyone who wanted in, you too would underperform." He was dead right.

In any case, index funds are terrific. But now we need to look at yet another level of how funds are organized. You could buy an old-fashioned index fund from a great, low-fee company like Vanguard, or you could buy an exchange-traded fund that represents the same exact investment. On average, ETFs will be slightly less costly than old-fashioned index funds, but we're talking about 1 basis point or 2 lower, a small fraction of 1 percent, and over time, though it might add up, it won't add up to much. So what exactly sets an ETF apart from a traditional mutual fund, or even another recent development, what are called "closed-end funds"? From the name, you probably understand that ETFs are listed on a stock market; for example, in this country most are on the American Stock Exchange, the AMEX. But that doesn't get to the heart of the matter.

A regular open-end mutual fund does not trade on the open markets. At the end of every trading day, it uses the closing price of its assets to determine the price of one "share" in the mutual fund. If you want to invest in the fund, you can contribute money at that price, known as the net asset value, and if you want to withdraw money from the account you can go to the fund and ask for your investment back. It's very simple: you bought a certain number of shares in the fund at some point, and the value of those shares was based on the net asset value of the stocks or whatever your fund owns. When you withdraw your money you pull out the same number of shares, but because the value of the assets in the fund has changed, so will the value of your shares. Open-end funds are constantly creating and retiring shares, but that has no effect on the value of your investment with the fund—it's not as though these are actual shares of stock or anything remotely like that. Every new piece of money invested in an open-end fund just goes into the same assets everyone else is invested in and doesn't dilute the yield your mutual fund pays you, or your upside, except in the sense that it's harder to manage larger amounts of money.

Closed-end funds and ETFs are very different. With a closed-end fund, the guys running the fund will sell huge blocks of its shares as it starts up, use the money to buy whatever assets they intended to buy, and then stop selling shares. The funds rely on the brokers who buy their massive chunks of shares to sell them in the secondary market to regular investors. So shares of a closed-end fund can be traded during the day because they're listed on an exchange, and these funds are essentially closed to new investment, which in my opinion is terrific for investors because, as I've said, running more money will always hurt even a great manager's performance. Closed-end funds tend to have lower fees too, because the funds don't have to spend any real time issuing shares or dealing with investors. If everyone wants to bail on a closed-end fund, then the price of the shares will trade at a big discount to the fund's net asset value. In fact, shares of closed-end funds always trade at a premium or a discount to their net asset value, except when the funds end and cash out of their investments, redistributing the net asset value to their investors. Usually, the shares of these funds will head back toward their net asset value, so you can catch a great opportunity to buy into a closed-end fund at a large discount should the price go significantly lower than the net asset value, which happens frequently.

An ETF is very similar to a closed-end fund, but with one very important difference: ETFs issue new shares and retire old ones priced at the net asset value per share, but only in huge blocks. That guarantee, even if it's something only big institutional investors can take advantage of, makes a huge difference for the ETF, because it keeps the ETF valued the same way as whatever benchmark it's following. That's another point about ETFs: they're almost always index funds. I know that ETFs are the flavor of the month right now, but as long as you buy an ETF that represents a diversified index (the S&P 500 comes to mind) it's actually a great deal because the fees are so incredibly low, and because it's so easy to get in and out of an ETF. Lately, ETFs have become more specialized as they've popped up all over the place. My attitude about that is the same as my attitude toward any of the "specialty" mutual funds that focus on only a single sector: there's no reason for anyone to own these. The banks love to create new ETFs because they're new products and bring more new fees. Many of them are totally useless to individual investors. Do you really want an ETF that tracks the price of pig bellies? When mutual funds first started to become very popular, all the asset management companies, banks, and brokers started issuing as many mutual funds as they could get away with. The same thing is happening now with ETFs, so what we see are a lot of hyperspecialized funds. There are country-specific ETFs, sector-specific ETFs, and it's getting even more detailed as you read this.

I think any fund that focuses on something as narrow as a sector or a country is a bad investment. It might do incredibly well one year, but how can you keep up with the homework necessary to understand an entire sector or country of stocks if you have no time to manage your own money? The more sophisticated an old-line mutual fund or ETF, the more specific, the less reason there is for you to own it. People buy funds so that they can stop worrying about diversification, stop worrying day-to-day about the performance of their investments, and generally let an expert make the decisions. That's not the best way to get rich, but it's the best way available to most people. If you never buy a fund that's devoted to a single place or sector and instead buy only diversified funds, you know you're doing something right.

As for funds that don't invest in stocks, you could put your money in a money market fund or in a fund that covers any other type of bond. Bond funds are important, and what I would do to build up bond exposure with age is find a bond fund with low fees that invests in U.S. Treasurys. If you're incredibly rich, put your money into a bond fund that invests in municipal bonds. Your tax savings will still come through even though they briefly pass through the fund, but still look for low fees.

Now what about the different types of stock funds? These all call themselves different names, and the ratings agencies have different classifications for them, so my description of them is just that: a description. An actively managed mutual fund will tend to invest in companies of a given size—so it's a large-cap fund if it has most of its investments in the stocks of very large companies; a mid-cap fund invests primarily in stocks with a range of market caps in the low billions to the 10 or 20 billions; small-cap funds focus on even smaller stocks. I wouldn't listen to a word of this garbage. A great fund manager will care only about making money, not whether the stocks going higher fit into the description of the fund. If it's going higher, then it is a good stock. Any manager who says, "But we invest only in companies of this size" is a fool whom you shouldn't trust with your money. I have seen all of these fund descriptions violated by different managers over time and there are no mutual fund police to stop managers who do this.

Mutual funds will also get divided up by whether they invest in domestic or foreign stocks and whether they're "value funds," "growth funds," or "aggressive-growth funds." These too are labels that tell us very little about the quality of the fund, the quality of its manager, the risk the fund actually takes on, or the profits it's able to generate. I know "value" sounds more conservative than "growth," but it isn't.

Again, lots of value managers own growth stocks and vice versa. Anyway, it's all about the fund manager, and unless you're sure the fund manager is good, don't try to pick one of the rare mutual funds that beats an index fund. Just get an index, either through a regular mutual fund or an ETF. I know, you want me to tell you who is the best mutual fund manager, and I will do that later in the book, but for now you need to know that the best way to use mutual funds, unless you're sure your fund has a great manager—and it's hard to be sure—is simply to invest everything in a low-fee S&P 500 index fund. You won't want to allocate all of your capital to that fund as you get older, but though it's not creative, it's still a great investment that doesn't take much in the way of homework. If you're investing in funds, you don't want to do homework; that's why those terrible target-date or life-cycle funds I wrote about in the previous chapter have become so popular, despite being such inexcusably awful funds with exorbitant fees and bad asset allocation.

You need stocks and you need bonds. Never go for individual bonds; always use a fund. I hope you can take advantage of individual stocks because you've got the time and think it might be fun—it is—but even if you don't, you have a lot of options, many of them in the form of index funds, that will still make you money and give you plenty of stock exposure.

5

FAMILY FINANCES

This is not just a book about making money. Growing your capital is only step one. Plenty of people score big and then can't afford to pay for the truly important things because they never thought about how to preserve their gains. I've told you how to fund your retirement, but what about all the other big stuff?

As far as I'm concerned there's nothing more important than family, and while married couples, especially those with children, are in tax-break heaven, raising a family is an expensive proposition that comes with a lot of other costs. Raising a child and paying for college can easily cost half a million dollars over the first twenty-two years, and that's if you don't continue helping out your children with money after they graduate. Good parents don't need to shower their kids with money, but raising a child will never be cheap, and I think most parents would like to be able to help out if their adult children ever got into financial trouble. But I am not about homilies; I am about money. Teaching your children about money is perhaps the single best thing you can do for them. Paying for the things they need is just as important, which is why I'm trying to make you as much money as possible using any technique that allows you to pay lower taxes and shelter the money for as long as you can, while teaching your kids how to do the same!

And then there's buying a home. Obviously, home ownership isn't just for families; it's practically built into the American dream. Once you start a family, though, owning a home seems a lot more important. Not so long ago, buying a home was considered the perfect can't-lose investment, the ideal way to build equity. Everyone wanted a piece of the action because the housing market was on fire. Starting no later than 2005, people who never would have been able to get a mortgage because of their credit at any other time began to qualify because the mortgage issuers—typically brokers, who didn't have to worry about burning their deposit base as a bank would, because they sold the loan immediately—became too confident and lowered their lending standards. It was so easy to make money in real estate. Whenever you heard about "subprime" on TV or in the paper, you were hearing about these people with bad credit buying homes. They typically either didn't have a lot of money in the bank or had no documents, or, alas, were undocumented themselves! Many of these buyers took out really bizarre, exotic mortgages that had fixed low rates or even no interest for the first two years, and then switched to an adjustable rate for the next twenty-eight years. That didn't seem like a big deal at the time, when interest rates were really low, but when these mortgages started resetting in 2007, rates were a lot higher, courtesy of the seventeen straight interest rate boosts put through by the Federal Reserve after it encouraged people to take these kinds of mortgages to get a piece of the American dream. The Fed was as irresponsible as the home buyers who took this toxic stuff.

People with a 2–28 mortgage, as they're called, thought they could just refinance their home with a second mortgage once the first mortgage switched from a fixed rate to an adjustable rate, and, to be fair, they thought that because that is what many of the mortgage brokers and banks were telling them. But higher rates made it impossible for these subprime borrowers to refinance, and the additional charge from the piggybacked home equity loan turned many homeowners into squatters who are just now, as I write, getting evicted. While it looks like some of them may get some help from the federal government, there could be as many as 7 million people who might end up defaulting on their mortgages and losing their homes. Yes, that's how many home buyers took these risky propositions when they bought their homes between 2005 and 2007.

The sharks who offered these mortgages and the brokers who packaged them and sold them, mainly to hedge funds that wanted to make more money than they could by investing in Treasurys, speak of the 2006 vintage as the worst ever, as if it were just a case of wine. It's people's lives, a point I have tried to drive home whenever I speak on this subject. Mostly it has fallen on deaf ears. That is why I never want you to be in that position. In fact, I want to do everything in my power to make sure no one who reads this book ever loses a home. So in this chapter I want to tell you how to pay for kids, how to pay for college, and how to buy a home, mostly by taking advantage of the federal government's generosity in creating enormous tax breaks for families, homeowners, and people paying college tuition. In fact, I'll cover a lot of tax breaks that might apply to you, because every extra dollar counts. I've never had a moral problem with paying taxes. I know many people, probably many of you, do have strong political objections to taxes, and that's a legitimate position. I've always felt that as a rich guy it would be obscene for me to complain about paying my taxes, or paying for anything else for that matter, even if my tax rate is higher. I have been a huge beneficiary of all the protections and opportunities that this great nation offers. That said, only a real masochist *likes* paying taxes, and if there are provisions in the tax code that let you pay lower taxes, I think you should go for them.

I'll start with how you can save money thanks to your children, then how you can pay less for college, and after that how you can benefit from home ownership. I know that for many of you, even most of you, owning a home may be at the top of your list, especially if you don't have any children and don't plan on having any, but as a parent I can't help but give kids top billing here.

Children

The best and easiest way to save on some of the expense of having children is by taking advantage of the child tax credit. A tax credit is subtracted directly from your tax liability, so a $1 tax credit means a $1 reduction in your taxes, regardless of what income tax bracket you happen to inhabit. If you have children and your household income doesn't exceed $110,000 if you're married and filing jointly, you can take a $1,000 tax credit per child. That's $1,000 of taxes you don't have to pay, practically money in your pocket. Unfortunately, there's a phaseout if you and your spouse together earn more than $110,000, which means that the credit becomes smaller and smaller as you earn more than that amount, and eventually dwindles down to $0. Then again, you'll be making a lot more money, so it evens out.

If you have child care expenses, you can get a tax credit or an exclusion. An exclusion is when the government makes a certain amount of your income tax-free, as long as those expenses are incurred in the process of earning an income. So, for example, if you need to pay for child care in order to go to work, that expense qualifies for a credit. Here's how this one works—and I should mention that this credit is for all dependents, not just children. You can get a tax credit of up to $2,100 a year for these expenses, but that credit gets reduced once your adjusted gross income hits $15,001. Your adjusted gross income isn't your total income; it's a tax term that refers to your income after certain deductions. Basically, if you look at your 1040 form, which is what most people use to file their tax returns, your adjusted gross income is reported on the last line of the first page of the form. Even though this tax credit starts to become smaller once you have $15,001 in adjusted gross income, it's never completely phased out. If the company you work for pays for child care or dependent care expenses, you can take an exclusion of up to $5,000, depending on your income. Again, an exclusion means that as much as $5,000 of your income becomes tax-free.

If you adopted a child and had to pay out-of-pocket expenses relating to the adoption, you can get a really large tax credit. You can claim an adoption credit of up to $11,390 per eligible child, which is a pretty fantastic credit, but this one also starts to phase out. If you're married and filing jointly for 2007, this credit starts to phase out if you earn $170,820, and will be totally phased out if your joint income is over $210,820. That's a pretty high limit, so if you do adopt you can likely take advantage of this credit.

Here's one that's not so terrific. Parents who receive child support payments, or the children who receive them, don't have to pay taxes on those payments. However, the parent who pays child support can't deduct child support payments from his or her income.

There are some things you can do with income shifting as long as you play by the rules. If you give one of your children investment property, he or she will pay lower taxes as long as he or she is in a lower tax bracket than you are. This doesn't work too well if your kids are under 18, because then they'll have to pay a "kiddie tax," and that eats up most of the tax benefit. You need to be careful about this sort of thing because the more money your child has in his or her name, the less financial aid your kid can get for college.

It's important to teach your children about money while they're still young. That means teaching them good habits and teaching them how to make money. Since many people don't have good spending habits and don't invest, it can be hard for them to teach their kids either one of these things. It's really important to recognize that talking to your children and telling them how to handle money isn't enough. Kids aren't dumb, and they learn as much by observing their parents as they do by listening to them. That's why it's crucial to make the process of shopping for anything with your children long and tedious. Even if you're well off, you need to teach your children how to comparison shop. If you're buying them toys or clothes, or anything else for that matter, make your kids consider the price of what you're buying and have them look for better deals, even if you don't end up taking them and even if the price doesn't matter to you. If there's something your child really wants, make him or her do some research about it online before you agree to buy it. Just getting your kids into the habit of being careful with their purchases can really help them later in life. I like debit cards too as a method of teaching. Nothing teaches kids to budget better than to run out of money on a debit card.

Of course, I think the most important thing to teach your children about money is the value of investing. Many parents teach their kids about the value of saving money, often by setting up a bank account under the child's name and showing them how interest works. This is fine because the compounding of interest is like the eighth wonder of the world and I want everyone to see it. But I think you can do better than that: set up a brokerage account for your children and buy one share of a stock that I recommend later in the book. Try to pick one that your child might actually be familiar with, such as McDonald's. The trick here is to get the child interested in the stock market so that he or she has a heads-up about what it is all about. Recently I taught a high school class—a sophisticated one at that—about stocks, and I was shocked that most students had no idea how stocks work. Owning one share will change that. For those who think that's excessive, you don't actually have to set up a real brokerage account. Instead, you can create a rotisserie league of stocks, where you draft some stocks and your kids draft some stocks using a limited amount of play money. The winning stock gets bought and put into the child's account. This is a much more powerful lesson than starting a bank account. Investing in stocks will make you a lot more money than keeping your money in the bank, and when your kids see how much they can make by investing, especially if you teach them about this at a young age, they'll be really impressed. You don't want your children just saving money, because saving isn't all that valuable if you don't invest. Plus, this is an opportunity for them to learn about losing money without it being too costly.

One more thing: many parents exclude their children from family discussions about money, and I think that's counterproductive. I admit I have been guilty of this. I have never wanted my kids to know my financial status. But when I give them an inkling about what I do with the money I make, they are fascinated. If you can talk to your children about the family finances, they'll get a much better understanding of how money works and how real people go about paying for the things most children take for granted. I also think that when you buy one share of a stock for them, it allows the discussion to go much easier. It also gives them a place to save when they make a little money besides what is in the passbook. I am grateful that my local bank, Commerce Bancorp, actually gives kids passbooks, but I would rather they had stock accounts to get rolling in the greatest investment possibilities we have in this country.

When I talk about getting kids involved in the market, I mean getting them involved in things they know and may get excited about. I can't stress how vital it is to get your kids excited about their holdings. I used to grab that newspaper out of my dad's arms each night when he came back from work just to see the closing prices of stocks that I was following on paper. What I wouldn't have given for those stocks to be the real thing. If it were possible back then, I would have gone online at each close to chart how my stocks were doing.

But to capture the fancy of little kids, kids as young as 6 years old, you need to find some top-notch brand names that you know and like and that your kids will naturally be able to follow. That way you can constantly refer to your child's holdings and get him or her comfortable with the idea of actually owning a piece of a company. You will be ingraining the process and making it fun. I have come up with a list of six stocks for kids under 6. I would buy one share of one of these the moment your child is born, and add another share a year later, or perhaps pick another one of the stocks and buy a share of that. I don't know a soul who is doing this, and that has to change, right now. Any unearned income less than $1,700 can qualify for UGMA (the Uniform Gifts to Minors Act) status, which allows your kids to make money owning stocks without paying the same level of taxes that you pay. That's why buying your kids stocks in small increments is so great; they'll get the gains without having to give them back to the government.

Stocks for Children Under 6

1. Disney. Here's a company that every child will recognize, from its dominance of animated films courtesy of its Pixar acquisition, to its Disney Channel full of programming. All children like to go to the parks, and this will become a much bigger deal over time if you buy a share now. Disney foundered for a long time under inferior management, but the change a few years ago to Bob Iger, the new CEO, has meant the world to this company. He instituted a buyback, solved the animation woes, and backed incredible franchises like *Pirates of the Caribbean, The Chronicles of Narnia,* and *High School Musical.* The TV division, including the amazing ESPN franchise, has been a huge cash cow even in a time when everyone records the programs and skips the advertisements. You just can't record ESPN and play it later. This is a premium name that can get a kid more involved than just about any other publicly traded company.

2. Viacom. This is a cheap stock that has been down on its luck ever since it split from CBS. It has some fabulous properties that will appeal to children, notably Nickelodeon, the foremost place for cartoons and kids' entertainment. MTV, which your kids could catch onto pretty early, has developed some programming about teens that young kids want to watch. Meanwhile, the Paramount film studio has some pretty remarkable kids' movies, including the ones that take advantage of characters that will be familiar to your kids, Jimmy Neutron and SpongeBob. The stock is cheap, management is emboldened to meet goals—they just had their first head-count reduction because the company had become fat and bloated—and they are buying back stock aggressively. You want your kids to own shares in SpongeBob for certain.

3. Hasbro. Kids love toys like Mr. Potato Head; they love Parker Brothers games; they like Tonka trucks and Milton Bradley products. Monopoly, Sorry!, the Game of Life, Twister, My Little Pony, *Toy Story* toys, everything that you will be playing with them from day one. I believe 2007 will be the year that Mattel took itself out of the running because of issues with its Chinese toys. Hasbro doesn't have that problem. The stock has been cheap despite consistent growth. I don't know about you, but board games were the way I connected with my folks. I would love to own a piece of Boardwalk or Park Place; so will your kids.

4. Gap. Gap is in the midst of one of the biggest turnarounds I have ever seen, and one look at GapKids tells you that they have at last gotten it together. I think that the new management, brought in from outside Gap, is engaging in a long-term turn that will mean you and your kids will be shopping there together. Plus, you need to have some stock that's down on its luck, and where I think a turnaround is at hand, so the risk is out of the stock. The worst that can happen is that Gap gets taken private before your kid gets to shop there—but certainly after you've bought a ton of infant clothes for him or her.

5. Gymboree. Not just clothes—that's how I look at Gymboree. It has play programs for children that make the company money. It also has play and music and art classes, something that first-time moms have fallen in love with. This is a company that also understands fashion; it's like an Abercrombie or American Eagle for little kids, with truly fashion-forward choices. Gymboree has always had a strong reputation with girls, but recently its boys' clothes have come on strong. Meanwhile, the chief competition, Children's Place, has been hurting, in part because of a chilled relationship with Disney that had previously spurred sales. Just as Hasbro is profiting from Mattel's misfortunes, Gymboree is benefiting because of weaknesses at Children's Place. This company may be the most likely stock to own if you, like millions of others, are a mall shopper.

6. McDonald's. This is one of my favorite stocks, one that I consider to be great for the ages. I don't know a parent who hasn't taken a kid to McDonald's, if only just for their clean bathrooms. When I was growing up, McDonald's stood for bad food; now it has tons of healthy offerings. Its kids' promotions make it a rival of Disney as the first company name that kids think of.

Any of these companies will work. I urge you to buy one share of one of these, and perhaps talk your parents into doing the same for their grandchild. If only baby showers would get registered with E*Trade, TD Ameritrade, and Schwab! And don't forget to reinvest those dividends. I can't ask you to explain compounding to a child, but the brokerage statements will help you do that.

When I was little, the first thing my folks got me was a passbook. The second thing was a savings bond. These yawners never encouraged me to do anything or follow anything. They should be banished as bad alternatives to stocks.

One more thought about stocks for children. I want to encourage you to speculate with a stock that seems like a highflier, whatever the highflier might be at the time. Why? Consider the five best performing stocks in the past twenty years, the time frame I use to make decisions for my kids: Oracle, the software company, up 13,064 percent; Harley-Davidson, motorcycles, up 7,603 percent; Microsoft, software, up 7,308 percent; Paychex, the payroll service company, up 6,838 percent; and Amgen, the biotech company, up 5,850 percent. Let's look at it another way, the price a stock would have been twenty years ago considering all the splits: Oracle, 15 cents; Amgen, 64 cents; Harley-Davidson, 71 cents; Microsoft, 38 cents; and Paychex, 65 cents. In other words, don't freak out if you pay $40 or $50 for a stock that is speculative. Look 'em up; look where the speculative stocks of twenty years ago got to!

More important, consider the categories worth speculating in: software (Oracle, Microsoft), biotech (Amgen), leisure (Harley-Davidson), and services (Paychex). You match one of these blue-chips with a speculative stock that could be a flier like every one of those best-performing stocks, and your kids could end up using their profits to pay for an education that you thought you'd get stuck funding.

Paying for College

There are a lot of great ways to save on paying tuition. I know that many personal finance authors advise parents not to pay for their children to go to college until after they've taken care of their own retirement fund. I agree that retirement is priority number one, but I don't see why you can't save for retirement and help out your children with college tuition at the same time. The best thing you can do for your children, at least financially, is to pay to send them to college. That way your kids won't be burdened with student loans when they graduate, and because they've gone to college they'll be able to get better-paying jobs. It's important to teach your kids about money, and I'll explain how I would handle that after I tell you how to save on tuition, but even if your children don't grow up learning how to handle money perfectly, giving them a free ride through college—which

I admit doesn't do much to teach them the value of a dollar—will really help with their future and perhaps aid them in taking risks that could produce much larger rewards later in life than if they were worried about every dime when they're in their 20s.

To make college more affordable, you've got two great savings plans, Coverdell Education Savings Accounts and 529 Savings Plans, two plans that I sure wish my folks had had when I was planning to go to college. Both of these plans have a lot in common with a Roth IRA, in that you contribute to them with after-tax income, but once your money is in the account it grows tax-free and distributions from the accounts are tax-free. With a Coverdell, you can contribute up to $2,000 a year, and you decide how to invest the funds you keep in the account. You can withdraw money from a Coverdell at any time, but withdrawals are tax-free only if you use them to pay for qualified education expenses. That covers more than just college expenses. A qualified education expense can include any costs related to attending a primary school, a secondary school, or college. If you withdraw money from a Coverdell and spend it on noneducational expenses, it will be taxed at ordinary income tax rates, and you'll also pay a 10 percent penalty, just as you have to pay for withdrawing money from a retirement account before retirement. Clearly, you shouldn't start a Coverdell if you don't intend to spend every penny you put in there on paying for education. Money in a Coverdell Education Savings Account isn't considered by colleges when they calculate the level of financial aid they're willing to provide. That's a really important, really terrific benefit. Unfortunately, you can't contribute to a Coverdell account if you're too rich. For a married couple filing jointly, the phaseout starts when your adjusted gross income hits $190,000, and once it reaches $220,000 you won't be allowed to contribute anything. You also can't use a Coverdell to pay for education expenses once your designated beneficiary turns 30, so make sure your kids go to college on time. There's one more problem, which is that some of the provisions that make Coverdell accounts helpful are set to expire in

2011, but I really don't believe Congress will let this happen. This is the kind of plan that gets bipartisan support because it appeals to everyone. Republicans see these plans as lowering taxes and Democrats see them as giving lower-income families a better way to pay for education. If you don't take advantage of a Coverdell plan, you really are costing yourself a lot of money.

If you've got too much money for a Coverdell account, you can use a 529 Savings Plan. These plans come in two different forms. There are 529 Savings Plans and 529 Prepaid Tuition Plans. The savings plans are run by states, and the prepaid tuition plans can be run by states or educational institutions. With a prepaid tuition plan you can buy tuition credits at today's rates and use them to cover tuition when your child goes to college. We all know that college is becoming more expensive, but I'm not sure that the price of college is increasing fast enough to justify prepaying tuition rather than contributing to a 529 Savings Plan. In a 529 Savings Plan you can invest your contributions, which are made with after-tax income. You pay no taxes on your gains and no taxes on withdrawals from the account that are used to pay for college. Compared to Coverdell accounts, 529s have a lot of drawbacks. The only thing about a 529 plan that's better than a Coverdell is that it lets you contribute a whole lot more money. Maximum contribution levels vary by state, and you want to start a 529 in your state of residence because you'll get more tax advantages that way, but the maximums are always quite high. You can contribute at least $230,000 a year to a 529 plan, and some states allow you to contribute up to $300,000. However, there's a drawback to contributing this much: you might have to pay a gift tax because this account names one of your children, not you, as a beneficiary. But even with a gift tax, you get a break from 529s, although a much smaller amount than those gigantic contributions. For 2007, you're allowed to give individual gifts worth up to $12,000 tax-free, and you can give twice that amount as long as you're married and file a joint tax return with your spouse. But in a 529 plan, you're allowed to contribute a lump sum of up to $60,000 in one year, and you won't pay any gift tax on that contribution as long as you take no gift tax exemptions for the next five years. You can use the money in a 529 to cover tuition, room, board, books, school supplies, and any other costs necessary for college, and you can always change the beneficiary of your plan without paying a fee. Don't blanch; school is a lot more expensive than when you went! (If you are a student now, you know exactly what I am talking about.)

While 529 Savings Plans do a great job of letting you contribute huge sums of money, they're like the 401(k) plan of the college savings world. Just as with a 401(k), you don't get to manage your own 529 account. Instead, your state of residence will offer a set of investment plans that are run by mutual fund companies or other financial services companies. The offerings in 529 plans are similar to the mix of undesirable mutual funds you might find in a 401(k) plan, which is a definite drawback. Plus, many states allow the companies that run their 529 programs to charge enormous fees. States will offer more than one plan, and they're all required to offer a no-fee, low-cost plan, but that plan might not have many good options. My advice is to first max out your contributions to a Coverdell Education Savings Account, and only after you've done that should you look at a 529 plan. You should use the plans offered by the state you live in, because they'll typically give you state tax breaks for the money you contribute. Look through all the plans your state offers for one with low fees and some decent funds. You're probably best off looking for a low-cost index fund rather than hunting for an actively managed fund that will consistently beat index funds. Once again, a good S&P 500 index fund is the right default option for most of you. You'll have the opportunity to contribute to bond funds as well, but I don't think that's necessary for an account designed to pay for college. Remember, this is basically money for your kids, and they're going to be young when they go to college. I don't recommend owning any bonds until you hit your 30s, and you shouldn't have your kids invested in bonds through their 529 plans. Sure, stocks are more risky than bonds, but it's not the end of the world if your children have to take out some student loans or rely on financial aid to fully pay for college. That was my ticket: scholarships and loans. They can be your kids' ticket too. This isn't like retirement, where you have few other options if your retirement fund gets wiped out (which is why you have to invest more and more of it in bonds as you get older).

Beyond tax-favored savings accounts, there's a whole universe of scholarships and fellowships that your children can apply for to cover the cost of college. I can't possibly go through all of these here because there are thousands of them offered by a whole range of institutions. I've heard of one scholarship that you can get for being left-handed. Your employer might offer some scholarships to your children, their high school might offer some, and so will colleges. You can find all of the information you need about various scholarships and fellowships online, as there are at least a dozen free websites that let you search for scholarships. There are also many sources of need-based financial aid that you can access by filling out a Free Application for Federal Student Aid (FAFSA) and submitting it to the federal government, your state government, and the college your child will attend. Some private schools will also make you fill out a supplemental form to get their financial aid. You have to fill out a new FAFSA every year if you want to keep receiving financial aid. The federal government has a whole range of grants and subsidized loans for lower-income students, and even if you have plenty of money you should still try to apply for financial aid. The vast majority of students in both public and private colleges receive some form of aid, and it's worth finding out if you're eligible in order to save money on education. More than 80 percent of students attending private colleges, which are much more expensive than state schools, receive some kind of aid, so don't be too proud to go looking for it. When I went to school thirty years ago, there were very few places to turn to for money. That's no longer the case, yet I still hear plenty of people complaining that there isn't enough money around to go to a good school. That's nonsense, and that's ignorance and laziness. Sorry to be blunt, but I am known as a guy who calls it as he sees it.

There are three really big tax benefits you can get from the government in order to cover the cost of college, but you can use only one of the three. Your choices are the Hope Credit, the Lifetime Learning Credit, and the Tuition and Fees Deduction. Anyone with a dependent who is a freshman or sophomore in college, or anyone who is a freshman or sophomore and is not claimed as a dependent on someone else's taxes, can claim the Hope Credit, which is a credit of up to $1,650 on the first $2,200 of college tuition and fees as long as your modified adjusted gross income is less than $55,000 if you're single, or $110,000 for a married couple filing a joint return. The credit becomes smaller if your income is over $45,000 if you're single, or over $90,000 if you're married and filing jointly. Remember, a tax credit is basically money in your pocket because your tax bill is reduced by a dollar for every dollar's worth of tax credits you get. Then there's a Lifetime Learning Credit, which applies to anyone taking college classes. You can claim this credit if you or a dependent is in college and you make less than $55,000 a year if you're single, or $110,000 if you're married and filing jointly. This is a credit of up to $2,000 on the first $10,000 of undergraduate or graduate school tuition and fees. If you're not eligible for either of these credits, you can take the Tuition and Fees Deduction. This is technically an adjustment, which is a tax deduction that you're eligible for even if you don't itemize your deductions. (In any year, you're allowed to take a standard deduction from your adjusted gross income, or you can itemize your deductions by looking at a list of available tax deductions. I suggest trying to itemize your deductions every year, and then taking whichever deduction, itemized or standard, is greater.) If you or a dependent is in college and you're paying for it, you can deduct up to $4,000 that you've spent on tuition and fees in a given year. That means you don't pay any taxes on the $4,000 of your income you deduct, which isn't as good as a tax credit because a deduction of $4,000 will result in only $1,000 of savings if your effective tax rate is 25 percent. At any rate, the Tuition and Fees Deduction starts to phase out if you make more than $130,000, and disappears once you make more than $160,000 a year, as long as you're married and filing your tax return jointly with your spouse.

Beyond these three big tax breaks, there's also the student loan interest deduction, which is available to everyone with a modified adjusted gross income under $65,000, or below $135,000 if you're married and filing jointly with your spouse. This deduction too can be claimed by either the student or someone claiming the student as a dependent, whoever took out and paid back the loan (this could be a parent or a child). This is a great deduction for anyone who's recently gotten out of school and is still paying off student loans. You can deduct up to $2,500 of interest paid on student loans when you file your taxes.

There are other ways to save money on college. Going to a state school rather than a private school is obviously much less expensive. Going to a two-year junior college and then transferring to a four-year college will also save you money. That said, getting a great education is more important than getting an inexpensive education. If you have to pay a lot of money for your kid to go to a great school, trust me: he or she will earn it all back after graduation. If you're paying for your kids to go to school, keep this fact in mind. I don't think that parents should be obligated to pay for their children to go to college, but many parents want to pay, and if you're one of them, you should know how to do it in the most cost-effective way possible.

The American Dream

Enough about children, let's talk about the American dream. Buying a home can be a great investment, but it's important to realize that it's not just an investment. Sure, owning your home is a great way to lower your tax bill, and generally speaking property values tend to go up over time, but you buy a home because you want to live there. Too many people treating homes as investments is a large part of what led to the housing bust from 2005 to 2007, when I'm writing this book. Speculators bought homes that they didn't intend to live in. They were going to hold them for a brief period of time and then flip them to someone else at a higher price. But when the bottom fell out of the housing market, those speculators got crushed. Plus, there were all these extra houses that had been bought as investments, but the buyers dried up and the home builders, strapped for cash, kept pumping them out. They became their own worst enemies by increasing the supply. A lot of these people were acting as if real estate always went up, something I can't blame them for because the only period of sustained declines in homes occurred during the Depression. Until now. Values started to decline in 2006 and continue to decline as I write these words in 2007. I'm not saying buying a home can't be a great investment, but I am saying you can't think that investments in real estate will always go higher. It's not a law of physics. The great thing about a house is that even if it declines in value, you can still live there. The bad thing is that if you have to sell soon after you bought, either because you have lost your job or you need to move, you can no longer be assured that you will even break even, let alone have a gain.

That said, if you can't pay your mortgage, you're out on the street. Considering how many people were hurt recently by taking out mortgages they didn't understand and couldn't afford, it's important that you take out the right kind of mortgage when you buy a home. For most people this is very simple: get a fixed-rate mortgage. Your monthly payments will stay the same until you pay off the mortgage. If interest rates decline and you can refinance at a lower rate, then do that. Don't be tempted into getting an adjustable-rate mortgage, or ARM. If rates go up, your payments will go up and you might not be able to cover the cost. Right now, many people with ARMs are losing their home because they can't make payments at those higher rates. This is your home; you don't want to mess it up. For the same reason, you should stay away from any kind of exotic mortgage. The worst example of these is the mortgage that has a fixed low rate for the first two years, then swings to an adjustable rate that can go much higher over the next twenty-eight years. Many people got these loans thinking they could refinance after the first two years, but by then the housing market had fallen apart and credit had gotten tighter. These people couldn't refinance, and many of them lost their home. And *never* count on a piggyback loan, a home equity loan, to pay your actual mortgage. That's a sucker's game, although many of the mortgage companies, including some of the ones that went under, encouraged that. If you get a fixed-rate mortgage, none of these shenanigans will happen to you. You could still lose your home if you lose your job and can't pay the same rate you've been paying, but as long as you keep earning the same amount of money, you should be fine.

As for tax savings, there are many different ways being a homeowner helps. If you sell your home and your profit is less than $250,000, or $500,000 if you're married and file your taxes jointly, then you don't have to pay tax on the sale. Keep in mind, this is just for qualified homes, meaning your main home or your second home. When you buy a home, the interest on your mortgage is tax-deductible, but again, this is true only for qualified homes. However, you can deduct all of your mortgage interest only if you have less than $1.1 million in the combined amount of your acquisition debt (which is the mortgage you used to buy, build, or improve your home) and your home equity debt (which is any kind of loan secured by the equity in your home that you used for other purposes, on the same qualified home). When you buy a home, you can deduct from your taxes what are called "fee points." The mortgage lender will usually charge you a loan fee, which is often 1 percent of the value of the mortgage. One percent of the value of the mortgage is considered 1 point. So if you took out a $100,000 mortgage, you would pay a $1,000 loan fee to the lender. That $1,000 fee is tax-deductible. You can deduct part of the interest on a home equity loan. You can deduct the interest on a home improvement loan as long as you don't use that loan for repairs. You can deduct the amount of money you pay in property tax from your income tax, and you can deduct water and sewer taxes too. And you can deduct any costs relating to selling your home.

Owning a home is a tax-deduction gold mine, which is why, despite all of the frightening talk about homes, they will always be a good investment if you buy them wisely. If you buy a home, you can get bountiful tax credits that aren't available if you rent. For example, there's a tax credit for energy-efficient home improvements. As long as you buy new, qualified energy-efficient equipment and keep it for five years, you can get a tax credit of 10 percent of the purchase price, up to $500. If you buy a solar panel—and I don't know why you'd do that because those things are hideous—but if you do, you can get a tax credit for 30 percent of what you paid for the solar panel, up to $2,000.

There is a downside, though. If you sell your main residence at a loss, you can't claim this as a capital loss and deduct the loss from your taxable income. With stocks, you can deduct your capital losses, and this can really help to lower your tax bill, although I don't recommend making tax deductions a priority when you invest, because focusing on avoiding taxes rather than making money can compromise your ability to be a good investor.

There are many other important tax breaks out there related to getting what you want. They can help you start a family, buy a home, and send your children to college. As far as I'm concerned, these are some of the most important things in life, not just the most important financial aspects of your life. Saving money when you're supporting someone you love or buying something you want more than anything else in the world is almost as good as making money. I regret that I didn't say more on this subject in *Real Money*, but that book was meant for trading and investing your way into wealth. *Stay Mad* is about making and saving money every way you legally can.

At this point, you know enough about personal finance to get rich and stay rich, but all of that can take you only so far. If you really want to try to get rich, you need to know not just that you should invest, not just what kind of tax-favored accounts to use as an investor, but also what you should actually invest in, and how you can become a better investor. I've already written a great deal about the specifics of being a great investor in my previous books, but now I'll teach you things you've never learned before, and I'll reveal my favorite stocks and mutual funds for long-term investors. That way you can put away as much money as you can and grow that money far beyond what you ever dreamed possible. In an era when houses are no longer a sure thing, that's the real American dream.

6

TWENTY NEW RULES
FOR INVESTING

For twenty years, I managed money professionally, taking the funds of rich people and trying to make them richer. I was in a performance business; I got to keep 20 percent of the gains, even if they were only on paper. There are two kinds of gains in the business: realized and unrealized. When you sell a stock for profit, that profit is a realized gain. When you own a stock that's up from where you bought it, that's an unrealized gain. At the fund I took 20 percent of both realized and unrealized gains. I also received 1 percent of the assets as a management fee. I initially reported to my investors once a quarter, but increasingly they asked for monthly, then weekly, and ultimately daily performance figures. As my assets grew and my performance fluctuated by the hour—I needed to make $430,000 a *day* just to continue my yearly returns—some clients asked for my numbers hourly.

With that kind of pressure, I began to focus entirely on short-term returns. If I could have a good day, I could satisfy the investors who checked in by 4 p.m. A good morning, and I didn't dread the hourly calls. In my last two years I installed software that flickered reds and greens along with down and up arrows every tenth of a second, all the better to see whether I was making or losing money at that *very moment.*

Needless to say, I felt like was on a daily treadmill from 4 a.m. until 4 p.m. as I traded early morning in Europe and then the U.S. markets right until the closing bell. Thank heaven my investors didn't demand nightly returns. I used to trade from 4 a.m. until 11 p.m., breaking only for a quick dinner before Tokyo opened. I was able to stop that insanity only after Tokyo peaked in 1989, and I never looked back.

I give you all of this information because I could not wait to retire from such an insurmountable minute-to-minute challenge. Although I have had a love of stocks my whole life, I do not have a love of report cards, and I was being graded with every tick of the symbols in my portfolio.

And I wanted to resume another passion I had, journalism—this time not just print, but Internet and television journalism. I wanted to stay in the game, but I couldn't be a legitimate journalist and a serious investor of my own money at the same time. To be a journalist I had to agree to provisions in my contract that wouldn't let me profit from any securities. That led to a wholesale sell-off of every stock I had, a retreat from all hedge funds, and a charge into real estate and cash.

And you know what? I was miserable. Just miserable. My beloved stock market was marching on without me and I wanted to get back into the band!

I struggled mightily for a formula that wouldn't let me profit but that would let me show others how the game is played, and I came up with a charitable trust model. I would put money into a trust that would distribute the profits to charities of my choosing at year-end. None of the gains could accrue to me.

Very quickly, through mention on TheStreet.com and CNBC, people wanted to know what I was doing with the trust and whether they could follow along. So I created a website and an electronic newsletter, ActionAlertsPlus.com, which you have no doubt heard of if you watch *Mad Money* or read TheStreet.com's RealMoney.com section, where my blog appears. For a fee, I would show you how I would manage my personal stock portfolio. In order not to profit, lest the product become a big success—which it has, the largest paid subscription e-newsletter anywhere—I let you buy the stocks ahead of me and sell them ahead of me. Unfortunately that has skewed performance down for me, but it doesn't matter because it skews it up for those who subscribe to the newsletter.

The business of running money personally, not being in the hedge fund world, has been incredibly eye-opening for a number of reasons. First, I am, at last, able to think longer-term, which is incredibly liberating and refreshing for me. In fact, I'm forced to think longer-term because of a whole variety of restrictions on the charitable trust that prevent me from trading stocks in the short term. I love the idea of being able to buy something and let it work over time, which is good because that's all the charitable trust lets me do. I try to have a six- to eighteen-month time frame for all my buys, which gives them a chance to truly percolate and blossom. As you will soon see, when I don't let them do so, I don't make as much money at best and perform quite poorly at worst.

Second, I think I have become a much better investor. That's because when I was at my hedge fund, we were in a very different world, an unregulated world where the big boys—including me—could always outperform small investors. We were able to call managements any time up until one month before the quarter—the so-called quiet period when they knew approximately the results of the quarter and weren't allowed to give them away—and ask how things were going. That allowed us to have a better idea than anyone else whether a given company was going to beat the estimates, meaning it would report a better-than-expected quarter or a worse-than-expected quarter. Given that the biggest determinant of a company's stock, besides its sector, is whether or not it will beat the estimates, these calls were money in the bank.

But at the end of the 1990s, the government ruled that such contact was illegal and the only way anyone could communicate with executives was through public forums—no more one-on-one insights. After a series of prosecutions by the government, the rule, Regulation FD, or Fair Disclosure, was interpreted to mean that unless the information was released and on the company website, it was not considered legal.

This rule and its interpretation changed everything. It made the whole concept of trying to game short-term movements in stocks almost impossible—not just for "home gamers," my term for non-professional investors, but for hedge fund managers. So the new style of my trust suited the times well.

Third, my charitable trust allows me a rare and *brutal* look back at why I bought or sold a stock. I am on record about what my thought process was. Which is why what I am about to teach you is the single best set of lessons I have ever come up with. Most people never set down contemporaneously why they do something. If you want to minimize the mistakes you make, you should keep a diary and at that exact moment when you buy or sell, write down why you did it. You will be struck by how many of the same patterns you repeat. The charitable trust forced me to invest like an ordinary person, and that's given me a lot of insight into the kinds of mistakes that regular investors often make, not the kinds of mistakes that hedge fund managers often make.

It is my sincere hope that you will not have to make those mistakes, not have to take the serious pain that I have had, because I have taken it *for you!*

With that introduction, let's explore the twenty most valuable lessons you will ever need for investing—*not trading*—your personal money. Both *Real Money: Sane Investing in an Insane World* and *Mad Money: Watch TV, Get Rich* have more than adequately addressed the best ways to trade. When I wrote the sets of lessons in those books, I still had my head stuck in the world of professional money management and hedge funds, of daily performance checkups, not of sensible long-term investing over a twelve- to eighteen-month horizon.

Here are my lessons from running ActionAlertsPlus.com, my charitable trust:

Twenty New Rules for Investing

1. Don't invest like a hedge fund manager. You don't have to worry about the quarter, so don't play it for the quarter. Free yourself from that mentality. There are so many services and websites and programs devoted to moving quickly and taking advantage of short-term movements and events that it's almost as if all of the financial services media were set up as if you are or wanted to be a hedge fund manager.

But as I have indicated, such thinking does not allow you to perform over a long period of time—not just because the tax consequences are higher for short-term trading but because the best ideas are the ones you own and continue to do homework on, investments that you're confident have long-term potential and don't require minute-by-minute analysis. After all, if you're reading this book you probably don't have time during the day or even during the week to trade stocks and constantly monitor them.

That's one of many habits that cost people so much in 2000. And when I went over my trades from ActionAlertsPlus.com I found that so many of my gains were truncated and much smaller than they could have been because I wanted to show good numbers, quarterly numbers, as if I were under pressure to continue to perform the old way. We are inundated with stocks and tables each month that show who is doing better or worse than someone else. I am sure you fall prey to wondering, "How am I doing?" Take it from someone who has suffered the lumps of being too competitive: It's a big mistake, especially when it's all in your head.

Foster Wheeler was one of the best picks that I've had in many years, an infrastructure play, meaning it's a company that engineers and constructs giant projects like petrochemical refineries and power plants, both of which are in incredible demand. Soon after I bought it the stock went down about 10 points, from $50 to $40. (One of the great things about keeping a contemporaneous document is that you can see where you made all of these trades. If the stock went down after you got out, congratulate yourself, but if it went up, you'd better be prepared to explain how you left the gains on the table.) At $40 I bought more. It then dropped to $30 and I bought more still. Slowly it went back to where I bought it and then above to the mid-$50s. As the quarter came, I wanted to record that terrific gain. It didn't matter that I liked the stock as much as ever. I wanted to be sure I booked a winner.

Though I had sworn that I would run ActionAlertsPlus.com as if no one was looking over my shoulder, I booted it. Subsequently the stock doubled over the next year as my thesis about the stock's potential played out.

I had fallen victim to hedge-funditis. Had I not cared about the short term so much, I would have held on to a huge gain for at least some of my holdings. While you may not feel as if you are running a hedge fund, the focus on short-term performance has infected pretty much every investor I know. You don't need to show good days, good months, good quarters, or even good years. You just need to show great wealth over many years. Invest for the long term. Lose the hedge fund mentality.

2. Don't quit when you get back to even. My ActionAlertsPlus.com Alerts are littered with missives about how I am "battling" individual stocks as they go down to get a better cost basis and then quitting just when I get ahead.

In 2002, I decided that ABB, a Swiss engineering company that was one of the few companies on earth that maintained the ability to build nuclear power plants during the dry spell of construction, was making a comeback. It had been damaged by some serious exposure to asbestos lawsuits. I first bought the stock at $13, but every time an asbestos lawsuit hit the tape, even if it was the good news of a settlement, the stock got hammered back to $11. I was able, after a considerable amount of buying over many months' time, to get my basis—that is, what the entire position cost me—from $13 to $12 a share.

It was a classic siege and I was conscious of the heroic effort that it took to buy little increments each time it ticked at $11 and change. After five months, the stock finally got back to where I initially bought it. I declared victory, saying I had gotten back to even and then some! I was so proud and relieved that I had outlasted the stock. The fact that I had actually made a dollar despite the bad first buy was icing on the cake. I had won. I rang the register.

A year later, I bumped into a friend who had gotten the first Alert, but didn't see the second because he was on sabbatical for a year in Switzerland. He wanted to know if it was time to ring the register on ABB. The stock was at $24. He had done much more than get back to even. Oh, and the big orders for nuke plants? The reason I bought it? They finally happened, just as I had predicted. Usually when you get back to even, the stock you own has a lot more upside left. Don't get out at the ground floor.

3. Never say never when it comes to a takeover. One of the most unnerving parts of investing is missing a takeover that should have been yours after you left the stock because management and everyone else thought that the company couldn't or wouldn't be taken over.

Recently, Dow Jones, a company with two classes of stock, one that was meant to keep the company independent and family-run, succumbed to a takeover bid from Rupert Murdoch's News Corp. Pundits and analysts were adamant that this takeover could never occur, which is why the stock was at $35 before the $60 takeover bid.

It might seem an unusual case, but it isn't. In reviewing all my bulletins for this book, I was dismayed to see that I had purchased Alcan around $52 because I believed there would be an imminent consolidation of the aluminum business as various mineral concerns were buying up independents. The stock rapidly fell to the $40s, where I bought more, and then dropped down to $39, where I bought even more to bring down my average cost. (Unlike when you are trading, it is perfectly fine to buy a stock that's down, because when you are investing you are getting a company you like on the cheap.)

When the stock got back to $45, Phelps Dodge, another mineral company, got a very big takeover offer from Freeport-McMoRan, a gold and copper company. Alcan spiked in sympathy. Immediately, almost all of the analysts who followed the company either downgraded it or pooh-poohed the notion that it could be taken over or would be willing to be taken over. Management gave interviews in the Canadian press about how the company was not a target and had not gotten any inquiries, but it was definitively not for sale.

I read the articles and the analysts' reports, and even though I liked the fundamentals, I decided to boot the company for a small gain at $47. Less than a year later Alcan got not just one bid, from Alcoa, as part of a big consolidation in the aluminum business, but a second bid, for $101, by Rio Tinto, one of the largest mineral companies in the world. Alcan happily accepted that offer, which neither it nor the analysts thought was possible when the stock was at $47.

My conclusion: never say never about a potential takeover, even when management and the analysts point-blank rule it out. If a company has stock, ultimately that company is for sale. Don't get scared away just because the Street and the company's management don't believe it can be bought.

4. Don't let the market shake you out of a good long-term thesis. In the spring of 2005 it became amply clear to anyone reading the newspapers or watching TV that we were going to be in a shooting war in Iraq for a very long time. The United States has only one company capable of making all the ammunition needed for a long war: Alliant Techsystems.

After reading about the company, listening to the conference calls, reading analysts' reports, and noticing that the company had one of the most aggressive buybacks, retiring millions of shares a year off a very small base, I decided to buy some around $67.

It proved to be a prescient buy. The stock vaulted to $75 over the next couple of months. A few months later there was a downturn in the market because of worries of consistent and unrelenting Federal Reserve rate increases. These increases were wholly unrelated to the Iraq War, but I got shaken out and decided to take the quick gain.

Meanwhile the war raged on and so did the need for bullets. Within two years' time the stock rallied to more than $112 a share. I had let the market shake me out of a perfectly good position with a long-term thesis that, unfortunately for the U.S. soldiers in Iraq, played out. I made 7 easy points; I left 40 just-as-easy points on the table.

You must guard against selling a stock that you own for reasons independent of a market swing. Use the declines to build positions in stocks that don't depend on market momentum; don't be shaken out of your good positions. Throughout my investing for AAPlus I have seen this pattern: oil stocks sold because of market volatility that had nothing to do with the increasing price of oil; farm stocks sold even though the farm cycle is separate from the economic cycle; and mineral stocks dumped even though they are more levered to China than to the United States. If you have a good long-term thesis that is independent of the economic cycle, do not let yourself be faked out of what could be some terrific long-term gains.

5. Piggybacking can be a winning strategy if you remember to stay on the pig! If you like an idea suggested by a great stock-picker and you buy a stock, don't jettison it as long as the champion of the stock still loves it. In the past few years, I have come to love a website that identifies stocks owned by great investors and lets you cross-reference those stocks with those of other holders: www.stockpickr.com. It also allows you to be involved in a community of investors who have posted their own portfolios and given reasons to own the stocks. I find this an incredibly worthwhile way to get started finding a stock.

Not long ago I learned that Rich Pzena, perhaps the greatest value manager of our time, had purchased a big stake in American Physicians Capital. I reached out to Rich—he's an old friend—to ask him the story. He pointed me to the company's website, which showed that this malpractice insurance company was beginning to benefit from a tide that had turned against the plaintiffs in lawsuits against doctors. He told me to monitor those lawsuit verdicts through the company's website and to follow his holdings on the stock to know if anything needed to be done, but that he was in it for as long as his thesis played out. Tracking Rich and others like him is what Stock pickr.com was made for. The stock soon moved up 4 points and I figured, why wait to see if Pzena still owned it when I could take the terrific gain? Not long after I sold, I saw that Pzena had increased his position and become the largest holder of the stock. I didn't want to buy it back—I should have, but I was too proud (another lesson learned, but something you shouldn't have a problem with; I was hung up on buying back because every move I make is public). Over the next year I watched it go up and up until it had doubled from where Rich had bought it. I could have piggybacked all the way, but instead I got off *despite my desire to mimic this great investor.*

If you are in a stock because some great manager likes it and you monitor the story and it doesn't change and the manager doesn't sell off some of the holdings, why sell? While a gain is never "costly," it glares at me that I bought it for one reason, the piggyback, after he had done *all the homework for me,* and I acted, with my selling, as if I knew more than he did. I didn't! My belief was in him and his abilities. He never wavered. I did, and I left an outsize gain for him and his investors without me. Stay on the bull that brought you to the party.

6. Try to play with the house's money. A couple of years ago, Dan Rather decided to do a profile of me for *60 Minutes*. I decided I wanted to focus on a stock that would be good anytime the piece ran, because he told me that if it was any good, it would be a candidate to be rerun the following summer. I didn't want to recommend a stock that would blow up on me.

So I looked at my portfolio and estimated which stock would last the longest, which one I had the most confidence in. I had bought the stock of Anglo American UK (AAUK), a South African mining conglomerate that had said that over the next year it would break itself into parts that were worth more than the whole. I liked the sound of that plan and I liked its long-term nature.

So when Rather's crew filmed the episode I emphasized that you could own this stock for a long time, scaling out as it went up but ultimately holding on to some stock until you were just playing with the house's money. In other words, scale out of the stock as it goes higher. I bought 5,000 shares at $26 and my plan was to sell 1,000 shares every few points up until I had recouped my initial investment and was now playing with the house's money. I didn't want to be greedy, but I knew that I had the staying power and I knew that it is awfully hard to find another stock that is as good as one that's winning for you now.

Did I follow my plan? Nah, I got short-term greedy instead of long-term greedy. Anglo American's stock went up 3 points soon after I bought, and I sold not 1,000 shares, as I should have, but 2,500. It then went up another 3 points and instead of scaling out slowly over time, I sold the other 2,500. My original plan, made before the heat of battle, had been to sell 1,000 shares every few points up and instead I exited the position up about 6 bucks, for a gain of $22,500.

Sure enough, about eight months later CBS reran the program. There I was in full glory talking about how this was one you had to scale out of on the way up. I looked at the stock when the show aired again, and it had almost doubled. Had I followed my plan, I would have booked a $30,000 profit and then let the last 1,000 shares run.

And if I had done that, the house's money, the last 1,000 shares I held, would have produced the biggest gain of all—$50,000! That's double the whole gain I took on the position, not including the gains on the other 4,000 shares taken off earlier.

The compounding you get from letting a position run *knowing you can't lose* is one of the greatest concepts in investing. But you can't get to that Promised Land if you don't even try. Don't be so quick to sell. You made your plan; stick with it. At least you know you won't have to be embarrassed by a national TV rerun.

By the way, the stocks I bought with the capital I took out of AAUK did nowhere near as well as that winner. Ouch! Don't just mind your winners, mine them. Scale slowly. Stop selling when you are playing with the house's money. Remember how hard it is to find winning stocks and don't be so quick to sell them. You are most likely going to substitute a loser for a winner if you are so quick to sell.

7. Never turn an investment into a trade. In *Jim Cramer's Real Money*, I listed the Ten Commandments of Trading that I learned while running my hedge fund. The most important, the first, still rings true every day: "Never turn a trade into an investment." You bought something for an event; after the event occurs, don't hold on to it. Sell it either way, take the gain or loss, because you can't start justifying it as something else.

But I have learned something new from running my charitable trust, something more valuable for those of you who want to stay mad for life: never turn an investment into a trade. In 2004, my youngest daughter asked for an iPod for her tenth birthday. I was stunned. I reminded her that I had bought her an iPod for the holidays. She said that she loved that one, but it was blue and now she wanted a pink one. I said that was ridiculous, her first iPod was fine. She said something that made me stop what I was doing and think hard for a moment: "Dad, it's like having two pocketbooks or two pieces of jewelry. Just because you have one doesn't mean you shouldn't have another. No one would get mad at someone who wanted a second piece of jewelry if you knew that person loved jewelry."

It hit me like a ton of iPods landing on my head. Of course, it was a fashion accessory! That's what the kids liked it for. When I went through the research, it was clear that not a single analyst considered it as such. All the saturation figures assumed a point where everyone who was supposed to have an iPod had one already.

I had always liked Apple. I had been paying my kids' iTunes bills for several years and I had toyed with getting an iPod myself (I now have one with hundreds of songs on it). But I didn't have a thesis to explain why the iPod would keep growing. I had thought it was just another glorified MP3 player and that many other contenders would eventually get into the market. I had never thought of it as a fashion statement.

Now, I had listened to my kids many times for ideas about where they liked to shop: Hollister, which is how I caught a 40 percent move in Hollister's parent, ANF Abercrombie & Fitch; Google, which was easy because all the teachers had written at the top of their homework assignments "No Googling." But this time I realized I had something very big, an investment thesis that no one seemed to have: Apple as fashion accessory.

I bought the stock at $26 with a goal of owning it for as long as the fundamentals checked out and until others in the research grasped the significance of the Apple brand. But when the stock moved up a quick 5 points, I figured, okay, so much for the investment thesis. Let's take the trading gain.

Everyone knows the Apple story. It went up fivefold, in part because of the recognition not just by analysts but by competitors, particularly Microsoft with its disastrous Zune competitor, that Apple is fashionable and that fashion means more than just utility; it means you can charge more and you can sell more. Each time I read a new analyst's report that grasped the concept, I kicked myself. I had a fabulous investment thesis, from my kids no less, and turned it into a trade.

If you know something's going to be an investment, you have to be willing to sacrifice the quick gains.

By the way, the takeaway is *not* that your kids are always right. Not long after the iPod brainstorm, I brought home a pair of Crocs because the company was about to go public. My younger daughter despised them. She said they were the ugliest things she had ever seen. The stock then quintupled.

But my elder daughter got behind Under Armour shirts as both a fashion statement and an athletic one. She insists on wearing Under Armour under her lacrosse and field hockey goalie pads. Kids are terrific sources of ideas, but you still have to do the homework. Elder daughter, one for one; younger, one for two.

8. Trust your instincts, not your friends . . . There was a terrific water company where I grew up outside of Philadelphia, Suburban Water, and it had a great reputation for pristine water and for management. A fabulous guy, Nick Debenedictis, ran the company. He was someone I had met several times and someone I considered to be a friend of both *Kudlow & Cramer*, my old show, and *Mad Money*.

Suburban Water, which became Aqua America, had been a consistent grower, but one thing disturbed me: it kept growing via acquisitions but showed very little core organic growth. Also, every time it bought a company, the target company's insiders would sell Aqua's stock heavily. Nick convinced me that the company was not masking a lack of growth and the insiders just desired some liquidity. So I bought the stock heavily in the $25 and $26 range.

For seven months I held on to it. During that time it kept making deals and the insiders kept selling. And then it had a shortfall. Why? Not enough organic growth. My instincts had been right, but I had let a friend sway me. As I say every night at the beginning of *Mad Money*, the show's not about making friends, it's about making money. If only I had listened to myself instead of Aqua America's management. It's too bad too: Nick is a great guy! But this water company ran out of steam.

And of course, beware of any company that needs to grow *endlessly* through acquisitions. That's a sign that the core business is slowing, regardless of what management says. Never let someone talk you out of what you know to be right in companies where you don't know the management.

9. Don't let short-term bad news scare you out of a good long-term stock. I had always favored the business model of Aramark, a food service company that started in Philadelphia. I was a vendor for years at the now-demolished Veterans Stadium in Philadelphia—I must be old, because I was at the first game played there! And I could see how much a well-run vending company could make.

Aramark had consistent earnings from managing sporting events and stadiums and had branched out to providing food for corporate lunchrooms. It operated like a Swiss watch and it generated cash as surely as the U.S. Mint. That kind of consistent cash flow always catches the eye of the private equity folks, who know that companies like Aramark don't need to be public and can make a lot more money privately because of their regular earnings streams. So I bought four thousand shares over a matter of about a month, at $26.

Wouldn't you know it, but that summer I learned there would be a National Hockey League lockout. Aramark has contracts with a lot of arenas where the NHL plays. I decided that there was no reason to own Aramark if its consistent earnings were going to be jeopardized by the lockout. So I sold it for a dollar-a-share loss. Sure enough, there was a lockout, and Aramark announced that the lockout would cost it a couple of pennies a share. I felt vindicated—until a few months later, when it went private for about $10 more than I had sold it for. I had let short-term bad news knock me out of long-term gains.

10. If you buy a position to fill a need in a portfolio, don't jettison it because it's not working. I like owning a gold stock as a hedge against the world's craziness and instability. I often tell people who call in to my show that if I have a ten-position portfolio—as I say in *Real Money*, if you have the time and inclination to spend an hour on every position per week, you must have a minimum of five stocks to be diversified—there is room for a gold stock. I feel the same way about my twenty-something positions in my charitable trust. When I started ActionAlertsPlus.com in 2002, I decided to buy Barrick Gold as the hedge in my portfolio. As other stocks went up, Barrick languished and started going down, so I sold it *even though I'd bought it as a hedge.* Sure enough, as the Middle East turmoil bled on and oil soared, Barrick moved up substantially, doubling over the next three years from where I had sold it. Barrick would have been the perfect hedge against oil-spike inflation, which is why I bought it in the first place! When the inflation scourge flared, I had little to protect myself in my stock portfolio.

If you buy a stock because you want it to counterbalance a portfolio or hedge out risk, don't sell it because it isn't working. That stock's your insurance, and just because lightning hasn't struck lately doesn't mean you shouldn't have insurance. Don't boot it out because it's not acting well compared to the rest of your portfolio; it's not supposed to!

I made a similar mistake a year later, this time buying something for a dividend because I wanted income. I bought BP, which yielded 4 percent, and then when I made 7 points on the stock, I decided that I no longer needed it and wanted the gain. I didn't buy it for that reason, though; the gain was just an unexpected windfall. I had picked BP because it raised its dividend consistently each year, but did I stick around for the increase? Did I really want an income producer, as I said when I bought it? No, I was satisfied, wrongly, with the capital gain, which was simply a delicious piece of icing on the dividend cake—not reason enough to trade in the cake, though. Sure enough, the stock rallied another 15 points in the year and a half after I sold it, and it still yields 4 percent because of its bountiful dividend policy. (The dividend grew as the stock price grew, which kept the yield steady at 4 percent.) If you own a stock for hedging or for dividends, don't contrive reasons to sell it, and don't just take the gain. You've got valid reasons to hold it through thick and thin, unless the gold company becomes something else or the oil company slashes the dividend. Sometimes when you choose to preserve capital you also make money, but if you are buying security, don't sell a stock because you've made a quick buck. Remember why you buy things and the reasoning you went in with will not betray you.

11. Uninformed low-dollar-amount speculation can wipe you out. Those of you who have followed my writings over the years, and now you new folks, should understand the value of speculation. It makes you more interested, keeps you in the game, and gives you an incentive to pay attention, all of which are vital if you're going to manage your own portfolio. When I set up my charitable trust, I was true to my word, deciding to put on a long-term, low-dollar-amount speculation that could turn into something huge.

I had always been enamored of the cable television model. At the time I believed that once you had cable, you regarded it as a utility and would no sooner abandon it than give up your electricity. So I picked Charter, a debt-laden cable company that sold at $4, for my speculation. Given that I'm running $3 million and given my desire always to be diversified, I decided to make this speculation a little more than 7 percent of my portfolio, the outer limits of what I have deemed safe because it won't tilt the portfolio down in a meaningful way.

In a series of very public presentations, Charter outlined its plans to go from a company with too much debt with a high interest rate to a company with modest debt and a good footprint in some growth areas around the country. Charter had about $18 billion in debt at the time and was struggling to refinance at lower rates—just as you would try to refinance a 10 percent mortgage down to 6 percent.

I bought the stock in November 2003 with the presumption that I would give management twelve to eighteen months to sell off properties and fix the balance sheet. I buy stocks for that period of time because that's about how long it should take for an idea, a really solid idea, to generate a great return. Anything longer than that, particularly in a stock that has failed to appreciate or actually goes down, is too long and you simply have to give yourself a failing grade. I waited for quarter after quarter for Charter to make good on its promises to sell assets and shore up its balance sheet. But the company did nothing except bleed. One quarter, two quarters, three quarters, and all that happened was the stock went down.

Frustrated, I went to see Charter's management at a presentation and demanded that they fulfill their obligations to shareholders. (Although I don't expect you to do this as a home gamer, it is possible to go to a company's annual meeting or any public presentation. As long as you are a shareholder, the company has to let you in. It's not like the old days, when you had to be a big institution to attend these meetings.) Management counseled patience. In the meantime the stock continued to drop. After the fourth quarter the stock dropped to the low $2s. I refused to give up. I dug in my heels and told readers that I believed the company was finally waking up to its destruction of the shareholder base. But they just postponed again.

After the sixth quarter, the stock collapsed to $1 and change. On a strong market rally the stock managed to go back to the $2s, but I had had enough. The company simply could not grow its subscriber base. Plus, given its lack of capital, it could not keep pace with all the innovations cable companies were introducing: high-definition, pay-per-view, and triple-play phone service. It either had some of these but could not advertise heavily because it was so cash strapped, or it didn't have enough money to develop them in other areas and was beginning to get hurt by satellite and by more aggressive telephone companies. I was beside myself.

There has to be an end point to all investments when they don't work, when the thesis doesn't play out, and after eighteen months I gave up and took a $130,000 loss, *the biggest loss I have ever taken in my charitable trust.* The lessons were clear: (1) Just because it's a low dollar amount doesn't mean you can't lose a fortune. (2) If you speculate, do not speculate with a company with a terrible balance sheet; it may never come back. (3) When management makes promises and fails to deliver over an eighteen-month period, you have to accept defeat. (4) Indebted firms cannot compete with those that don't have as much debt, making them far more problematic stocks than those that are without much debt. (5) If you think you'll get bailed out, perhaps by a takeover because you think that the stock's price—the amount of dollars it costs to buy a share, which is meaningless, not the price-to-earnings multiple—is small, forget it. Other companies see the same thing you do. (6) If the stock had a higher dollar amount—if it had done a reverse split—I would never have been attracted to it. What drew me to it was its under-$5-a-share status. (7) It is irrelevant where a company came from to get to $5 other than to suggest that it didn't get there because it is doing well. At one point Charter was a high-flying $25 stock. It didn't matter that it had once been there. That was totally irrelevant. Good stocks don't travel to the single digits. I was foolish to be attracted to it just because it "looked" cheap.

All of these horrible investing mistakes give you some fabulous guidelines for the kinds of stock to *avoid* if you speculate. There are tons of companies out there that simply don't have any ability to fix themselves. While I am all in favor of speculation, it must be informed speculation with benchmarks and targets; otherwise you'll lose far more than you ever expected. When you ask yourself, "How low can it go?" think of this Charter situation. A stock can go pretty far down, enough to lose you huge money.

By the way, Charter never came back. It's about where I sold it, give or take a couple of dimes. Pathetic company, pathetic speculation.

12. Love the product, don't love the stock. You may be very late to the cycle and miss the upside. When I was doing my radio show, I had to do it remotely. Many radio hosts like to have someone on staff in their ear telling them the name of the caller and where he or she is from. I didn't want to be distracted by that.

One day, after a year of trying to deal with the incessant chatter in my ear while giving people good advice, I protested that I could not do a good job unless there was another way. My telephone board operator went to his top-notch tech guys and came back with what they said was a brand-new solution: "Go To My P.C." from an outfit called Citrix. I was able to download the program and on the other end the telephone board operator did the same thing. This software allowed me to access remotely the names of the callers.

It was miraculous. I couldn't believe such a product existed. I researched all the public filings on the company. It seemed very strong, and the product I liked so much was one of Citrix's most important contributors to the bottom line. So I leaped at it at $43 in the spring of 2006, expecting that others in the industry, and outside too, who also needed remote software that allowed them to hold meetings and all see the same thing at once, would snap up the product.

And you know what happened? The company reported its quarter and it showed a distinct slowing in this product line. Everyone who needed "Go To My P.C." seemed to have ordered it. Contrary to what I had thought to be the case, or my tech guys had thought to be the case, I was late to the product cycle. (You can't rely even on the tech experts in the field, because they may not know either.) I was on the tail end of the new customer base.

There was nothing I could do. The product had peaked, and after a tech product peaks it is all downhill. I had to sell the stock 10 points lower, as there was no reason to hang on. It subsequently went even lower before it was able to stabilize, but it never recovered to where I had bought it despite a huge rally in the market. I liked the product so much that I bought the company, not realizing that as great as the product was, I was coming in well after the product had been adopted.

The moral? You may think you are early in the development of something, but you may be late, much later than you think. Just because you discovered something doesn't mean it hasn't been discovered many times over already. Could I have recognized how late I was in the product's cycle? I think that I could have simply by asking how long the product had been on the market. At the time I bought, it was about three years. That's late in any tech cycle, whether it be the Pentium chip or the Motorola Razr. Without constant innovation in tech you will be passed by another company doing something better, or you will have a saturated customer base and only a few rare radio hosts will be left to sell to.

13. Never buy the best house in a bad neighborhood. About midway through my radio show's history I wanted to get picked up by Cumulus Media, the second-largest radio company in the country. So I called its terrific CEO, Lew Dickey, and beseeched him for a meeting. He obliged and came to the offices of TheStreet.com.

Dickey was energetic, charismatic, and enthusiastic, so much so that he could not contain himself about the coming renaissance of radio. He was talking about all the new formats and how radio was going to win back customers because, in the end, it was the customers' favorite medium when driving in the car. It was the spring of 2004 and radio had been in the dumps since the collapse of the dot-com era, when many companies had relied on radio to spur business. I said that radio seemed to be a dying business. He insisted that it wasn't, but more important, *his business was certainly not dying.* His business was generating huge net cash flow—what's left in actual cash when you deduct all the costs of doing business. He gave me no non-public information—remember that great equalizer between the pros and the amateurs I wrote about in the last chapter—but it did seem like a terrific story, even if the other radio companies were being shunned by investors.

I bought the stock at $19 over a series of months and readied myself for the renaissance. Meanwhile, Sirius and XM had different views and the auto companies began including them in new models. When I got my new car, satellite radio came standard. And my kids used the electronic jack in the car for the iPod. Commercial radio responded by running fewer commercials but charging higher rates, which they could not sustain.

Cumulus did better than the average radio company, but its stock performed just like the others. Six months later—that's how dynamic business can be—the stock was down 25 percent, part of an overall exodus from all radio companies. I had bought the best house in a bad neighborhood.

I realized the error of my ways—which was, of course, against my conviction to begin with—and took the big loss. The stock proceeded to get more than cut in half over the next two years and then, adding insult to injury, Dickey took the company private in 2007 at a little more than half of what I paid for it in 2004. I say this added insult to injury because had I held on to it as a classic long-term buy-and-hold investor, I wouldn't even have had a chance to get back to even. If the renaissance ever occurs, I sure won't be a part of it.

At least the radio execs believe. Cumulus was one of three companies in this terrible industry to take advantage of the declines in its stocks and go private. By the way, I think the execs are gravely mistaken about what will occur, but at least they won't hurt anyone but themselves this time around.

14. You are not an index fund. You don't "need" any one kind of stock in your portfolio. When I started running my own money, I was gripped by a fever: I was underweighted in tech. How can you not own some tech? I thought.

"Underweighted" is genuine Wall Street gibberish for not owning many stocks in a sector that is big in the S&P 500. Tech is a huge part of the S&P 500, and I owned nothing in it when I started AAPlus, because I though tech was dangerous. Didn't matter: I felt the need to own something simply because I didn't want my holdings to be too different from the S&P 500.

What a mistake! I bought EMC at $14 in the spring of 2004. I compounded the error by buying tech at the worst time on the calendar, which is right when the traditional summer slowdown occurs. If you insist on buying tech, wait until July or August, when tech has bottomed in fifteen of the past sixteen years. I felt satisfied that I had the representation I needed to show, and I no longer felt naked.

What did EMC do? Like the rest of tech, it collapsed. My judgment was right. At the very moment I was buying tech, the group became unfashionable in the great fashion show that is Wall Street. EMC plummeted to $10 as tech fell viciously out of favor. I had to punt it. The stock didn't come back for a long time and only recently has it moved above where I purchased it. I had violated one of the great tenets of individual investing: *you don't need to mimic the S&P 500.* You can own what you want, when you want, and you do not need to be constrained by the artificial nature of trying to pick the best stocks in sectors in the S&P 500. Doing that will lead you to buy stocks in sectors you don't believe in, and, given that 50 percent of a stock's performance is the sector, doing so is contrary to generating healthier returns than the benchmarks over time. Still, it's so easy to get sucked in, because all you ever hear in the media is professionals speaking of "underweighting" and "overweighting." It simply is irrelevant to you at home. No one is watching; no one is critiquing except yourself. Remember, there are plenty of good sectors to diversify into, so you don't need to be in the bad ones.

15. Be suspicious of high dividends—they often don't get paid. Two years ago, while reading the always valuable *Investor's Business Daily*, I repeatedly saw the chart of Fording Canadian Coal Trust on the list of winning stocks. Everyone knows I like winning stocks, and this one just called for more work because it yielded 14 percent. I like income-producing stocks because unlike bonds, which also produce a steady return, stocks with dividends can produce capital gains too. Oil was going up endlessly and with the United States having an abundance of coal, a little research showed me that Fording had clean coal that would not rankle the environmentalists. I figured I had a good one.

I didn't. One month after I bought it, the company announced a production shortfall that forced it to cut its dividend, and the stock plunged 6 points. Given that the company didn't even try to explain away the shortfall or project when the problems would be fixed, I quickly booted the stock. That damage control kept me from losing another 6 points as the problem only grew worse.

But I learned a valuable lesson: outsize dividends, dividends that are much larger than what other kinds of stocks are offering, are red flags. They are often a sign of worry, not a sign of safety. This Fording Coal experience kept me from buying what looked to be some terrific buys in the spring and summer of 2007, when many of the mortgage-related real estate investment trusts were yielding dividends in the low teens. This lesson saved me hundreds of thousands of dollars as even the stocks with the highest coverage of dividends, companies like American Home Mortgage, not only discontinued their dividends but discontinued their business altogether. Many people were attracted to these companies, particularly because managements continued to say that the dividends were safe right up to the last minute, when they were sliced or eliminated.

Remember: there is no free lunch with dividends. Could I have spotted that these dividends were in trouble? Not really, as the companies seemed to be making a lot of money. Sometimes, though, you have to take the market's cue: I don't want you buying stocks with ultrahigh dividends; I want you to sell them. Occassionally, a company can snap back. But we play the odds here and the odds say that a gigantic dividend isn't a sign of confidence or health, it is a sign of trouble.

16. Pay attention to local papers—the Web is your secret weapon. When I first started trading, I used to read the local papers in the towns where my companies were headquartered. They came three days late. Three days! So it was of limited value to read the Peoria paper to find out how Caterpillar was doing in its efforts to crush the union and bring costs down.

But that was nothing compared to what you can do now to find out about stocks you own. You can load them into Google and find stories about them and their sectors, which is how I was lucky enough to limit my losses with Lamar Advertising early in 2007. The story is a simple one: billboards are important venues for advertisers now that TiVo has made it easy to skip commercials and XM and Sirius have cut into commercial radio. You can't stop looking at billboards, but that ended up being the problem. Lamar has billboards all over the country, and with a new technique, liquid crystal displays, they were able to rotate the advertisers who rented the billboards, putting three different advertisers on each billboard.

The result? A windfall. Once the fixed cost of the lighting was in, Lamar could charge three times the price for the advertisements. It seemed like found money to me as Lamar rolled out one sign after another around the country. What I didn't realize, though, when I purchased the stock in the high $60s, was that the signs were *too* effective. They were causing car crashes. I would not have picked this up had I not done repeated searches for billboard stories to stay current about the industry. (Clear Channel and CBS were doing the same thing; they are the other two in the big three of billboard advertising.) Sure enough, in Providence, Rhode Island, highway safety officials were making noise about these billboards being a dangerous roadside hazard. I was able, quickly, to leave the position at a small loss.

Subsequently, the stock dropped $15 as the Providence concerns went statewide and then became a national problem. The LCD roll-out got crimped and the stock got crushed. While there are limits to what you can search even on the Web, let Lamar remind you that things can go wrong with major innovations and changes, but you can follow them and be ahead of the curve. The analysts who followed Lamar stayed bullish until the problems with these billboards surfaced nationally. Then it was too late.

17. Be suspicious of technical analysis. It tends to miss all of the big turning points. I have always had a use for technical analysis because others who run money do, and they can make decisions based on it. Technical analysis tends to divine future prices from how patterns in stock movements form. Typically, you can see tops from something that looks like a head and shoulders on a stock chart, and you can see bottoms when you get what looks like a reverse head and shoulders. I critiqued this analysis in *Real Money* and gave you examples of where I had been driven out of stocks by technical analysis right before take-overs.

I am going back over this kind of analysis to tell you that the major brokerages now make a big deal of offering technical analysis on all of their free sites as if it were value added. It is extremely seductive and feels scientific, even as investing is inherently psychological and doesn't lend itself to such hard and fast methods. Good stock-picking, or call it good investing, is much more an art than a science, and the certainty of these research tools can be misleading at best and outright dangerous at worst. Nevertheless, at times I attempted to pick stocks and follow them using this software because it is what many home gamers use. Also, part of the exercise of trying to run the charitable trust was to move away from the professional style I was used to and examine what *you* might be looking at *instead* of the fundamental research I prefer.

I point this out because at two crucial moments, when I was desperate to find bottoms in two stocks, Bristol-Myers Squib and Ingersoll Rand, I looked up what the charts said. The charts were miserable. In these two cases the lines indicated that the stocks, BMY at $22 and IR at $37—well down from where I first purchased them—would not bottom for at least another 4 points.

While I don't like to trade for my charitable account, I figured, why not sidestep the expected losses? I could sell now, then buy the stocks at the lower price that I expected to come. Sure enough, the stocks never got to those targets—targets, by the way, that independent charting services I looked into verified. Now here's the rub: because they never got to those targets, I had no ability to get back into them, which is what I'd intended to do. I just kept waiting and waiting for the targets to get hit. Meanwhile both stocks had bottomed and started sustained runs upward. Not only did technical analysis get me out at the wrong time, but it *never got me back in.* All my homework and assumptions were lost. Keep that in mind when you lap up the free research that the brokers provide. You get what you pay for.

18. Companies can change their stripes, especially when you least expect it. So often we regard companies as static victims of the vicissitudes of their business. We figure they say to themselves, "You know what? We are going to take a beating, no doubt about it. That's just the work we are in." It's one thing for a homebuilder to say this, or even a bank, although some banks have been able to augment their lines of business with some excellent fee income. But it is a whole other thing to believe that companies with diverse lines of business have to take the pain. If Textron sees that its commercial aircraft business is hurting, it can always jettison it. If Procter & Gamble feels that its gross margins are being killed by some boring old brands, it can

sell them. And most important, when a good solid American manufacturer is being weighed down by a line of business, it can change its
stripes overnight by selling the division.

That's what happened after I sold Ingersoll Rand in 2006 after the
stock took a true beating. As I just mentioned, I rode the stock down
and got out at the bottom in part because of technical analysis. However, the story of the turnaround is eye-opening. The company, which
has some excellent divisions involving transportation, biometric security, and refrigeration, was being weighed down by its most visible
division: Bobcat. Homebuilders employ Bobcats to grade property.
They are integral to the housing construction business. Because they
are so integral to the process of homebuilding, the analysts who follow the company couldn't envision any way IR could separate itself
from the housing slump. They simply took it as gospel that IR was a
housing company. They didn't listen to management, which was saying that it would do whatever was necessary to reward patient shareholders. The analysts kept downgrading and denigrating the stock as
a helpless doe in the lights of the eighteen-wheeler that was the housing slowdown.

One day the company announced that the Bobcat division was for
sale. The analysts were in total disbelief. But they recovered from their
momentary vision of possible scenarios that could go right and set-
tled on the notion that nobody would buy Bobcat for much, given the
housing recession. So wrong! A Korean company with a long-term
view stepped up and paid about a billion and a half more dollars than
even the optimists thought IR would get. Next thing you know, the
stock had jumped 16 points from the $38 price where I had sold it. I
had succumbed to analyst negativity. IR was now a home-free play on
global transport and security worthy of a much higher price-to-
earnings multiple because of the more consistent earnings growth
that could now be predicted without the Bobcat division. IR's management quickly put the proceeds to work, buying back stock to make
it one of the better performing stocks during the mortgage-related

slowdown. It was a total home run for those who believed, and there was no reason not to believe unless you listened to the negative analysts who followed the company.

Coincidentally, not everyone got this wrong: Warren Buffett accumulated a gigantic position in IR when the company signaled its willingness to make brutal changes to improve profitability. Never underestimate management's abilities to take control of its own destiny.

19. It just can't be this bad, can it? The curious case of Yahoo. Not long ago, I was the guest commentator in the postgame show after the Jacksonville Jaguars handed my beloved Philadelphia Eagles a brutal loss at home. I was particularly critical of the Eagles' defense in my postgame analysis. Some of the players must have been listening to this professional stock picker's amateur football digression, because when a reporter stuck a mike in front of Sean Considine, a member of the Eagles' riddled defensive backfield, he fired back that he may not have played well, but that Cramer had burned him worse with his stupid Yahoo pick.

The charge was true to the mark: I had owned Yahoo for a couple of years for ActionAlertsPlus.com. Originally bought in the high $30s, I had averaged down to the point that I had a decent $28 basis. But anyone who had listened to me earlier and not later would have definitely felt like Considine and been eager to clothesline me.

I was still on the air and had a split second to answer, so I simply blurted that I couldn't believe that Yahoo could be that bad. I had inadvertently hit on another lesson of what it means to publicly manage private money: things *can* be this bad. I can't tell you how many times in the past five years I have picked the stocks of companies in industries that were rocking, thinking that, despite a stumble or two, the company was in such great shape, it had such a good business, that it simply could not screw it up.

The experience I had with Yahoo forever puts the lie to that kind of thinking. But you have to understand first how I could arrive at what turned out to be a bogus and costly decision. As a founder of TheStreet.com I was aware firsthand of how powerful and successful Yahoo was. When we started, a mention of our site on Yahoo caused traffic to spike and we depended mightily on Yahoo to gain readership. Over the years Yahoo became less and less a factor for us, in part because we had more people coming from various places on the Web, but also because Yahoo had become less relevant. Throughout this period, though, and to this day, Yahoo has the most traffic of any site on the Web. When you have the most traffic, the most viewers, of a business where advertisers are desperate for space to advertise in and want robust searching to turn up their sites, you should be in the catbird seat. To be sure, Google did come along and take lots of search revenue, in particular because Yahoo was late with its search product. But I figured it didn't matter; Yahoo would right itself and the stock would advance higher. Yet, over the past two years, *no company* I follow has been as haphazard as this one in attempting to meet estimates the Street sets for it. It has missed more quarterly projections than any company I have ever seen. It has changed managements, booted people, brought in new people, and the results are always the same: disappointing.

Finally, when the stock ran up on a takeover rumor I was able to dump it for a small loss. It then slid down another 25 percent almost immediately. The whole time this sickening slide was occurring, I consoled myself with the simple alibi that it just couldn't be this bad; no company could mismanage such a golden goose with such a stunning lack of dexterity and such helplessness.

The moral here is that you can never fall back on something as ephemeral as "It just can't be this bad" *even when you own what had been the best of the breed*, that is, the best in its sector. Yahoo owned the Net, but its own terrible management made the stock uninvestable. When you say, "It just can't be this bad, can it?" think of my Yahoo experience and answer, "Yes, it can."

20. Don't let the media panic you out of a good holding. The media is not your friend when it comes to stocks, particularly the stocks of health care companies. It is fitting to examine this lesson at length, because *no other lesson has spooked me out of more money than this one.* In part this is because, as part of my job, I am such a close observer of programming, particularly when it comes to stocks I own. The media isolates the most negative story about medical issues and plays it in your face over and over until you can't take it anymore. When I say I can't take it anymore, focus: I am a seasoned pain-taker and if I can't take it, you can't either. Let me give you a couple of examples so perhaps you can develop thicker skin than I have and we can go forward knowing that there's more to every story than the media provides.

In 2006, I noticed that Bausch & Lomb had fallen a quick 10 points from a high. I always liked Bausch & Lomb as a gold-standard play on eye care and was devoted to many of its products for my eyes. It has a hammerlock on products worldwide for surgical eye care, such as for cataracts, and consumer eye care, such as contact lenses and solutions. It has been number one in these categories for years. So I took advantage of the decline and bought some stock in the mid-$60s. Sure enough, not long after, I found out what was ailing the stock: reports that its lens solution with MoistureLoc, a small part of its product line, was causing eye problems that could lead to blindness in a small number of patients. The media was quickly all over it and the analysts panicked, many taking it to a sell. I was beside myself with fear. How many people would get this eye disease? Where was it coming from? Would B&L get in front of it? We had almost no information on it, yet every time there was a new case of the disease, it was on the news. The stock sank right through the $50s to the $40s. When it got to the $40s the company recalled its products from the stores, gave out coupons, and assured people that the situation was under control. But then the media focused on some additional cases, no doubt caused from the same lots, and the company couldn't put its finger on which plants were making the contaminated solutions.

After what seemed to be myriad negative stories, I gave in and blew the stock out in the low $40s. Soon afterward the company and the FDA began to get their arms around the story: there were probably no more than two hundred cases and they were treatable. The stock began to move upward and the company got a takeover bid for more than $70 soon after. I had succumbed to the media's assertions of dire forecasts for B&L because of this one small product line. There were a host of businesses that were doing quite well for B&L, and though other companies grabbed some share, its core franchise was strong enough to withstand this recall and this negative publicity. By the way, the same reporters who kept hammering this story home never reported on the conclusion of the scare. It didn't matter; the opportunity to buy from those scared by the media was long gone. The money had already been made by others.

A second case of brutal media coverage came at the expense of Bristol-Myers. This fine company, with a host of truly great medicines, including some of the very best cancer drugs, had a very important heart drug, Plavix, under patent. Because of some quirk with a Canadian company, Apotex, management had somehow let a generic version come out without enforcing its contract. Consequently the drug, responsible for a good deal of the company's profits, was momentarily blitzed by a huge amount of generic pills before Apotex could be stopped. The media focused endlessly on the patent loss, harping on how Bristol-Myers was in huge trouble. The reality is that BMY had a strong franchise. If you believed in these media reports, you would have thought that all BMY had was Plavix.

Two quarters after the generic drug worked through the system, Plavix pricing went back to its premium level because the generics did violate BMY's patents. Plus, BMY applied for and introduced exciting new cancer drugs. Soon the stock rallied to $32. Too late for me, as I was stampeded out of it at $23, down $3 from where I had bought it. I was caught up in the media frenzy and didn't believe in my own homework. Of course, no one in the media regarded this momentary blip as a buying opportunity, which is exactly what it was.

Or how about Cephalon, a biotech company with a host of excellent, profitable products, including Sparlon? Cephalon had developed what looked to be a terrific product for attention-deficit disorder. It was important for the company that Sparlon be approved as a way to augment the 2009 earnings for the company. But when Sparlon came before the FDA, there was a high-stakes drama because a couple of patients in a study encompassing more than a thousand people had come down with Stevens Johnson syndrome, a rare skin disease that could be fatal if not detected. Because the disorder Sparlon was meant to combat was not life-threatening, this side effect was considered to be too negative to allow the drug to be approved. I had bought the stock in the $60s and it had run to the $70s on the possibility of Sparlon approval. That didn't happen, and the stock got crushed to the $50s. At that price it was absurdly valued compared to the rest of its product line.

But the stakes had been so high and the media coverage so vociferous that it obscured everything else that the company was doing right. I succumbed to the focus and dumped the stock in the $50s. Eighteen months later the stock had reached the mid-$80s as the rest of the product line just kept chugging along. I had been spooked by the media into thinking that Cephalon was a one-trick pony and the pony had come up lame. It was just the opposite: another buying opportunity because of a strong, stable product line. I can't tell you how often an FDA hearing seems make-or-break for a company. And it has been for true one-product companies like Dendreon with its Provenge prostate-cancer vaccine. But the opposite is true most of the time: there are many drugs humming in a diversified pharmaceutical company, including biotech companies, and it pays to remember that when the sound and the fury are focused on one product. Think of B&L, Bristol-Myers, and Cephalon before you succumb to the media's drumbeat against one of the drugs in what may be a strong breadth of products. That way you will realize what might be a time to buy, not to sell.

I hope these twenty lessons, gleaned from the many glaring mistakes I've made while running a public fund, will help you to avoid similar consequences. I don't want to imply for a minute that these stocks wrecked the performance of those who followed my recommendations. (Remember that my actions are restricted and some of the prices in these stories are lower than they would have been for my readers, who could have gotten out sooner as I apprise readers of my moves ahead of time.) Nonetheless, unlike the trading mistakes I describe in my other books, you can see that these bloopers are, in many ways, patterns that may be familiar to you or patterns you might not even realize yet. Just so you know, I spotted them in two ways that could help you. First, I went over every trade and bulletin I had issued over the life of the trust. Second, I also looked at the trust's holdings in snapshot fashion, meaning I looked at the portfolio as a whole every quarter and at the end of every quarter. I didn't do it to torture myself; I did it to remind myself that many heat-of-battle decisions have been wrong. Many positions would have worked out well in the end, but most important, many times I had let others disturb my thinking about what would have been sound decisions otherwise. Know thyself. You are better than almost anyone out there at picking your stocks. Rely on your stocks with my lessons, and I bet you will beat the market handily over time—perhaps becoming richer than you've imagined in your wildest dreams.

7

WHAT THE PROS DO RIGHT AND THE AMATEURS DO WRONG

Not long ago my good friend James Altucher started the first social networking stock site. It's a terrific place, Stockpickr.com, where professionals and amateurs gather every day to noodle on what to do next and what is happening in the market. It is also a great place to learn. But not just for home gamers anxious to pick up experience and lessons; for people like me too. Every day when I go into the "Answers" section of the site, I see questions addressed to me that show the tremendous gulf between amateurs and professionals, a gulf so great that, unless I do my best to help ameliorate it, will simply grow wider and wider, with beginners losing money repeatedly and even seasoned investors getting blown out because they don't understand what is happening and they don't know how to put aside their amateurish acts because they've never been taught by the pros. I have been a pro for three decades, but that doesn't mean it wasn't a continuing education course from the moment I got to Goldman Sachs to the moment I went on my own to start one of the first hedge funds. I never thought I would say that, but in retrospect it was a pretty gutsy thing to leave the friendly confines of Goldman to strike out on my own. It worked, but being a professional was something that didn't come second nature to me and won't to you either. So what can we do? After culling all the differences between what I see amateurs do routinely on Stockpickr.com and what I have been taught to do, I thought it might be a good idea to bridge the gulf right here and now by showing you the distances between us on a list of ten divides, and then giving you the tools to close them yourself.

Here are things the pros do right that amateurs insist on doing wrong when they manage their money:

Ten Things Pros Do Right but Amateurs Get Wrong

1. Pros always have cash. Amateurs are always fully invested. One of the most painful lessons I have learned is that when you run out of cash, you are truly in trouble. I always, always always keep cash around when I am running my trust, and if I ever find myself without 5 percent in cash, I consider that running on empty. This concept is alien to almost all of the amateur investors I have ever met. I can't tell you how many times I have responded to questioners with suggestions that they buy more of their favorite stocks and they say they are "fully invested," with no more cash on the sidelines. There's a simple reason for that: nonprofessionals think it is right to be fully invested. When I was a professional investor I was probably fully invested only after gigantic declines in the market. My rule of thumb was that unless you had a 10 percent decline, peak to trough, you should have cash on the sidelines ready to put to work, preferably as much as 10 percent, maybe more after a big run in the market. Yet I always see people and hear from people with no reserve.

How strongly do I feel about the need to keep the cash, not for a rainy day but for a monsoon? Even in my own 401(k) I don't commit

all at once. I commit one-twelfth of my annual allocation a month, changing my behavior and putting the rest in, only on a 10 percent decline. If I don't get a 10 percent decline, I will have committed the money on my regular one-twelfth-a-month schedule. What can you do to ensure that you will have cash for those great opportunities? And believe me, having that cash will be the difference between staying even with the averages and trouncing them. I want you to consider the cash you have to put to work like the gas in your car. Would you ever consider running it on empty? Don't you always like to have at least an eighth of a tank of gasoline? That's what I want you to do with your stock money. If you can fill 'er up there, that's fabulous. But if you can't, sell something you don't like as much as what you do like, or sell something to buy something better. Unless the market's down 10 percent, consider yourself fully invested until a huge decline occurs, and then you will be able to have a shopping list ready. When I write in *Real Money* or on Stockpickr.com or when I say on my TV program that it is time to get your shopping list ready, you won't be mad at me. You will be grateful. Oh, and by the way, if you are even tempted to use margin—borrow money from your broker—and if you are even contemplating a home equity loan for stocks, please go recycle this book; I wasted good paper on you.

2. Pros learn to start living and stop worrying about the quarterly report. Don't base buys on quarters—avoid them. And don't buy during earnings season. That's too hard. "Jim," the queries always begin, "do you like Intel ahead of the quarter tomorrow?" To which I say now, because I am no longer a hedge fund manager, "I think I like Intel *every day but* the day before the quarter." The pressure nonprofessionals put themselves under trying to trade quarterly reports is unbelievable. They take these totally unfathomable moments to put the gun to their head and pull the trigger.

You should know some things that have happened in the past decade. Every company tries to report at pretty much the same time.

Because of Regulation Fair Disclosure, no one can contact a company during the quarter to see how it is doing, which was formerly standard practice and was part of an investor's homework. This regulation made being an amateur an impossible hurdle to overcome. We are all equal now in the eyes of the law, so you can't get an edge. That means you have to listen to the conference call, match the expectations—what analysts were looking for—with what the company did, and then make a judgment. There are hundreds of people listening to these calls or to their replays and playing out this exercise. Then the analyst community scrutinizes the quarters and pronounces judgment. All this is happening at lightning speed because there are usually a dozen companies' calls that people might be interested in all taking place at the same time. I don't care how dedicated you are, how smart you are, how plugged in you are—this kind of rapid-fire moment does not lend itself to smart thinking. And you know what? It can be proved.

I sat down and looked at the periods when companies reported and saw how stocks did compared to when they don't report. The three weeks after the end of every quarter that companies report is almost *always* the time period when the *least* amount of money is made and the most is lost. That's why many of the professionals I know, including the best ones, have chosen simply not to buy *anything* during this period. They want to see the news, they want to retreat to their offices, they want to make decisions after everyone reacts, and they want to do it all on their own time with no pressure. Only amateurs pressure themselves. Professionals remove the pressure, remove the noise, and make decisions at their own pace. Will it cost them occasionally not to get in front of a good quarter? Of course. But it is much better to do the work on the quarter, watch and listen, and then pounce when the market gives you that break. You don't have to take action. I don't want you taking action. I want you to make your decisions with as many facts as are available after the quarter, when everything there is to know is known. That answer is always

disappointing to those who want to make the quick trade. But I want the bigger bucks, and the biggest bucks cannot be made betting on the direction of a given quarter. After all, if the company is that good, this won't be its last good quarter.

3. Pros try not to invest in things they don't know. They are not anxious to risk their hard-earned capital on something that sounds cool. Taking passes is the best thing I do. So many people ask me about different stocks, but many stocks are beyond my ken. I just recognize they are not my strength. I am a generalist who takes pride in knowing more stocks than anyone in the universe. Hardly a day goes by when someone doesn't ask me about some stock that has a miniaturization method, a nanotech derivative. I know better. I recommended one, Tessera Technologies, and the week after my recommendation it lost 20 percent of its value on something that, frankly, I simply did not understand, some piece of technology that was just too hard to know unless you were using it as a client. Same thing goes for a lot of the wide-area network stocks—stocks that help remote workers tie in with headquarters. These are jargon-filled black holes that you need an information technology expert to walk you through. Lots of the biotech stocks leave me cold; I don't understand how the medicines they make are special or different and how the companies themselves can be sure that they work. I also never think I can get an edge in commodities, even though so many people want me to tell them what I think of the direction of wheat or corn or soybeans—yes, I actually get asked that. I just accept the fact that I don't know it, that it is too hard for me to learn, and I take a pass. Too many people feel embarrassed to take a pass. Not me. I am always willing to say, "Nope, I don't get it, I don't understand it, and I don't want to trade it." Don't think that everything has to be traded or owned. Some things are genuinely too hard for you to know. In *Magnum Force,* Clint Eastwood summed it up well: "A man's got to know his own limitations." I know mine. Do you know yours?

4. Pros recognize that not everything is analyzable. Amateurs think that everything can be explained, graded, and traded. Not that long ago, a persistent questioner on Stockpickr.com kept asking me about a company called Clean Energy. He would not let up. Finally I told him it was not analyzable. That wasn't enough. He said that the legendary oilman T. Boone Pickens owned a big piece and he wouldn't do that if he couldn't analyze it. I told him I didn't know anything about why T. Boone Pickens liked anything but I did know that the company didn't file financials and it based its so-called earnings on the amount of natural gas it pumped into gas tanks. I kid you not! That was the metric. You couldn't even tell what the darned revenues were, let alone the earnings. Sorry, I think it's irresponsible to invest in something like that. This lesson is quite different from knowing your own limitations. There isn't anyone in the world, including T. Boone Pickens, who can make sense of that stock.

Tons of people call in to my show and ask me about Chinese stocks. Again, the financials are not only often opaque, they are often nonexistent. I can't tell a thing about them. I also am a firm believer that if you can't figure out what a particular bond is, such as a collateralized debt obligation that batches mortgages into a bond, you should *never* even be invested in a fund that has this junk. I believe that no one should own a fixed-income instrument or be in any hedge fund or mutual fund that owns something that can't be priced online from a Web service. The bonds that wiped out so many hedge funds and some banks were unanalyzable and unquotable. No one even knew what they were worth. And that's the bottom line: if you can't figure out what something is worth, if you can't compare it or match it to something else because you can't understand the financials or don't know where it is trading, forget about it.

I will leave you with a story. Recently, a very nice man who had read all my books stopped me in a card store and wanted to know what I thought about a certain Chinese airport stock. He said it was

going great guns and that I should look into it. I did. There wasn't even a fact sheet on the thing, just a name of a stock, an address in China, and a price, around $1.50. Sure, maybe it could go up. But checking it out was impossible. If you can't check out a stock, which means listening to the conference call, making sense of the filings, reading the releases, and comparing it to other stocks, forget about it. That's the basic information you need to make a decision. Without that, you just don't have enough to act on.

5. Pros want to know the downside, not the upside. That's why dividends and buybacks are so important. Whenever I meet or am in contact with a nonprofessional and I am pressed for an opinion, I always turn the tables and ask, "How much do you think this stock can go down?" People don't want to know that. They just want to know how much it can go up, or they want to tell me how much it can go up. They never want to hear about the downside. They don't even think it *will* go down. I think that everything will go down, everything. I always want to know what can cushion me. How big is the buyback? Is it a genuine buyback that shrinks the float? (A "buyback" is when a company purchases its own shares, reducing the number of shares on the market and thus making each share more valuable as it represents a slightly larger piece of the company. The "float" is the number of shares that actively trade on the market.) Or is it one of those bogus buybacks that retires some of the stock the company is issuing to employees? Is the dividend good? Can they pay out more? Is it possible that, even though the dividend seems small as expressed by the yield (dividing the stock price by the amount of the dividend), it may be bountiful if we think of it is as a moving target?

Consider that Procter & Gamble, for example, has traded for some time with a 2 percent and change dividend. But that's because the value of the stock keeps going up along with the dividend. The same dollar amount of the dividend it paid in 2007 would have been a 5 percent dividend if the stock were still selling at its 2000 price. Dividends that grow are fabulous cushions; dividends that grow fast are trampolines.

If a stock can't be saved by a buyback or a dividend, can it be saved by the multiple to earnings? You need to figure out if the company's growing faster than the average stock but sells at a lower price-to-earnings ratio than the average stock (as expressed by the average of the S&P 500). If you have a company with a high price-to-earnings multiple and no dividend and a buyback that is not meaningful, to me that means you have a stock that could really gaff you if things go wrong at the company or things go wrong with the stock, even if the growth rate is high. Watch for stocks that grow at a double-digit rate, but sell at single-digit multiples, and have big buybacks and good dividends. What—you don't think those exist? Consider that was precisely the situation of all the major oil companies before and during their remarkable runs in the past decade. Often a stock that has a limited downside will gain tons of adherents, letting the upside take care of itself!

6. Pros always look; they never avert their eyes from a downturn. Amateurs turn off their computers, stop watching CNBC, and don't even read their statements! I have always thought that ratings should go up on CNBC when the market goes down. But usually they don't. You know why? Because people don't like to watch themselves lose money. But that's a total loser, amateur reaction. When the market is down big, pros shine. When you see the market down a couple percentage points, I want you to turn on *Mad Money with Jim Cramer* that night so I can set you straight. Do you know how so many people lost money from peak to trough in 2000 to 2002? Because they put their statements in a drawer and turned the market off. If they had just paid attention anytime until the end of 2000 and sold their declining stocks, they could have saved themselves a fortune by sidestepping the even worse declines in 2001 and 2002. I know this because many gave up but did *not* sell—and lost considerably more. But they didn't dare look! They didn't want to see how much money they had lost. Pros, however, look at the market as a place where there is always mismarked merchandise, always something cheaper than it should be, and they shrug off the losses as part of the game. You can't make big money unless you are willing to lose big money, and the time to buy is exactly when the amateurs choose to run.

I always say that the good stuff—the runs, the market highs—takes care of itself. But when you stop looking, you stop caring, and when you stop caring there is no way to make any money in the market. Steel yourself against the gloom and consider this: when I got into the game, the Dow Jones average was at 1,200. I have watched it go to 14,000. If you had gotten out after the stock market crash in 1987, you would have left 12,500 points on the table. If you had left in October 1998, another dark hour, you would have missed 6,000 points. What more evidence do you need that it is time to turn on CNBC, not turn it off, when things get ugly? And they always do get ugly.

7. Pros accept that not everything works or is going to work at once. The price of diversification is owning losers. When I first started trading aggressively for my own account, my old friend Jack Shepard, my partner at Goldman Sachs, used to hear me on an up-market day swear, "Why the heck does my Exxon have to be down?" He would always look at me and say, "Jimmy, they can't all go up at once." I have had it drummed into me so many times that I have recognized that the price of a diversified portfolio is that they can't all go up at once. Yet I hear people kicking themselves that they own a stock that is down on an up day. They want to get rid of it, or curse it. But if you are running a diversified portfolio—and remember, I insist on it—you are going to have some loser stocks on up days. In fact, if they all go up at once, you probably aren't diversified enough, and when the down days occur, you are going to get clocked something awful. You own insurance, right? Do you wish that the insurance kicked in along with all the other things going right in your net worth? I didn't think so. I think that's how you have to feel about your stocks. Something won't be working if you are doing things right. Don't kick yourself; take it as a badge of prudence that will propel you much higher than the other guys over the long term.

8. Amateurs are worried that they aren't making enough, but pros are worried that they are making too much. I know it seems ridiculous to believe that you can ever make too much money. You can never be too thin or too rich, right? Wrong! Portfolio risk, the overall amount that your stocks can swing, is vital to understand and identify. If you are gaining 2 percent when the market, as represented by the S&P 500, is up 1 percent, you are taking on way too much risk. I am quite confident that when the market subsequently has an inevitable 1 percent correction, you will lose *more* than 2 percent. You can't swing more than the market without risking too much. Given that we want to beat the market incrementally, not trounce it daily, we have to measure risk. The best way to measure risk is to calculate the reward on these up days. Use those days after the big swing—unless you follow the market intraday—to cut what we pros call "exposure," that is, exposure to risk. That means raising some cash to swing less and cutting back on the number of stocks and percentage of stocks that are doing most of the swinging. Sure, you'll be limiting your upside, but I never stop: it is the downside we need to worry about because if we do, the upside will take care of itself.

When I was running my hedge fund I was most worried, most frightened, when I was making huge money. Anybody can make a ton of money all at once by taking on too much risk. There were people in 1999 to 2000 that were coining money daily, making more than they had ever dreamed. You never hear about them anymore, though. They don't pay attention to the market. They don't care about making money anymore. They've been blown out of the game. That's because they were making too much money. Whenever I had a streak when I was beating the market, sometimes by as much as 1 percent a day, I knew I was doing something wrong. I knew I had too much exposure. I had to cut back. Almost every time I took money off the table after I had been making too much money, I was able to avoid a real debacle. It *never* cost me any money when I did that. The secret to great professional money management is to get out before you blow yourself up. Look at your holdings. If you are killing the averages, making much more than you ever dreamed, you are doing something very wrong. You are setting yourself up for a huge fall. Go take something off, and as my late mother always said after a particularly productive day at the ponies or the casino, "Go buy yourself a nice sweater!" Or put it in some stocks with higher yields that will not swing so much. You will sleep better *and* make more money.

9. Pros know that cuffing it without doing homework can reduce you to—well, no offense—an amateur! Not long ago, *Barron's,* a publication that in my lifetime has made me no money, decided it wanted to find some way to discredit me. It spent weeks trying to find out if I bought the stocks that I mention on my show ahead of time, or if I have money in hedge funds that bought the stocks. Of course, neither is the case. Then it decided to focus on my performance, on the performance of the stocks I recommend. Of course, I thought I should be judged by the stock recommendations I prepare every night in what I call the "researched" blocks on my show. Those are the ones I work on ahead of time and have real conviction in. I also thought it would only be fair to include the stocks I constantly re-recommend, including some terrific ones like Apple and Research In Motion and Google. Nope. That would show me in too good a light. But what really galled me was that *Barron's* decided to weigh everything I said equally, putting the Lightning Round picks on par with the research blocks. I didn't even have to calculate it; I knew that I would not look good with those Lightning Round picks included. Those are snap judgments, where, as I said in the book *Mad Money*, I simply try to steer you toward what I think is the best of breed in a sector. Sure enough, by including those stocks and by choosing to judge my research stocks from the day of the spike that occurs so often after I recommend a stock (even though I repeatedly say wait five days before buying), *Barron's* said I failed to beat the market. What does all of this mean? To me, it is the empirical evidence that if you don't do the homework, you will have an awfully hard time beating the market even if you are a pro. It is not enough to know the stocks, and I do know most of the stocks in the Lightning Round; you have to do the homework to beat the market. Come to think of it, I owe a debt of gratitude to *Barron's*. Although their goal was to drive me off the air, as befits a News Corp. publication taking on a program on CNBC, they did prove, once and for all, that even pros need to do in-depth homework if they are going to beat the market. So how can amateurs possibly stand a chance if they don't do their homework?

10. Pros understand the upside, but they know that things can go wrong. Amateurs go full-bore and think it wouldn't be a stock if things could go wrong. Perhaps the widest gulf that I see between amateurs and professionals is a belief among home gamers that a company wouldn't have a stock if it weren't the real deal. Amateurs don't have any concept that there are whole periods, like the one from 1999 to 2001, when almost every single stock was no good. Pros recognize that there is a lot of crummy merchandise that should never have been created. The fact that a company comes public is not a Good Housekeeping seal of anything. There is no endorsement by the government through the SEC, nor by the underwriter, which typically wants to take in the fee for bringing the company public, and certainly not by the company, which just wants the money from issuing stock. Worse, amateurs think that when a company comes public it is as good as any other company that comes public. Pros are much more skeptical.

Take the case of Crocs versus Heelys. When Crocs came public, the company had a vision. It wanted to create a whole new category of shoe; it wanted to brand it, take it worldwide, and make it so that it would thrive for years and be a moving target to the competition. It turned out to be a fabulous stock and one I am glad I got behind early. Soon after, Heelys came public. This is the company that makes the shoe with a wheel in its heel. Because of the excitement around Crocs, the public bid the Heelys stock way up. It looked like it was the next Crocs. But the professionals I know and those who watch my show called it a short from the get-go. There were no plans to make Heelys big, to take it global, to make it a moving target. Heelys went public only because of its shoe, and the popularity of the shoe was just peaking when the stock was issued. I had person after person call me in the Lightning Round about this one, wanting me to bless it. They wanted to hear that it was the next Crocs. They were not skeptical. They thought it would not have come public if it were going to be a dud. Of course, what really happened, and what pros understood, is that Heelys took advantage of the Crocs halo to come public. Unseasoned individual investors couldn't believe that anything could go wrong. But the pros know that many, many stocks should not have been created, let alone been bid up. Heelys is Exhibit A of this era's lack of skepticism.

It took me years of hard work and emotional agony to learn how to invest like a professional money manager. You can have the same experience, or you can skip a lot of it by taking my advice on doing these ten things right, and let the amateurs keep doing them wrong.

8

FIVE BULL MARKETS
AND TWENTY STOCKS
FOR THE LONG TERM

Watchers of *Mad Money* know that I end my show every night with the mantra "There's always a bull market somewhere and I promise to find it just for you." Most people think of the stock market as one big market, a monolith. Nothing could be further from the truth. The market is made up of numerous submarkets and sectors, some good, some bad. At all times, something's working, something's making you money. The trick is to find out what that something is and stick with it, exploit it, and build a diversified portfolio around it.

On *Mad Money,* we have spent a great deal of time trying to find those bull markets. I want to reveal now, for the first time, the ones I think will last, maybe not for life, but certainly for the next five years. These are sectors that have some tremendous secular growth trends behind them, meaning that regardless of what's happening in the domestic economy, regardless of all of that chatter you hear endlessly about what the Federal Reserve might do or what the growth of the nation is or what the next quarters look like, these bull markets will hold up on their own. They are all different sectors so you can pick a stock in a sector and be sure that you have my blessing for the stock, as 50 percent of a stock's performance is its sector. Or to put it another way, you want to buy a house in a good neighborhood, because even the worst house in a good neighborhood is better than the best house in a declining neighborhood.

So what are those fabulous neighborhoods? What areas do I think will be great, not just for this year but for many years to come? I have five of them, and I will tell you why you can buy stocks in these sectors regardless of the chatter and how they will stay strong for many years to come.

I always say that I am a tease on TV, that I make you wait the whole show, including the Lightning Round, before you find out what I really like. But I don't want my *Stay Mad* readers to be mad at me. So here we go: (1) aerospace and defense, (2) agriculture, (3) oil and oil service, (4) minerals and mining, and (5) infrastructure.

Before we take them one by one, I want to let you in on the secret behind why these bull markets can be bought regardless of the U.S. economy and the Federal Reserve's attitude at a given moment: these are ROWers. That's right, they are Rest of World stocks, meaning they don't depend on the U.S. economy to propel them higher. We no longer want to be hostage to the U.S. economy, because our nation has entered a slow-growth phase that I believe will last for many, many years, certainly the period that you can count on this book to help you in. Believe me, I wish it weren't the case. But I have to be realistic; we are not in a position in this great country to grow at the pace of other countries, particularly less-developed countries, or countries in the Middle East that are linked to oil, or countries with high-growth populations that need to put money and people to work in order to keep civil order, such as China, India, and most of Latin America. The ROW category is what all of these bulls have in common. Given the growth paths outside the United States, I am highly confident that

American companies in these bull markets can compete with and beat foreign companies on their home turf.

Now that you know the secrets behind why these mini-bulls keep stampeding, let's explore why each market has "legs," as we say in the business.

Aerospace and Defense

When we think of the airlines, we think of companies that seem to go in and out of business, companies that have labor problems, companies that fight each other for routes and gates and can't seem to make any money unless the planes are full to the gills and jet fuel is low in price. That's why American investors have such a hard time understanding the bull market in aerospace. They are too U.S.-centric.

Around the globe in every newly industrialized nation, there is a booming airline company, often state-run, that is growing the way our airlines grew in the 1940s and 1950s, when this sector was hot, hot, hot. This growth can go on for years. As is so often the case, the epicenter of this bull market is China, where many of the major cities, cities that in the United States would have two or three airlines serving them, don't even have airline service. China could use ten times the number of planes it has and *still* not offer airline service to cities of millions of people. That means there will be demand for planes just for China that could fill order books for generations.

The countries in the Middle East, flush with oil money, want to expand their airlines. So do the newly wealthy nations in South America. Same with Central and Eastern Europe. That's where the growth is coming from. When I list twenty stocks for the future, you will read my case for Boeing, but there are only two major aircraft companies capable of meeting these worldwide needs: Airbus and Boeing. Right now only one of them, Boeing, can produce the planes. As with all bull markets, the components of the bulls, the suppliers to the end markets—in this case, Boeing and Airbus—can boom right alongside the customers. That means a company like BE Aerospace, which makes seating, and Honeywell, which makes precision instruments, and Spirit, which makes wing assembly, and Precision Castparts and Allegheny Technologies, experts in the "skin" of planes, can all boom right along with their clients.

On Wall Street, we often group aerospace with defense. That is done because the analysts who understand planes can follow the defense plays that have an aerospace component. In this particular case, there's more than just convenience to the marriage. The United States is home to most of the world's major defense contractors and we have become a giant exporter of the tools of war. We are arms merchants, financing billions and billions of dollars to arm Saudi Arabia and Israel and Egypt for many years to come. Plus, in our own country post-9/11, both political parties have remained committed to military spending, something that will continue even if we eventually wind up our efforts in Iraq. That means Raytheon, Lockheed Martin, General Dynamics, Northrop Grumman, and L-3, the major defense contractors, have what is known as "visibility," meaning they can see orders many years out. Oh, and don't forget that Boeing is one of the top five defense contractors too. Boeing could stay in bull-market mode just from defense for years to come. There are lots of smaller defense plays, such as Alliant Techsystems, the nation's largest bullet maker, that will make sense as long as the Iraq War continues, but I prefer to go with the larger defense contractors that have far more overseas business than the smaller ones, which are almost entirely dependent on the U.S. military.

Agriculture

Energy independence is a goal of both American political parties. The farm states have tremendous political power. That combination has produced one of the most amazing booms that our nation has ever seen: the agricultural boom, which is still in its infancy. You may not be filling up with ethanol yet—you may not even believe in renewable resources—but the commitment's been made, and being a farmer in this country is going to be lucrative for years to come. Throw in the fact that the federal government has proven to be completely incapable of reining in farm subsidies and you can see why "farm" replaces "pharma" in this generation's raging bull markets. Most people on Wall Street are skeptical of this group. They view it as a boom-bust sector, a cyclical sector with good times and bad. They fail to realize that the commitment to domestic fuels that don't destroy the environment (hence no coal) is irreversible and growing.

I like to look at the stocks in the ag bull market as secular growers, immune to the economy's vicissitudes. They should be viewed not as companies that help bring food to market but as companies that are the new oil-service companies, suppliers of energy at less and less cost each year, as the companies improve their products. The ag bull market is a tight-knit one. There's Deere for farm implements, Monsanto and Bunge for seeds—each is amazing at producing strains of vegetables that can generate more and more fuel per stalk of corn or soy—and Agrium and Mosaic for fertilizer. It's not a big cohort, but it is one that has become a market leader and has proven to go up no matter how the stock market performs. Deere is the best in show of this group, but Monsanto's the sleeper. The market values it as if it were a stodgy old chemical company, its legacy. In reality, it is a company that produces patents to develop better and better seeds. I consider it a biotech company for fuel, and that's something that will be in demand for years and years to come.

Oil and Oil Service

We are running out of oil, yet it will still be our fuel of choice for at least the next twenty-five years. We aren't producing enough renewable energy to satisfy demand. We are trying to expand nuclear energy, but the power plants are expensive and, in this country, still considered too dangerous and difficult to build. (As someone who for a spell lived next door to a power plant in Sacramento, I find this outlook odd, but then again, who else would willingly live next to one of those scary cooling towers!) Coal is just not attractive anymore, and the technology to make coal clean is costly. That keeps sending us back to black gold, and it is something that a whole host of companies benefits from.

When we speak of oil we think of the majors, the Exxons and Chevrons and Conocos. These are giant companies that produce stable cash flows and dividends; they are and will remain great investments for years and years. But, as in any mini-bull market, there are tons of other stock subsectors that will do great because they are involved in energy. We don't have enough refiners, which means that Valero and Marathon (which also has substantial oil properties) are going to be buys whenever they come down in price. We have plenty of natural gas in this country, which will increasingly have to be relied on as we run down our crude resources. Natural gas has been cheap in this country because we haven't been able to store as much as we would like. Still, I believe that companies like XTO, Devon, Apache, and Anadarko are all fantastic long-term buys.

For years, we starved the drilling and oil services businesses because oil was priced too low by OPEC to make alternative fuels profitable enough to develop. (OPEC's own inability to produce enough oil was responsible for much of the recent surge in oil prices, which I think will last for years.) Now there are only a handful of companies with the expertise to drill and harvest the oil that is found. National Oilwell Varco is the only major company left that can build drilling rigs. Schlumberger is the only company with worldwide ability to find and drill oil. Halliburton, its smaller rival, has similar skills, but linked more to natural-gas drilling. The remaining big prospects for oil and gas are all in deep water in remote areas, and only Transocean has the rigs—and the might—to hit pay dirt in those areas. Core Lab and FMC Technologies have the brainpower, the intellectual capacity, to get the most out of wells thought to be spent. All of these service companies work for publicly traded oil giants and nations that are eager to exploit their resources. If I could invest in only one sector, if you put a gun to my head and said, "Promise me you will not diversify," I might just let you pull the trigger, that's how important diversification is to me. But in the end, I would relent and say, "If I have only one sector to give to my portfolio, let it be oil and oil service."

Minerals and Mining

For years, the minerals and mining group of stocks was perhaps the worst group of stocks to own. They were never "investable" because they frequently needed financing; they were poorly run; and any time the U.S. economy sneezed, this group got pneumonia. I can't tell you how much money I lost at one time or another on Amax, Asarco, and Phelps Dodge, to name some terrible stocks of yesteryear. These were serial cutters and omitters of dividends that would then catch a few years of warmth and institute new dividends and buybacks, only to suspend them again the moment the U.S. economy slipped into neutral. Those days are over, totally over. We always hear about the pull of China, how China is going to reshape the world and become a global power—with India not far behind it—and investors—pros and amateurs alike—just can't stop looking for ways to play these markets. Stop looking: minerals and mining are the way to play them.

Let me give you one quick anecdote about how this group has ceased to be levered to the U.S. economy and a Federal Reserve Bank that cares far too much about inflation and not enough about growth. Ten years ago, the United States used 30 percent of the world's copper and China used 10 percent. Now China uses 30 percent of the world's copper and the United States uses 10 percent. And that is not because we've ceased to grow. As in the ag, oil service, and aerospace bull markets, there was so much starvation for so long that many players merged or were driven out of business. That left just a few powerhouses, all of which are totally investable.

Countries like to have a one-stop mineral shop, like a supermarket, to produce their goods. That's why, when I think of minerals and mining, I think of CVRD, the Brazilian powerhouse linked to low-cost nickel; Freeport-McMoRan, a U.S. gold and copper producer; and BHP and Rio Tinto, which mine and smelt just about everything. A portfolio without a mineral or mining company will miss the greatest secular trend of our lifetime, the growth of what we used to consider Third World or less-developed countries into countries that can compete globally or eventually exceed us in the production of goods and services.

Infrastructure

Most of the mini-bull markets I have described specialize in one aspect of business—producing weapons or energy or fuel. This last bull market is more complex. Once again, because of starvation of orders for multiple years, it doesn't have enough players to satisfy investors so they can keep rallying as new dollars come in. Infrastructure is and will be an era of gigantic projects to tackle major needs: (1) the need to refine oil and gas; (2) the desire to replace oil and gas with other complex fuels that have to be harvested, cleaned, and refined; (3) the need to repair and replace our aging highways before they become too worn out or too dangerous; and (4) the need for more power as poor consumers in foreign countries become wealthier. Remember, the first thing that a poor person in a newly industrialized nation does with his or her paycheck is buy an appliance that needs power, so you have to build plants to service them. Power plants worldwide are in short supply.

A small group of companies excels at just these kinds of projects and tasks. You want to build new roads and bridges or fix them up? Call AECOM or Chicago Bridge & Iron. You need to build power plants that run clean energy? McDermott, ABB, and Foster Wheeler can do that, including coal and nuclear. You need to make sure that urban infrastructure, sewers, levees, and piping are working? Call URS or Shaw Group. You have to build refineries or factories in hard-to-get-to places? That's Fluor, or KBR, the old Kellogg Brown & Root subsidiary of Halliburton. All of these companies, with the exception of ABB, are based in the United States but do tremendous amounts of business overseas because of their reputation for quality work and expertise. The projects they get called for are long-dated projects that give these companies exceptional visibility to the "out years," where they can make projections for earnings that can last far longer than what other companies can project. For these companies I've mentioned, the foreseeable future extends well into the next decade.

At any given time, the leaders in these mini-bull markets can change. It's hard to pick a best-of-breed infrastructure or oil play that I can guarantee will stay that way for life, so to speak. But the sectors I outline are going to stay strong, and if you call me when I play "Am I Diversified?" on Wednesdays on *Mad Money,* you will hear me say that you should swap out of that lame financial stock or that boring drug company and pick a stock in one of the five sectors I just outlined that you may not have exposure in. It's a trick of the diversified trade, but it will ensure that your stocks live in the best neighborhoods possible for years to come.

Beyond the five bull markets, you want specific stocks, ones that should hold up for eighteen months, or even years, longer. You might think it's impossible to find stocks that are truly good for the long term, but that would be a mistake, as long as you stay in touch with them and make sure that the things that I like about them hold up. I'm really going out on a limb here and doing something that's quite unusual for any book about money, especially one that's geared toward long-term financial planning. I'm giving you my list of stocks that work for the long term. A year from today, not every stock on this list will still be worth owning. This list is good, but it's tentative by necessity, because not everything that looks good for the long term right now will stay that way. That's why this list goes beyond the five bull markets.

How do you start? First of all, of course, you must start with diversification. That means you need to pick sectors, sectors that have a long-range thesis and very little overlap with each other. The five bull markets are all strong sectors, but we want a list that gives you more choice and diversification in case the five bulls get mauled by bears. Then you need to pick stocks in those sectors and make sure they have long track records of doing the right thing for shareholders, along with strong managements that have been able to pass the baton effectively. You don't have to have the same weightings as the S&P 500 or any of that Wall Street gibberish, and you don't have to keep track of these stocks day-to-day or even week-to-week, because this portfolio is not meant to be traded.

Impossible? I thought that when I wrote *Real Money*, which was the handbook of my old hedge fund and had a trading orientation to it that required quick-wittedness and a sense of what was happening *now*. That's always been my code on CNBC, to the point where I used to be referred to as Reverend Jim Bob Cramer of the Church of What's Happening Now. But those times are past. I have switched to a strategy that is far more like what I am asking you to do at home, picking stocks with an eighteen- to twenty-four-month perspective and trying not to feel that I have to sell them unless I am being so piggish that one or two stocks just become too dominant in my holdings. I'm picking twenty stocks for the long term for you, and I want you to consider this as a menu. I am loathe to give you just ten, because I fear that you simply might not like enough of those—if you recall, you must be comfortable enough and care enough about each stock that you'll enjoy following them. Some stocks simply aren't for everyone, so you have to know yourself. If you think that you can't keep up with them, remember that I manage to keep up with these stocks myself on a daily and weekly basis as part of my charitable trust, ActionAlertsPlus.com, which is affiliated with TheStreet.com. It may be the lazy man's way of staying in touch with the stocks, but I still encourage you to follow these names on your own.

So here it is, my list of great stocks with long-term potential:

Twenty Stocks for the Long Term

1. Caterpillar. Caterpillar is the world leader in the production of heavy industrial machinery. It has the most sales, is in two hundred countries, and has the largest dealer network in the world. Despite a yield of nearly 2 percent and a constant buyback, usually in the range of $7.5 billion at any time—one-fifth of the company's capitalization—the stock has traded for roughly twelve times earnings, which is only two-thirds of the historic market multiple of the S&P 500. Caterpillar is the foremost large engine and infrastructure play worldwide. Its machines are used in everything from road-building to residential and commercial construction to alternative energy products to the mining of just about anything. Management has been able to transform this once largely American company into a global powerhouse that is respected on all continents and by all government and private contractors. It is the lowest-cost producer and yet is able to charge the highest prices because of its reliability and its brand name. Any portfolio needs a company that is known as a "cyclical stock," meaning that it does best when economies are strong. Given the nature of the worldwide economy, where nations are going from being underdeveloped to being part of the twenty-first century in what feels like days, CAT is the best way to play this longer-term trend. I suspect that this stock can be virtually a lifetime stock given that the most important trends in the world, from alternative energy to the buildup of the world's infrastructure—buildings and roads and homes—need Caterpillars to make it all happen.

2. Goldman Sachs. Okay, call me biased. I worked at Goldman Sachs in the 1980s and have been enamored of the place ever since. It is a gathering of the best financial minds worldwide and has always been a leader in stocks, fixed-income securities, mergers and acquisitions, corporate finance, trading, and private equity. This is a company that has been run by legendary players in the industry, everyone from the deans of finance John Weinberg and John Whitehead when I worked there, to Bob Rubin, the former Treasury secretary; Jon Corzine, the governor of New Jersey; Hank Paulsen, another Treasury secretary; and Lloyd Blankfein, a friend for many years. Once perceived as a strictly American company, Goldman now derives 50 percent of its income from overseas. It makes most of its money advising companies, issuing stocks and bonds for them, merging them, and taking them private. These businesses are going to be strong for years and years ahead, and Goldman is the market leader in every one of them. I like Goldman more than the other firms because most of them have had some turmoil at the top or have not been able to capture business away from Goldman, no matter how hard they try. Plus, bizarrely, this stock has been cheap compared to the rest of the market almost since it came public despite its massive outperformance, meaning it has done so much better than the rest of the stocks out there. It is the bedrock financial stock, and that's a group I believe you must have a position in. This is the best one there is. It will be for many years to come. While financials are a big part of the stock market, I am not willing to put more than one of these stocks in your portfolio for fear that you will end up stuck in one that is too related to American housing or to the Federal Reserve's whims. Goldman makes money in any environment.

3. ConocoPhillips. I am a huge believer that energy will be in short supply for most of the rest of our lives, so not having a couple of energy plays in your portfolio is a giant mistake. I like this group so much that I am including three of them. ConocoPhillips is one of the world's largest integrated oil companies, with operations in oil, exploration and production, midstream, refining and marketing, and chemicals. Despite its leadership status, the stock trades for less than ten times its earnings, a significant discount compared to its large, integrated peers like Exxon Mobil and Chevron. In addition, the company has one of the largest buybacks, a multiyear one for $15 billion that I expect won't be complete until 2009. That's more than 10 percent of the company! While most energy stocks have had a big run over the past five years, including Conoco, I believe much more upside remains. The world economy is growing rapidly and there just isn't enough supply to keep up with demand. Any new oil that is being found comes from increasingly unstable locations, and supply disruptions are common. These stocks are still discounting a steep drop in oil prices that I think just isn't in the cards. With a low valuation, huge share buyback, and tremendous exposure to oil and gas prices, I believe Conoco is tremendously undervalued.

4. XTO Energy. XTO, a domestic oil and gas company, is among the best-run companies that I follow—not just in energy, but in any sector. Since coming public in 1993, the company has grown its proved reserves 30 percent a year, an amazing achievement that no other oil and gas company comes close to matching. The stock has gone up more than fifty times its IPO price. The company's finding costs are consistently among the lowest in the industry. It also uses a disciplined capital strategy to grow production through low-risk acquisitions and investments in high-return projects in "safe" areas immune to geopolitical problems, something almost no other large oil and gas company can claim. XTO has allocated $3 billion for more acquisitions over the course of the next couple of years. It expects to grow production 10 percent a year for the foreseeable future. Most recently, the company has proved reserves of 6.94 *trillion* cubic feet in natural gas, 52 million barrels of natural gas liquids, and 214 million barrels of oil. Pretty good for a business you have probably never heard of. To produce more predictable cash flows so it can wildcat more than most companies (meaning drill for oil in places where none has been drilled for before), XTO uses derivatives to hedge some of its production at what have been really favorable prices. It has sold forward about 65 percent of its natural gas production for several years into the future at prices that are dramatically higher than anything near the current price of natural gas, a brilliant move considering the fact that almost every other company I follow is stuck producing gas at the current low prices. It has also hedged out about 40 percent of its 2008 oil production at $74.26, a very, very smart decision that makes XTO far less hostage to the ups and downs of oil pricing. These above-market prices are a prime example of good management in action. All of these factors make XTO a best-of-breed name in the oil and gas space—and a great investment at these prices. It's another stock that is at a huge discount to the S&P's market multiple, the benchmark I measure all stocks against, even though it grows much faster than the average S&P stock.

5. Transocean. No portfolio can be considered complete if it doesn't have a driller, a company involved in the exploration of oil. Given how adamant I am about the importance of the long-term shortage of oil, especially without any real economic alternatives to crude, I want a driller that is worldwide and has expertise in finding oil in hard-to-get-to places, which is pretty much all that's left in the world to explore. That's why I have picked Transocean drilling, which is a combined entity that includes GlobalSanteFe. This company operates the largest fleet of deepwater drillers in the world. The company works in the sweet spot of the drilling market overseas, particularly in the 10,000-feet-down and deeper category, with experience in every kind of climate. While North America has seen a significant slow-down in drilling from the Gulf of Mexico to Canada, the worldwide picture is quite different, with furious drilling globally as countries and companies try to replenish dwindling reserves. The demand for Transocean's rigs is so great that it has been able consistently to raise what are known as day rates—the rate it can charge for drilling each day—pretty much at will. Because of the long-term nature of Trans-ocean's contracts, the company produces very steady and predictable cash flows. These contracts don't allow for a tremendous amount of upside, but I value the stocks I am picking here for their long-term consistency, and RIG (Transocean's stock symbol) has much more than many drillers. The company has been extremely shareholder-friendly, buying back a tremendous amount of stock and awarding shareholders large cash payments, including a recent one of more than $30 a share.

6. Hologic. With the huge cohort of aging baby boomers, health care is too important for you not to have several positions in the field. This area will be growing regardless of the economy, which is a huge plus given our nation's endless commitment to stopping inflation instead of worrying about growth. With that in mind, I think you should start a position in Hologic. This company recently merged with Cytyc, another health care company, to become the best of breed in women's health, with a specialty in early and improved detection of cancers and less invasive treatments for illnesses. Hologic is the leader in diagnostic and medical imaging for mammography and osteopo-rosis applications to hospitals, imaging clinics, health care organiza-tions, and pharmaceutical companies. Improving women's health is a noble undertaking and a profitable one too. According to the company it should produce 2008 earnings of $2.35 to $2.45 a share, which means the stock sells for just a little above the price-to-earnings multiple of much slower-growing companies. What an opportunity given that this company will be able to grow its earnings at a 20 percent rate for the next several years *and* yield substantial cost savings from the merger with Cytyc. The company believes that there will be $75 million in revenue synergies because both companies sell to the same clients. This is the kind of company that is ideal for any environment, but will really excel in a slowdown.

7. Inverness Medical Innovations. Inverness is another health care diagnostics company, with both professional and home diagnostics. It is also a manufacturer of vitamins and nutritional supplements. The vitamin business provides the company with a stable revenue stream. But what excites me are the incredible opportunities for Inverness in the diagnostics field. (This is the single most important growth market in the world, so I am willing to have more than one of this kind of health care company in a portfolio for the long run.) In 2007, the company acquired Biosite and Cholestech, which have improved Inverness's product portfolio and distribution capabilities, specifically in the fast-growing cardiology diagnostics market. The combined company offers incredible financial synergies from both a cost-cutting and a revenue perspective. I think analysts' estimates are way too low for the coming years, and companies that beat estimates have stocks that go higher. The professional diagnostics side presents the greatest opportunity, but Inverness's consumer diagnostics group, set up as a 50-50 joint venture with Procter & Gamble, is also compelling. The P&G transaction provides Inverness with a much-needed cash infusion of around $300 million to help offset the debt it took on to finance the buys it made. It also allows Inverness to leverage P&G's substantial marketing and distribution capabilities. Look for a new digital pregnancy test under the Clearblue label, with a lot more to come, including the first over-the-counter strep test.

8. CVS Caremark. Rounding out my explosive health care choices is CVS Caremark, a fantastic retail and pharmaceutical sales company that was created in 2007 through the merger of the drugstore chain CVS and the pharmacy benefits manager Caremark. With the acquisition CVS has increased its growth rate to well beyond Walgreen, its principal competitor, but you pay much less for it than for Walgreen. We want to be in this business because the major pharmaceutical companies are facing an unbelievable challenge as more and more drugs come off patent between now and 2012, and no real replacements are coming because the pharmaceutical houses have bare pipelines. Why should we care? Because big companies use CVS to manage their pharmaceutical bills and CVS can switch to generics for drugs and capture some of the differential between the price of the generic and that of the patent drug.

You might ask why I am not suggesting owning any major pharmaceutical companies. It is precisely because we can't trust their pipelines, with the possible exceptions of Schering-Plough and Celgene, the former because it just completed a European acquisition that gives it strong new drugs and the latter because it has a fantastic blood cancer (leukemia) franchise that keeps growing. Still, I would much rather play this segment with diagnostics and cost controllers because disease prevention and saving money on drugs are probably the two biggest growth opportunities for the next five years.

I also considered including Allergan because of its strong anti-aging vanity portfolio, including Botox and artificial breasts and a device that combats obesity, but, again, the competition could become swift, so great are the opportunities in that field. I want my companies to have as little cutthroat competition as possible so I can own them for a very long time. Still, Allergan is a best of breed if you like that segment, and I update its progress all of the time on *Mad Money*.

9. McDonald's. One of the most recognizable consumer brands in the world, McDonald's has undergone an incredible makeover in the past few years. For many years at my old hedge fund I was short McDonald's, because its food and service were both subpar. But the company has now refurbished its locations worldwide, added new items to the menu, made the food healthier, and serves premium coffee and popular snack wraps. It has also extended hours at many of its stores. McDonald's has also taken significant strides to improve the financial side of the business by moving stores from the company to franchisees. Franchised stores require lower capital expenditure and generate higher returns and cash flow, which the company continues to return to shareholders at a rapid pace. McDonald's has one of the biggest buybacks of all public companies—something I find to be quite important when you are buying an old-line business like this one—and is committed to paying a good dividend, which I expect it to hike this year as it has in the past.

Like many of the companies in this potential portfolio, McDonald's is seeing its most robust growth overseas, where it derives about 60 percent of its revenues and 40 percent of its profits. I call it a "ROWer," meaning it is a dominant Rest of World player, which is so important when you are based in a company that no longer has much growth left in it. Oddly, despite its long-term run over the years, McDonald's sells at a much lower price, when you look at its price-to-earnings multiple, than its competitors Wendy's and Burger King, even though I consider it a much better company. I expect McDonald's to get to a much higher multiple and then a much higher price over time. This stock is an ideal stock in a portfolio where you might want to get your kids interested in the market, because everyone knows McDonald's. I know a lot of people like to choose Disney for that reason, but Disney does not have the long-term growth profile that McDonald's has and is hostage to old-line media, which I expect to be challenged for many years.

10. Freeport-McMoRan. This resource company is one of the world's largest copper and gold miners, with the lowest cost of extraction for both precious and red metals. For a long time Freeport lagged other mineral stocks, but last year it stole Phelps Dodge, paying much less than it should have, making the company the world's largest copper producer, a terrific place to be as more and more people worldwide can afford homes. FCX trades at less than *nine* times earnings despite a multiyear growth rate that I think will far exceed that of most of the companies in the S&P because of voracious demand for copper from China and for gold from India and China. There simply isn't enough easily reached copper in the world, and FCX has access to much of the cheap supply. Plus, I like a portfolio that has a long-term inflation hedge in gold, as well as a hedge against geopolitical craziness. This stock, like the others, should be good for years to come.

11. Hewlett-Packard. I don't like to have much technology in my portfolio. There are too many brilliant companies going tooth-and-nail at each other. Why own them when there are so many other companies in other sectors that don't have much serious competition? But to overlook tech entirely is to lose some possibilities of explosive growth at times, and that's why I like Hewlett-Packard. This company, run by Mark Hurd, has emerged as one of the biggest players in the PC market, which sells about 60 million computers a year. It is also the dominant printer company. It used to go neck-and-neck with IBM and Dell, but IBM gave up this market and Dell's management troubles allowed HPQ to power ahead. For a long time I liked Intel as a PC play, but Advanced Micro wrecked its monopoly. I also like Microsoft, but the company has not been able to innovate away from its staid software business. All the other products that go into a PC, the components, are always losing value, as the competition among their manufacturers is some of the most intense in the world. You're getting an opportunity here to own the dominant PC company, with sales around the world that dwarf its U.S. sales, at a price so much cheaper than the average company in the S&P in spite of its excellent growth, that the opportunity is too good to pass up.

I debated including Cisco, but the company, while best of breed in networking, is an expensive company that has made a major move off its bottom. If the stock were to sell off into the $20s again, I would consider it for my trust. I also debated including Apple because of all the special qualities it has aside from personal computers, but much of the upside has been taken away by speculators plowing into the stock. Finally, I considered Research in Motion, which is a terrific consumer gadget play. You might know it as the maker of the Black-Berry, an addictive product that is still growing like wildfire. But once again, it is an expensive company and my goal here is to provide you with a list of *inexpensive* companies with rapid growth rates. RIMM is an expensive company with a rapid growth rate and that's too dicey in a book about staying mad for life. I don't want you to stay mad at *me* for life!

12. Corning. This is a very inexpensive play on two of the best long-term trends out there, liquid crystal displays for TVs, of which it is the lowest-cost producer, and the much more exciting fiber optics business, where it has a hammerlock on the actual fibers. In 2008, it will begin to ship in volume the most exciting new product in the company's history, a bendable fiber that allows telephone companies to string up clients for voice, data, and video. Verizon and AT&T are committed to becoming serious challengers to the cable companies over the next ten years, and they will all be using this product. You will need plenty of bandwidth in the future for the Internet's growth, and Corning's the way to play it.

13. Google. As a dot-commer from way back, having started TheStreet.com in 1996, I am acutely aware that having Internet plays is the way of the future. Unfortunately for just about everyone else on the Internet, there is really only one dominant company: Google. This company is considered too expensive by many who say its price is high, meaning you have to pay a large dollar amount to buy one share.

That's nonsense. Google is actually cheaper than most of the companies that I track when you look at its growth rate. It sells at less than thirty times earnings but grows at 33 percent, and in my book that's a great deal. Why do I like Google? Simple: it is an advertising play, the best one in the world. The advertising market is a $600 billion market and I think that GOOG will take close to 10 percent of that in the next five years. That's phenomenal growth, just phenomenal. The management is exceptional; it is pulling away from all of the other Internet plays; it can pretty much buy any company it wants, since everyone wants Google currency—better than the U.S. Mint's—and I believe that it can own the phone market in a few years' time, which is one of the reasons why I am *not* recommending two of my near-term favorites, AT&T and Verizon. I just trust Google to stop them at their own game through a wireless handheld device. GOOG is the quintessential growth stock from the point of view of its user base, as the next generations regard it as their newspaper, their reference, their TV, and, soon, their way of communication. I am willing to bet that by 2012 it will have the programming that youth watches, which is why I can't possibly pick any media company for the long term. Google's stock will always cost a high dollar amount; you might want to buy just one share to get started.

14. International Game Technology. Gambling is a worldwide addiction, and every country suffers from it. We make no judgments here in *Stay Mad*, which is why for a long time, before it split up, I liked Altria. IGT is the largest manufacturer of computerized gaming equipment and systems, including slot machines and video poker. The company is benefiting from the massive explosion of gambling worldwide, most notably in Asia. While Las Vegas has long boomed for IGT and state governments nationwide are encouraging the construction of casinos to stimulate jobs and taxes—all of which need IGT machines—it is the Macau opportunity, where the number of slot machines is expected to quadruple in the next four years to

50,000, that will be the best source of IGT's growth. That's in addition to the 114,000 gaming machines that I expect to be added in the United States, although that's a number that is already expected and factored into earnings estimates. There's much more upside in Macau, and also from a partnership IGT has with China LotSynergy, which gives it access to the Chinese video lottery market. I expect big orders for the rest of the decade from Japan too, where it sells pachi-slot, a hybrid slot machine that is immensely popular in that country. If everything goes as planned, I believe that IGT should double by the end of the decade.

15. Pepsi. For many of you, this soft drink and snack company may seem too boring. Not for me. This is a play on the person I believe may be the smartest CEO in the world, Indra Nooyi, who took over recently and wants to make this consumer company into the world's best beverage and healthy snack business. It's with the latter that I think she'll make the most strides, as Frito-Lay is the true driver of the company. I am a passionate believer that in four or five years' time there will be only a handful of food and beverage companies. One of them will be Pepsi.

There are three great franchises here: Pepsi, which, while not growing that well in the United States because of an endless price war with Coca-Cola, is growing in the teens in the rest of the world; Gatorade, which is a fantastic double-digit grower worldwide; and Frito-Lay, which under Nooyi has begun to break out from its low-single-digit growth to something far more spectacular. I normally do not want to own too many pure defensive stocks like this, as the growth in health care and minerals and oil should be far superior and the price tag for safety is often too high. But this company sells right in the middle of the pack of the defensive names—ones that grow regardless of the strength of economies worldwide—*and* it might be the only one trading domestically that has accelerating growth. (Nestlé, from Switzerland, might be the other.) Pepsi is also the company I follow that is most concerned with the environment and energy efficiency; it rates number one on the latter in many surveys, which I believe will allow it to have a premium multiple over time, much the way Starbucks and Whole Foods have, although their growth rates are slowing and PEP's is moving faster. Nooyi believes; she is taking as much cash as she can and buying back stock. This is and has always been a very pro-shareholder company.

16. Procter & Gamble. Besides Pepsi, there is one other consumer products company that is innovating and growing and attempting to be a dominant worldwide player, particularly in the less-developed nations: Procter & Gamble. I don't know if anyone who is outside of the business of consumer products recognizes that this is one of the most aggressive companies in the world, routinely trimming brands, cutting staff, and making sure that its businesses are all number one in their category. I preach homework, telling you to get on the conference calls of companies to hear how things are doing and how companies are able to fend off competition to keep their franchises intact. If you listen to only one company's call, I suggest you pick P&G's. After the company bought Gillette a few years ago, there was a sense that it had misstepped and perhaps had lost its ability to integrate large-scale acquisitions and wrench out costs and synergies. It is amazing to me that anyone would doubt these guys, because they are their own toughest critics. They cut and cut and cut the costs of Gillette until it became one of P&G's most lucrative properties. Still, the analyst community was reluctant to believe, so finally P&G announced one of the two or three largest buybacks in history. It has been lapping up stock ever since.

This is the most expensive stock I am recommending relative to its growth rate, but I am willing to accept that because P&G has another enviable record: it is the most consistent raiser of its dividend of any company in the S&P 500, with fifty years of higher dividends. That means you as an investor must reinvest this dividend and allow the growth to work magic for you. That should produce a phenomenal core holding that may be the most perfect stock for any portfolio.

17. New York Stock Exchange. Here's a controversial pick that I think, long-term, could be the biggest stock out there. The New York Stock Exchange wants to be the dominant global stock and futures exchange. It wants to trade everything everywhere and it wants to be the low-cost trader. It already dominates stock trading in both the United States and the far faster-growing European markets. It's been public for only a couple of years, and it's getting its costs in line so that it can add new business without adding a lot of cost. NYX is controversial because there are many doubters about its ability to compete with the Chicago Mercantile Exchange in the faster-growing world of derivatives and futures. My bet is that NYX, with its fantastic, recognizable brand name and scale from the Euro acquisition, will be able to wrest substantial business from the CME in the next five years. I believe analysts are drastically underrating this company's ability to cut costs—I suspect that there will be a smaller and smaller trading space in downtown New York over time—and its ability to increase both volume and companies that want to list in its valuable and prestigious ranks. I think the stock will see great gains in the next five years as it dawns on the market that this is the best brand name in the financial services industry. It would not surprise me to see this stock at $200 five years from now.

18. Union Pacific. For years the railroad industry was an awful industry, with terrible price-cutting and vicious competition from both other rails and trucking. That's all changed now. The road infrastructure in this country has been falling apart for years, and the declining ability of trucks to navigate traffic makes them far less reliable than in the old days. Railroads are now much more energy-efficient and they can compete on favorable terms with truckers. Plus, the rails have pretty much divided the country into territories and don't compete with each other any longer.

Why Union Pacific? It's the nation's largest rail, operating in twenty-three states in the western portion of the United States. That's the vital place to be because it handles the vast majority of the nation's voracious Chinese imports. Its rail lines also connect with Canada's rail system and all six of Mexico's major gateways. UNP is benefiting from strong demand for coal and agricultural products, particularly corn, as both are being used to supplement high-priced and dwindling oil supplies. It's been growing at double digits for some time, in part because of growing traffic but also because it can hike prices, given the lack of competition. If oil comes down in price, UNP might not have as much coal or corn to ship, but it will more than make that up in reduced fuel costs that it will most likely not pass on to its customers. It won't have to, because of the paucity of competition.

19. Boeing. Few companies dominate their industry like Boeing, yet it fails to get the credit it deserves for that domination. This is a quintessential double-digit growth story that sells below the average stock, because big money in the United States looks at domestic airlines and figures they are unlikely to have the orders to make Boeing a great stock, despite the fact that it has a new plane, the Dreamliner, that should boost earnings for at least the next five years. Why am I so confident? First, because the big orders are going to come from overseas, particularly China, which could have ten times the number of planes it currently uses just to service its own country's growth. But there are many nations with growing populations and solvent airline companies, particularly in the Middle East, Asia, and Latin America, that I believe will be buying Boeing planes for many years to come. Second, Boeing's new planes carry far more people and use far less jet fuel per passenger than the planes currently in use. That means airlines that upgrade over the years can increase profitability at a time when energy is the biggest wild card facing the industry. Third, Boeing's blessed with a competitor that at one time was all-powerful but now can't even produce its own planes: Airbus. Over the next three years, as Dreamliners come out of the factory in the state of Washington and Airbus stutters to produce anything, let alone a competitive plane, I expect you will see more and more orders of a far greater magnitude going to Boeing.

Boeing also has one of the largest defense businesses in the United States. I expect the defense budget to continue to grow as a percentage of the gross domestic product, no matter who is in the White House.

Boeing's management has been wildly pro-shareholder, plowing everything that is not needed for R&D into one of the best buybacks in the Dow Jones average, exceeded only by the likes of P&G and Exxon Mobil.

20. Sears Holdings. Am I saving the best for last? Some would argue otherwise, mostly the people who haven't gone into Sears lately or who think the one-two punch of Sears and Kmart is an anemic play that will never recover. I urge you to think differently about this stock. Longtime viewers of *Mad Money* might know this story, but let me tell it to you so you know the faith I have in Sears. The company's vision is set by Eddie Lampert, someone I met at Goldman Sachs more than twenty-five years ago. He sat next to me in a place we called "the swamp," a sweltering closet of an office where all trainees huddled during Goldman boot camp. We would work hard and play hard, most of us going out for beers after a solid twelve-hour training day. Every night I would ask Eddie to join us, but he always said no. Finally, one day, frustrated as all get-out, I asked him what was so wrong with me that he kept dissing me. The answer: "Jim, I'm only 15." Well, now Eddie's in his 40s, having worked for Bob Rubin for years at Goldman and these days running his own hedge fund, which has the best long-term gains after all fees are taken of any fund I know. (When I was in the hedge fund business, Eddie and I were vicious competitors and frequently were neck-and-neck in performance numbers before I retired in 2001. We are now good friends.)

Eddie backed into owning this retailer. He had taken a position in Kmart and then attempted, with a group of banks, to buy the whole company. At the last minute, Eddie was kidnapped and the banks walked away. Eddie ran from the kidnappers, who are now serving life in prison, when he got the chance. Without the banks, Eddie bought the rest of the company himself with his partners. He quickly rationalized the business and then merged it with Sears. People are concerned that Eddie hasn't been able to implement the changes that would stabilize sales, which is where the leap of faith comes in. Sears looks a lot like Berkshire Hathaway did in 1981, when you could buy it for about $200 a share. The business seemed pretty dowdy; I know I passed on it. But the bet was on the manager, Warren Buffett, who turned a $200 investment into a $100,000 stock twenty-five years later through sheer investing prowess. I believe Eddie Lampert will do the same thing with Sears Holdings.

I do not believe this is a stock for the squeamish, and Eddie has far more doubters than Buffett had. I don't know if Eddie can repeat what Buffett, his idol—and mine—was able to accomplish, but I turned down a chance to be with Buffett once, and I am not going to ignore the chance to be with the next Buffett, even if I have to hold my nose when I go into a Kmart or a Sears. I think that the real estate alone is worth the price of the company, and the brands—Craftsman, DieHard, and Lands' End—have a great deal of value too. In the end, though, it is a play on my friend Eddie, and I am betting on him.

Some would sneer at this list. Why so few financials, given that 20 percent of the market is made up of banks, brokers, and insurance companies? Where are all the utilities? How about more tech? More drugs? Where are the big conglomerates? I believe that you have to pick sectors that will be great for many years and then pick the best of breed in those sectors. That's what I have done here. I skewed them to the sectors I like, because if you can pick only five stocks—my original formulation for the minimum number of stocks you need to be diversified—then you will at least know the sectors I care the most about. I have often emphasized that if you know a company that is local—a local bank or a local retailer—then I can get behind a decision to invest in it, but I cannot help you do the homework, as I will be doing for years to come on these twenty stocks. These are the stocks that I invest the most time in, the ones I follow the most closely, and the ones I think will offer far better returns than you will get from an exchange-traded fund or an S&P 500 or total return fund. In the next chapter, I list the best mutual funds for all occasions, but if you want to pick stocks for yourself, if you want to stay with me, mad for life until we're rich, pick from this list and play along with the *Mad Money* Man.

9

MY GUIDE TO MUTUAL FUNDS

Finding the right mutual fund is a notoriously difficult and confusing process. You can find ratings for funds all over the place, but who has any idea what those mean? You might find a fund that has five stars at one place, a B+ somewhere else, and a three with yet another service that claims to rank mutual funds. What are you supposed to do with those ratings? Some of the more basic attempts to rank funds just throw in the towel and rank them by past performance. A rating source might tell you they've got the top twenty-five funds over the past year, or the past five years. I have to tell you, that information is next to useless. Everyone warns you that you can't pick mutual funds based on their recent performance. People love to pile into the mutual fund with the best performance over the past year or the past quarter, under the assumption that a big win says something about the quality of the fund. That's certainly a mistake. As I've said before, making too much money usually is a sign that you're doing something wrong.

You could have made a killing in the late '90s by keeping your money entirely in tech stocks. Anyone who did that had enormous gains for a couple of years, and then, because having all your money in one sector is the height of folly, that same person would have taken enormous losses as the market deflated. Most of the time, if everything you own is making you money so that you're dramatically outperforming everybody else, you aren't diversified. A portfolio without diversification is a portfolio that will eventually lose you money.

The same goes for a mutual fund. It could be that the fund isn't diversified, but many funds are designed not to be diversified. For example, there are all of these so-called select funds that focus entirely on a single sector; they must be avoided at all costs. There is absolutely no reason to put your money in a mutual fund that invests only in stocks that are part of one industry. Why?

Let's go back a few steps. The best way to make money, and the best way to keep it, is to invest in a portfolio of stocks (no more than ten stocks) that you yourself have selected and researched, doing at least one hour of homework on each stock every week. That's your best option. I know this from what I have seen myself as a broker at Goldman Sachs, handling dozens of wealthy people who built their own portfolios; I know it as hedge fund manager who interviewed hundreds of people trying to get into my fund over a fourteen-year period; and I know it from the thousands of people I have interacted with on TheStreet.com and *Mad Money*. But a lot of people don't have the time to manage their own money well, and even among those who do have time, there are plenty of people who just aren't interested enough in stocks to make managing their own money a worthwhile decision. Those are the determinants, although the industry as a whole makes you feel you are too stupid to do it yourself or that you aren't getting enough "technical" help in picking stocks, or the right charts and graphs. That's all pablum. It's the homework that's difficult, and now that I have demystified the process you can see that picking stocks isn't that confusing. Then again, you might not want to pick your own stocks even if you understand the process. And if you're investing in your 401(k) plan, as you should, you won't be able to invest in individual stocks or manage your own money. A 401(k) will let you choose only between different fund managers and index funds that aren't managed. So two kinds of people want a good mutual fund: everyone who wants to get rich and doesn't have the time or inclination to pick stocks, and everyone with money in a 401(k) plan who isn't allowed to pick stocks, only funds.

Let's assume that most people who want a good mutual fund are in the first category. The odds are good you're one of them. So many people ask me about mutual funds. They'll say, "Jim, we love what you do, but could you please recommend some mutual funds because we feel comfortable only with a professional managing our money?" Despite years of underperformance by mutual funds and revelation after revelation about how high fees and hidden fees can eat into your mutual fund gains, people still trust actively managed funds. What an amazing PR machine this industry is—almost as good as the hedge fund industry, which takes on a massive amount of risk and pretends it doesn't! Investing in a fund with a manager to look after your assets makes an intuitive kind of sense. Passive investing, meaning simply putting your money in an index, is brainless investing. Shouldn't a fund that's run by an actual person, and someone with years of experience no less, do better than a fund that isn't run at all? In fact, most of the time, index funds will outperform actively managed funds, especially after fees, because a fund with a manager obviously costs a lot more to maintain than a fund that's simply tied to an index. But the idea that a fund with someone at the helm making the decisions should really do better than a fund that's basically headless is an appealing one that fits in perfectly with our common sense. We have been raised to think that if some people are average, that means there are others who are better than average. Plus, despite the fact that most actively managed funds fail to beat the indexes consistently, there is a small group of funds run by expert managers that *do* consistently outperform the market. The existence of these people gives everyone in all the poorly run mutual funds hope that they can find a really great fund if they just try harder.

Going back to the question of why we shouldn't put our money in funds that specialize in only one sector, we now have an answer. You invest in an actively managed mutual fund so that someone else with more experience, whose full-time job is money management, will take care of your investments for you. People like mutual funds because they don't have the time or the inclination to manage their own money, and they appreciate that a pro is handling it. The whole point of putting your money in mutual funds is to find one fund with one manager who will invest for you. You might put your money in two funds, one for stocks and one for bonds. But beyond that, investing in multiple funds makes no sense at all. Some people have five, maybe ten mutual funds in their portfolio. That's preposterous. You're a mutual fund of mutual funds! You're a giant fee-spouting, underperforming machine! To be an effective mutual fund investor you still need to spend time researching your fund, at least one hour a week, to make sure everything is running smoothly. If you're going to own half a dozen mutual funds, you might as well just manage your own portfolio of stocks, because to be a good mutual fund investor in that many funds takes just as much effort as owning stocks does. If you're investing in a fund that owns stocks in only one sector, that cannot be your only investment. Sooner or later, that sector will fall, and you'll lose money. Remember, 50 percent of a stock's movement is determined by its sector. You can't have a really great bank stock if the banking industry is struggling. Owning a mutual fund that's exclusively invested in one sector is like owning a stock, not owning a diversified, actively managed mutual fund.

To be honest, I don't even know how someone would go about managing a fund that invests in only one industry. Just think of the poor guy running the fund that invests only in airlines. Lately these stocks have come back, but historically they've been some of the worst-performing stocks I've ever seen. How could anyone possibly manage a fund that's allowed to invest only in airlines when all the airline stocks are going down? It just doesn't make sense.

Because so many people have had so much trouble picking the right mutual fund, and because many of them have come to me asking for help, I've done something out of character. It has always been my policy not to rank funds; I would only steer people toward mutual funds that I was very familiar with, to the point of being personally acquainted with the fund's manager. In *Real Money* I recommended five mutual fund managers, and their mutual funds, with whom I was familiar and whose performance I trusted. That's the thing about any fund: it's the manager who matters. Forget everything you've ever seen about different fund categories; that's not what truly differentiates a good actively managed fund from the rest of the pack. You're paying such high fees for the manager when you invest in a mutual fund. When you evaluate the performance of a fund, you're evaluating the performance of the manager. So in *Real Money* I recommended four managers whom I knew personally and one manager whom I hadn't met, but who clearly does a fabulous job running his fund. These five funds were good selections, but there was nothing methodical about how I picked them. I just used my knowledge of twenty years of investing, at that time, to pick the guys that I thought were in the Big Leagues and who came to play every day. Yes, that was, alas, anecdotal.

I have never favored investing in mutual funds, but I realize there's a huge need for good mutual fund advice, and it's one that's not really being met. So I decided I would take my perspective, my years of money management experience, and come up with a truly rigorous method for evaluating mutual fund managers and, by extension, the funds they manage. If you're going to invest in mutual funds, you should at least have some good advice before you do it. As I was telling you before, most of the companies that rank or rate mutual funds do so either in a way that's easy to understand and totally without value—for example, by looking only at the performance of a fund over a certain time frame, or in a way that's much more comprehensive but also totally opaque. You can devise a system to rate mutual funds based on performance, risk, consistency, fees, taxes, you name it—a really comprehensive method—but if you tell people only the end result, what grade the fund gets, you're not really giving them very much information. What does a high rating mean? Does it mean you should invest in the fund? Does it mean that within its category the fund is better than its competitors? Is it predictive or not? These are questions that don't get answered.

To give you a comprehensive list of well-managed mutual funds, I had to come up with my own methodology, one that would consider the variables that I believe are of the utmost importance when evaluating a money manager. I put my system together (I'll explain it momentarily) and I compiled a list of actively managed mutual funds with their managers that I believe will not only make you money over the long term but will outperform the benchmarks. That's what really counts.

Before I discuss my system and my list of funds, I have to give you all the big caveats. First, nobody ever got upset because he or she invested in an index fund. I know that many of you want an actively managed fund anyway, but if you haven't even considered investing in an index fund, take a minute to think it over. Your fees will be much lower, which means that you start with a big advantage. Index funds also outperform the majority of actively managed funds in any given year. They are a good, intelligent investment. Second, I believe that it's the fund manager who makes or breaks the fund, and if the manager at any one of the funds I'm listing in this book leaves, you should leave too. You'll need to do homework to check on this, because mutual funds are notorious for not alerting you when they replace your fund manager for whatever reason. Third caveat: I have a talent for picking stocks; I've done it successfully for decades, and my record at my hedge fund of compounding at 24 percent annually after fees speaks for itself. But this is my first time taking a truly rigorous look at mutual funds. I believe this is the first time anyone has taken a rigorous crack at mutual funds using my criteria, so I might not be a great picker of money managers. I think I'm better positioned to evaluate money managers than are the vast majority of the people who write about funds, but there's still a chance that I'll be wrong. With that in mind, let me explain my system and then I'll show you the results.

When you're looking for a good mutual fund, focus on performance: how much money will the fund make you? The people who rank funds to extrapolate from past performance try to give you a picture of how a fund might perform in the future. The smart ones who try to do this realize that recent performance is not a great indicator. The period being considered is just too short to get any kind of decent idea about a money manager's prowess. Instead of using a fund's results over the past year, what we usually do is look at its five-year and ten-year returns. That's a long enough time to give you a pretty good idea about the fund manager's abilities. That way we eliminate the hot funds that tend to burn out right when you put your money into them.

My method is a variation of looking at past returns to assess a money manager's abilities and predict how he or she will do in the future. Because I myself was a money manager, I have my own unique perspective that I believe makes my system better than any other that I've seen. I wanted to find funds that made money when the market was going down. The ability to make money in a down market is the true mark of a great manager. Some people think that you invest in an actively managed fund because you hope it will beat the S&P 500, or whatever benchmark you decide is relative. I don't think that's quite true. You don't get a money manager in order to outperform the indexes every year, although that's great if you do. You get a money manager in order to avoid declines. If you invest in an index fund, it goes down when the benchmark does down; there's nothing to be done about it. But when you put your money in an actively managed fund, you expect your manager to sidestep at least some of those declines. Mutual funds with managers exist to protect your capital against downside risk. It's not so important that they deliver additional upside. Anybody can make money in a bull market. You probably remember the late '90s when everybody decided to be a so-called day trader and regular investors were making a killing left and right. It seemed as though stocks always went up, right? Well, in fact, that's pretty close to the definition of a bull market. Stocks go up and it's easy to make money. You don't need a pro for that. You get a pro to make sure you're still making money, or at least not losing it, when we're in a bear market.

With that in mind, I decided that I would weigh the performance of mutual fund managers in the off years, the years the market was down, more heavily than their performance in the good times. I think this method makes a lot of sense because it measures what you actually want in a money manager, or at least what you really should want in a money manager: someone who can hold off the downside. From the beginning of 2000 to the end of 2006, we had three bad years, 2000 to 2002, and four good ones, 2003 to 2006. I believe that the managers who outperformed in 2000, 2001, and 2002 deserve much more credit than the managers who outperformed in later years. If the S&P 500 is down double digits for the year and your mutual fund is up at all, let alone up double digits, you've got a good mutual fund. Over the long term, the fund managers who can make money in any kind of market will do a better job running your money than the guys who perform well only when times are good, or an index fund. If you don't take big losses when the market's hurting, then even if your gains are smaller when the market's strong (this is just hypothetical; the vast majority of the funds and fund managers I've selected continued to beat the market from 2003 on), you'll outperform over the long term. Consider what would've happened to you if you put $100 into a great low-cost S&P 500 index fund, the Vanguard 500, at the beginning of 2000.

You were down 9.06 percent in 2000, another 12.02 percent in 2001, and then in 2002 you went down even further, by 22.15 percent. After three years of losses, that $100 would be down to $62.28. Then, in 2003, things turned around, and you would have been up 28.5 percent, which translates into a $17.74 gain. Suppose you had a good money manager who simply kept you from losing money from 2000 to 2002. Even if that manager underperformed the S&P 500 in 2003, he or she could still make you more money because a 20 percent gain, worse than the S&P 500 did in 2003, translates into a $20 win off a $100 base. Those who have more money make more money. That's why preservation of capital is so important, and why you want a money manager who knows how to win when everyone else is losing.

Here's the nitty-gritty explanation of how I got my list of thirteen mutual fund managers with their mutual funds that I think are worth your time and money because I believe that they will, on average, outperform the benchmarks over the long term. First, I looked at only actively managed stock funds. There are two reasons for this: performance in a bond fund is a lot more uniform, and it's really difficult to compare a fund that's all stocks with a fund that's a mix of stocks and bonds, an apples-to-oranges comparison. I wanted to build my mutual fund list on apples-to-apples comparisons. I have three lists: one for aggressive-growth funds, one for growth funds, and one for value funds. To some extent I think these categorizations are silly and unhelpful, but they're already widely used. I wanted to produce fifty great mutual funds, but as it happened only thirteen met my criteria. I could have loosened up my standards to generate a larger list, but I didn't feel comfortable putting my seal of approval on funds that probably don't deserve it. You have to admit: it is saying something about an industry when you set out to find fifty great products and you can't. If we set out to find fifty great restaurants, we would probably have to start by cutting five hundred just to make the list manageable. But then again, that's food; this is only money!

I took lists of the fifty best-performing funds in each category for every year from 2000 to 2006. By the way, these are all diversified mutual funds, and any one of them could be a place for you to invest all of the money you want to put into stocks. Within these lists, I isolated the funds that made money in 2000, 2001, or 2002, or at least outperformed the market in these years and were among the best performing funds in their category at the time. These are the funds that made the core of my lists. Then I considered their performance from 2003 to the end of 2006 to rank the funds, excluding from my final lists any of the initial funds that did not perform well during this period. Because I believe that a fund's performance is the manager's, not the fund's (even if a good manager is gracious and willing to give full credit to the team), I looked only at funds that had the same manager over this entire span of time. It would be unfair to give one manager credit for gains that the previous manager had actually racked up just because they were at the same mutual fund. I used data provided by some very helpful people at TheStreet.com Ratings, which is a great service that rates everything from stocks to funds to HMOs, and Morningstar to do my analysis.

After this process I arrived at thirteen actively managed mutual funds that were up to my standards, or, I should say, that have managers who are up to my standards: five aggressive-growth fund managers, two growth fund managers, four value fund managers, and two honorable mentions. Because it's not important to me how a fund performs within its category (I want to know only how it performs compared to the market), I didn't try to come up with the same number of funds for each category. My method does not compare aggressive-growth funds only to other aggressive-growth funds, or value funds only to other value funds, but compares all funds against the market. My standards are objective. You don't need to know the ten best funds in each category. You just want the best funds with the best fund managers.

. . .

Before I dive into the list, I want to give you some pointers about mutual fund investing, because it's a subject that confuses a lot of people. One mistake most mutual fund investors make is putting their money in too many funds. Ideally, you don't want to spend hours and hours looking through funds to try to find the best five or six managers and "diversify" your mutual fund holdings across different fund categories. That's the wrong move. You want a mutual fund because you *don't* want to spend so much time thinking about where to invest your money. You want someone else to do that for you. With any advice in this book and the great fund managers I've picked out, you're in good shape. So how many mutual funds should you actually own? If you can find one well-diversified fund—and the actively managed funds I'm giving you are all diversified by sector, meaning they don't have too much concentration in any one industry—then the answer is *one.* I realize that makes some people a bit nervous, and there are certain situations and times when you would want to own more than one fund. For example, many of the funds on my list focus on small-cap stocks, and one is a micro-cap fund, which means that these funds own stocks of only small and tiny companies. You don't want to put all of your eggs in one small-cap basket. So if you see a small-cap fund on this list that you really like, you shouldn't invest all of your assets in it. Instead, give no more than half of your assets to any small-cap fund. If you like a fund that invests in large-cap stocks, big companies, you don't need to diversify into a small-cap fund. The reason you should avoid exposing yourself 100 percent to small-cap stocks is that they're inherently more risky than larger companies, although they also tend to have more upside.

Remember, when you're picking mutual funds, you still have to do research on the fund once you are in the fund. You can't forget about it. You don't have to follow it as closely as a stock, but if you are in too many funds, you will end up spending more time following them than you care to. If you want to diversify across different approaches— so that you own one aggressive-growth fund, one growth fund, and one value fund—you can, but I should caution you that these investing styles aren't as important as the quality of the fund manager and the stocks your manager picks.

In my list of funds, I've got everything you need to start being a great mutual fund investor. I've included the symbol for each fund so that you can look it up on any Internet site that you'd normally use to look up stocks. This is your one-stop shop for mutual fund investing. If you're attracted to one of the funds I've picked, look it up and you'll be able to see which brokerage houses sell that particular fund. You can either call one of those brokers or use their website to set up an account and invest in the fund of your choice, or you can talk to your own broker or access your broker's website to see if they can help you.

This is not just a list of funds with great managers. I'm also including my observations about who these funds would be good for: which funds would be best for young investors, which ones for older investors who are more conservative, which fund is the best one to give your mother-in-law (if you get along with her), which fund you should buy for your kids thanks to the Uniform Gifts to Minors Act—it's all in there. (UGMA, by the way, is a law that lets you give assets like stocks and mutual funds to a minor, such as one of your children, without having to set up a trust fund. You just have to appoint a custodian for the money, which your child can access as soon as he or she turns 18 or 21, depending on your home state. You can give up to $12,000 in gifts a year to any one person without having to pay a gift tax. It used to be the case that UGMA was great because when you gave one of your kids stock or shares in a mutual fund, he or she would pay lower taxes on the gains, assuming that your kid doesn't have nearly as much income as you do, or any income for that matter. Unfortunately, the rules have changed. In 2007, only $1,700 worth of a child's unearned income can avoid being taxed at the same rate you, the child's parents, pay. Still, $1,700 a year isn't chump change, and if you want to give your children some exposure to mutual funds, the gift that truly keeps on giving, you should definitely take advantage of UGMA.)

One last point before jumping into the list: many of you don't have time to read through this whole list, or aren't interested even though you want to make money. For you, I'm including a quick guide to being a good mutual fund manager that won't take you more than a minute or two to read, right after I tell you about these great funds and great managers.

These funds are all in roughly descending order, because they appeal to different investors. You can't just say, "This fund is the best," unless you take your age and risk tolerance into account. But to the extent that you can ignore those two factors, the best funds are at the top of the lists, becoming less great as you go down the lists.

Aggressive-Growth Funds

1. CGM Focus Fund (CGMFX), run by Ken Heebner. Heebner is one of the best, perhaps simply the best, mutual fund managers around. I think his style has a great deal in common with my style when I was at my hedge fund. Heebner's returns are spectacular. His performance in 2000 and 2001 was simply awe-inspiring. His Focus Fund is all stocks, although he can invest in fixed-income instruments and he can short stocks in this fund, which gives him a big advantage. Heebner made a killing shorting tech stocks in 2000, which is exactly what I was doing at my hedge fund at the time. Very few mutual funds actually short stocks, even though many are allowed to. According to Morningstar, only forty funds that hold long positions also have more than 20 percent short exposure. Short-selling is when you borrow shares of a company, sell them, and then buy them back at a later date to return them to whoever lent you the shares. If your short is good, the stock will go down after you sold it, allowing you to buy the same number of shares at a lower price and pocket the difference. Rather than buying low and selling high, shorting is when you sell high and then buy low. Most mutual funds won't short stocks because it's much more risky than simply buying. If you buy a stock, the worst that can happen is that it goes to $0 and you lose all of the money you invested in it. If you sell a stock short, you can have much bigger losses. You could short a stock, and then if it triples you'll be down 200 percent on that trade. Heebner's unique in that he's willing to take on this risk, and he consistently shows that it's worthwhile even if he is sometimes wrong.

Heebner got into the great real estate market early and got out in 2005, because he could see that borrowers with wacky mortgages and poor credit would pull everything down. He made a big bet on copper in 2006 at the same time I was advocating owning copper producers on my show. The guy knows how to make money. He knows how to win. He likes a lot of the same stocks I do, but the proof is in the performance. Heebner's CGM Focus was the best performing aggressive-growth fund in 2000, when it was up 53.93 percent, and again in 2001, when it was up 47.65 percent—keep in mind that the S&P 500 was down double digits in 2001—and he was number one again among aggressive-growth funds in 2005. Heebner has a record of outperforming when the market is taking a beating. Although he was down 17.79 percent in 2002, a rough year for everyone, he still came in ahead of the market. And he bounced right back with a stellar 66.46 percent return in 2003. Before the great tech bull market in the late '90s, Heebner's other funds were some of the best in the business, and he was producing similarly great returns, but he didn't make a lot of money in the late '90s, when everyone else was practically printing it. That's because Heebner does his homework. This is a man who clearly has the right kind of work ethic and who relies on his research and his good judgment. He couldn't get behind radically overvalued tech stocks in the late '90s because he had no conviction in them. I was more cynical, but over the long term Heebner was right, and he made his investors a lot of money. This is not a fund that never goes down, and it's not a fund that gives you the same consistently solid return every year. But Heebner does know how to make money, lots of it during the bad times, and though his returns vary wildly, most of them are wins, and really big wins at that. Heebner and CGM Focus are not for the faint of heart, but if you want to make a lot of money and you don't mind risking losses every now and again, this is the mutual fund for you.

Heebner appears on TV once in a while. My friend Erin Burnett at CNBC likes to feature him. I turn the volume up and tell everyone in the room to shut up and listen and learn something. This is the mutual fund I would recommend to people in their 20s, along with every investor who's still young at heart and willing to take on a bit of extra risk to produce extraordinary returns. CGM Focus is not a fund for your mother-in-law, but it's definitely a fund for your 18-year-old. I believe that you should give your money to Heebner unless you're getting closer to retirement or you really want an investment that will generate stable returns from year to year. In that case, you still might want to invest with Heebner, but give him only 20 percent or 30 percent of your money, splitting the rest between a more conservative value fund and a bond fund that will invest in U.S. Treasurys, or municipal bonds if you're rich.

2. Dreyfus Premier Strategic Value (DAGVX), run by Brian C. Ferguson. I know, I know, it's a value fund, but it's on the aggressive-growth list. That's why I do not take these labels very seriously. What I do take seriously are results, and Brian Ferguson has them. Here's another manager who has some experience making money in a down year. Ferguson's fund was up 21.49 percent in 2000, his first year running it, and although it was down 2.5 percent in 2001 and lost bigger than the S&P 500 in 2002, a 26.81 percent decline, Ferguson made it up to his investors by gaining 43.54 percent in 2003. Since then, his fund has continued to beat the S&P 500—by 7 percentage points in 2004, 4 points in 2005, and again by 4 in 2006. That's a record of outperformance right there, and despite the fact that Ferguson didn't consistently make money in the down market, he came in well ahead of the pack in 2000, and that's more than most fund managers can say for themselves. I'm much more familiar with Ken Heebner at CGM Focus than I am with most of the funds and managers on this list, because I used a rigorous, empirical method based on the data rather than relying on anecdotal evidence that I'd culled from my experience on Wall Street. The numbers and my method say that Dreyfus Premier Strategic Value is a fund that works, and Ferguson is a manager who knows how to protect you from losses. Investors of any age looking for capital appreciation will appreciate Ferguson's results, because his fund is less risky than the other aggressive-growth funds on my list.

3. Bridgeway Aggressive Investor (BRAGX), run by John Montgomery. Montgomery's goal is to beat the returns you'd get from investing in the market as a whole, that is, investing in an index fund, while maintaining the same level of overall risk that you would have if you went with the index fund. In *Real Money,* I recommended mutual fund investors go with Will Danoff, who runs Fidelity's Contrafund. Unfortunately, Will did the smart thing and closed off Contra to new investors, so if you're not in it now, you won't have the chance to join in the future. I called Contra an index fund with a brain. Bridgeway Aggressive Investor is like an index fund with a brain and an attitude. What impresses me about this fund and its manager is that in 1999, they were up 120.62 percent. That's the kind of big win that you usually associate with a fund that is not diversified. That type of win, more often than not, is a signal that the manager doesn't have a clue. I would expect any fund that was up 120.62 percent in 1999 to be down big in 2000, and that's not just my spite toward and envy of Montgomery's great year. In fact, Montgomery was up 13.58 percent in 2000, a year when the S&P fell 9.11 percent, but he was down double digits in both 2001 and 2002, although in both years he outperformed the S&P. The list of diversified mutual funds that were up in 2000, 2001, and 2002 would be a very short one, but so is the list of funds that were up in any one of those years, which is an important characteristic all by itself. Montgomery's another manager who had a huge 2003, up 53.97 percent, more than taking care of his two years of losses. Bridgeway Aggressive Investor then beat the S&P by 2 percentage points in 2004 and 10 percentage points in 2005, and then fell behind by 8 percentage points in 2006. Over the long term, Montgomery is a winner, with an average annual return during the past five years of more than 18.13 percent, much better than the market and far better than most actively managed funds. That five-year average performance makes me like this fund for middle-aged investors who still want some risk, but with a bit more reliability.

4. Rice Hall James Micro Cap Portfolio (RHJSX),* run by Thomas W. McDowell Jr. As you can tell from the name of the fund, McDowell invests in micro-cap stocks, which are stocks with a market cap of anywhere from $50 million to $500 million. If you remember, market cap, short for market capitalization, is one widely used way to value a company. You take the price per share and multiply it by the number of shares to come up with a figure that's a good proxy for how much money the market thinks the company is worth. Investing in micro-cap stocks is a pretty risky proposition, which is why I asterisked this fund. Even though it meets the standards I set down in my methodology for picking funds with great managers, the fact that it's all micro-cap stocks makes me slightly uneasy. Companies this small can make you a lot of money, but as you can imagine they're more risky than larger companies. I think this would be a terrific fund if you wanted to use a part of the money that you intended to invest in stocks to speculate instead in mutual funds. Granted, McDowell's performance is reassuring, but I have to accept the conventional wisdom and say this is a fund that invests in some pretty high-risk stocks. There's a place for that in every portfolio, but it shouldn't be your entire portfolio. Still, looking at the numbers, I see a manager with a strong record. McDowell made money in both 2000 and 2001, up 11.24 percent and 16.41 percent, respectively. He lost big in 2002, but still beat the S&P by a little less than a point. Again, what's unusual is the outperformance in 2000 and 2001. I would have liked to see better numbers in 2002, but for an aggressive-growth fund that invests in high-risk stocks during a bear market, it's almost surprising that McDowell didn't do much worse than the S&P in 2002. At any rate, like everyone else on this list so far, McDowell had a grand-slam 2003, when he was up 56.62 percent. He continued to outperform in 2004 and 2005, but came in 2 percentage points behind the S&P in 2006.

Because this fund invests only in micro-cap stocks, it might make more sense to compare it to a different benchmark, the Russell 2000, which consists of 2,000 stocks with market capitalizations that skew slightly larger than McDowell's micro-cap investments. The Russell 2000 looks much more like McDowell's portfolio than does the S&P 500, which is made up of large-cap stocks. At any rate, the Russell 2000's average annual return over the past five years was only about 16 percent, while McDowell averaged 18 percent. Even taking into account this fund's expense ratio of 1.19 percent, McDowell still beat the Russell 2000.

This is another fund that you definitely don't want to give to your mother-in-law, and even if you're giving it to a kid who rides a motorcycle and sky dives, a real risk-taker, it shouldn't be more than 30 percent of total assets, because micro-cap stocks are just too risky.

5. Legg Mason Partners Aggressive Growth (SHRAX), run by Richie Freeman. I highlighted Freeman in *Real Money* as a stock-picker's stock-picker, a man who lives and breathes stocks, someone who cannot stand to fall behind the benchmarks. In *Real Money*, my mutual fund analysis was based as much on my firsthand knowledge of the fund managers as it was on the numbers. I think both perspectives are invaluable, especially because so few people have the knowledge to express either one. But my current endorsement is based on Freeman's record, on the data, and not on my personal knowledge of the guy. Still, Freeman is another manager who made money in 2000, a lot of money actually; he was up 19.12 percent. He was down in 2001, and then down 32.75 percent, worse than the S&P 500, in 2002. Because the man is so driven it looks like he's been trying to make up for it ever since—up 36.57 percent in 2003, up 10.61 percent in 2004 (a hair's breadth behind the S&P), up 12.55 percent in 2005, 8 percentage points better than the benchmark. Then last year Freeman gained only 7.98 percent, compared to over 15 percent for the S&P. I've written before that I like to bet with Richie after he's had a worse year than the benchmark, because he's such a competitive guy. You've got another chance to take advantage of his nature, and his ability to make money when others lose. Richie Freeman is a fund manager for all ages; whether you're in your 20s, 30s, 40s, or 50s, his tenacity will serve you well.

Growth Funds

Before discussing the two growth funds on my list, I should say a little more about the methodology I used to generate these mutual fund rankings. This method originally produced five growth funds and ten value funds, but three of the growth funds and five of the value funds were closed to new investments. This isn't great in terms of your options, but it does help validate my analysis. Only the best funds that attract the greatest money have to close themselves down to new investors. The fact that my methodology picked out eight growth and value funds that had been closed and only seven that were still open makes me believe that looking at the off-years, the years when the market is down, and selecting funds that were up (or down less than the market) in spite of the market's weakness, is the right way to go when hunting for a good mutual fund.

1. Buffalo Small Cap (BUFSX), run by Kent Gasaway. Buffalo is a growth fund that invests entirely in small-cap stocks. Gasaway's annual turnover is only 15 percent, compared to 116.18 percent for other growth funds. The turnover is the amount of buying and selling that your fund manager does in a year: a fund with a 100 percent turnover replaces all of its holdings once in a given year. When your fund manager sells stock at a gain, your fund pays capital gains tax, so if a fund is good, a higher turnover will really eat into your return. Gasaway's low turnover suggests that he's a longer-term investor who has real conviction in his stock picks, which I think many of you can appreciate. For those who would be more attracted to a sizzling hot fund run by a more aggressive trader, allow me to show you Gasaway's magnificent returns. Remember, the entire reason to invest in an actively managed fund is so that the manager can sidestep losses that the market takes. You're not paying for additional upside; you're paying to avoid the downside that comes with stocks. If you want both the additional upside and the protection from downside, Kent Gasaway is your man. His performance during 2000 and 2001 was tremendous. He gained 33.69 percent in 2000 and 31.18 percent in 2001. He mopped the floor with the benchmarks. In 2002, he lost 25.75 percent, but he made up for that with a 51.23 percent gain in 2003. He followed that up with a 28.82 percent gain in 2004. In 2005 and 2006, Gasaway lagged the S&P by a little more than a point each year. The recent underperformance is not encouraging, but you're still looking at a fund manager who's got a five-year average annual return of 18.86 percent and a fund that's been down only one year of its eight-year existence. I will take Gasaway's recent slight underperformance in a heartbeat if it means he'll continue to deliver stellar performance in the years when the market is down big.

There is one big point here that you should keep in mind. Since

Gasaway's fund invests only in small-cap stocks, you probably don't want his fund to be the only stock fund you own. There are years when small-cap stocks do better on average, and there are years when large-caps stocks do better on average, although I believe there are more gains to be had among small-cap names. Nevertheless, you probably don't want all of your stock exposure in a fund that focuses solely on little companies. I wouldn't call Gasaway's fund speculative, but it's so concentrated in small caps that in the interest of diversification, you might want to put the same amount of money in a fund with more large-cap and mid-cap exposure. That would be the prudent and correct course, even though Gasaway's got a clear ability to win when others lose.

2. FBR Small Cap (FBRVX), run by Charles T. Akre Jr. This is another small-cap growth fund, that, just like Buffalo Small Cap, is characterized by fairly low turnover, meaning the fund buys and sells stocks far less frequently than the average growth fund, which, among other things, saves you money. When you see a fund with great performance and low turnover, you're looking at a fund run by a terrific investor, not a trader. I have nothing against trading—in fact it was one of the things I did best at my hedge fund—but I know many people have a built-in bias against trading that they will never overcome. This fund manager and his fund cater to you. Akre is a long-term thinker with a great track record of picking out small-cap stocks, those with market capitalizations of less than $3 billion, with great long-term growth stories. Akre's the kind of manger who seems to be terrific at finding long-term winners and riding them all the way up.

Akre's fund lost 8.79 percent in 2000, but then came back with a really landmark year in 2001, gaining 32.63 percent in a year when the S&P 500 was down double digits. That's the kind of thing that really turns fellow money managers green with envy. Luckily, you can turn green with dollars by giving Akre your money so that he can invest it in his FBR Small Cap fund. Akre's fund gained only 2.63 percent in 2002, but that was astonishing in a year when the S&P lost over 22 percent. And then the numbers just kept getting better. He posted a 45.77 percent gain in 2003 and a 30.67 percent gain in 2004. He had a paltry 2.31 percent gain in 2005, more than 2 percentage points beneath the S&P's return, but made up for that and then some by his 28.49 percent gain in 2006. Growth funds tend to be less risky than aggressive-growth funds, but I'm not convinced the evidence bears that out. What I do know is that Charles Akre's fund looks unstoppable.

This fund is for longer-term mutual fund investors, no question. But if you have the patience to stick with this guy through the lean years—it looks as though every third year or every other year is a dud, with gains in the low single digits or even small losses—he'll deliver the big long-term results. The reward of staying in this fund through the lean years is that they're followed almost inevitably by some really fat years, where the gains range from 28 percent to 45 percent, more than making up for the slow times. Akre's fund is a great place for more conservative investors who still want some exposure to growth. If you get along well with your mother-in-law, this would be a good place for her to invest. Akre is a manager for people who really want long-term outperformance and care less about year-to-year wins. So if you're a more conservative investor, or you're in your 30s and 40s and still have a long time before you retire, this fund is for you. There's a place for FBR Small Cap in anyone's retirement fund, but because it is a small-cap fund, it shouldn't be your whole retirement fund. Unfortunately, because 401(k) plans don't let you choose your own funds, you probably won't have the opportunity to invest with Akre in your 401(k). Instead, invest in his fund with the money in your IRA. Whether you're 25 or 55, this is a great retirement mutual fund.

Value Funds

1. Putnam Small Cap Value (PSLAX), run by Edward T. Shadek Jr. Shadek worked for one year, 1992, at Steinhardt Partners, led by Michael Steinhardt, who was one of the first legitimately famous hedge fund managers. Steinhardt has a phenomenal record in addition to being a really great guy. When I started my hedge fund, he actually let me operate out of his office until I got my feet on the ground. He also got Will Danoff his start and Fidelity's Contra fund has benefited ever since. At any rate, Shadek worked for the best, and now he's performing like a true disciple of Steinhardt's. I should point out that Putnam Small Cap Value is another fund that invests mostly in stocks with low market capitalization, and that means you should at least consider investing in another mutual fund on top of Shadek's to spread your exposure to different kinds of stock. Then again, when you look at this guy's record you might not want to. Shadek was up 24.43 percent in 2000. He was up again, this time by 18.95 percent in 2001. His fund did lose 18.69 percent in 2002, but that performance was better than the market.

As far as I'm concerned, any mutual fund manager who was up in 2000 and 2001 deserves some slack for taking the hit in 2002. It's not ideal, but considering that the vast majority of funds were down all three years (and did not beat any benchmarks at all unless they were competing for the biggest losses), Shadek's record starts to look quite impressive. He came back with a 50.67 percent gain in 2003, followed by a 25.67 percent gain in 2004, then a 6.78 percent gain in 2005, and a 17.30 percent gain in 2006. This guy has been one step ahead of the market all along. A fund with a manager who can make you money when other funds can't stop losing, and who can remain ahead of the market in good times, is a fund I want to be in. Sure, you could say that Shadek's fund barely outpaced the Russell 2000 over the past five years and delivered a substantially lower return after fees, but I have to point out that investing in an index fund pegged to the Russell

2000 would not have given you double-digit gains in 2000 and 2001. People really don't understand that fund managers are paid to take care of the downside. Once you've got someone good worrying about how to prevent you from losing money, you can let the upside take care of itself.

Shadek's fund isn't cheap. Most mutual funds have two or three classes of shares, with different fee structures, although one class is usually for giant institutional investors. If you want to invest in the Putnam Small Cap Value fund, you can take the A-class fund, which has a 1.27 percent expense ratio, no more than .25 percent in 12b-1 fees, and a 5.25 percent front load. I know sacrificing 5.25 percent of your investment for long-term gains is obscene, but in fact this is the cheaper, more sensible option. If you buy into the C-class fund, you'll have a 2.02 percent expense ratio and pay 1 percent a year in 12b-1 fees, making your annual fees almost double what you'd pay in the A-class fund. There's no front load in C-class, but there is a deferred sales load, a back load, of 1 percent, which you have to pay when you sell. I would take the 5.25 percent hit up front to invest here, as it's certainly worth it for the downside protection, rather than giving up 3 percent of my assets in the fund every year to management. As with all small-cap funds, this one can't be your only exposure to stocks, but I would recommend it for older investors in their 40s and 50s who are nearing retirement.

2. Heartland Value (HRTVX), run by William J. Nasgovitz. Small-cap funds have really done a bang-up job lately, but since we shouldn't count on that to continue, look through the funds in the aggressive-growth list for something with more large-cap exposure if you're going to put a sizable portion of your capital into a small-cap fund. The fact that it's a value fund doesn't make this fund any safer than other stock funds. However, the fact that Nasgovitz is at the helm does. This is a guy who's been in the game for thirty years, a really seasoned pro who knows what he's doing and who especially knows how to make money while almost everyone else is losing it. Nasgovitz was up 2.03 percent in 2000, and then a gargantuan 29.45 percent in 2001. His fund fell 11.49 percent in 2002, which would have been a great time for you to buy in because Nasgovitz came back with a 70.16 percent gain in 2003. That more than totally eradicates even the memory of his 2002 loss. Nasgovitz then had a couple of slow years in 2004 and 2005, when he gained only 9.10 percent and 1.99 percent, lagging the market. Then he came back with a stellar year: in 2006 his fund gained 28.02 percent. Nasgovitz is a seasoned guy, and I would trust his fund with money from older investors, and younger ones who want to feel safe.

3. Berwyn (BERWX), run by Edward A. Killen, another seasoned professional. Finally we're looking at a fund that invests in large-cap stocks, not just puny small-cap names, so if you want some diversification based on company size, and trust me, you do, Killen's fund is a good place for mutual fund investors more comfortable with value funds to go. Killen can keep 20 percent of his portfolio in bonds, but as of now he has no bond exposure. That would pull his returns down. He does have over 9 percent of his portfolio in cash as of late summer 2007, and I consider that the mark of a truly experienced investor. Like the good fund managers on my lists, who know how to protect you from losing money, Killen had a strong 2000 compared to the market and an amazing 2001, followed by a loss, albeit a single-digit one, in 2002. He was up 2.10 percent in 2000 and 28.93 percent in 2001, and lost 6.88 percent in 2002. Killen's 2001 performance should make most money managers jealous. His 2000 performance would also make most mutual fund manager jealous, since they largely lost money that year. Killen's had a good run since 2002. He posted a 50.01 percent gain in 2003, followed by a 22.83 percent gain in 2004 and a 12.18 percent gain in 2005, and then for the first time since 1999 he failed to beat the S&P 500 in 2006, posting a mere 6.71 percent gain.

If you choose to place your money under Killen's stewardship, I think you'll be in good shape. It's possible he's losing his edge, but then again, I also find that a good money manager gets better, if less intense, with age. The guy knows how to avoid the losses, although I do have to wonder about money managers who lost money in 1999. I'm willing to give Killen a pass for that, because you'd rather invest with someone who won't abandon his convictions to chase hot stocks that he doesn't really believe in. I have nothing against chasing hot stocks with no conviction—I became great at it—but it's a dangerous game to play, and you're probably better off with a more serious money manager. Killen is therefore an ideal manager for older investors looking for a steadier hand to guide their investments—your mother-in-law, or anyone looking to retire soon. Killen won't chase fads, and he'll protect you from losses in his terrific value-oriented fund.

4. Muhlenkamp (MUHLX), run by Ronald H. Muhlenkamp. Muhlenkamp likes to hunt for undervalued companies that nevertheless generate large profits and a lot of cash flow, which is what you'd expect from a value manager. His record with this large-cap value fund meets my basic criteria too, if in a more understated fashion than some of the other money managers. Muhlenkamp posted a 25.3 percent gain in 2000, followed by a 9.35 percent gain in 2001. Then, like most of these guys, he turned around and lost big in 2002, down 19.92 percent. That's a large loss, but the gains in 2000 and 2001 outweigh it significantly, and the 48.08 percent gain in 2003 also makes it seem less consequential. The really good value guys made money in 2000 and 2001 but still got hit hard in 2002, which is a lot more than you can expect from most fund managers, or most value managers, who also came up short in 2001. Since 2003, Muhlenkamp's gains have been solid but unimpressive. A 24.51 percent gain in 2004 looked promising, but it was followed by a 7.88 percent gain in 2005, which at least was better than the benchmark, and a 4.08 percent gain in 2006, which wasn't better than much of anything.

At the end of June 2007 Muhlenkamp was sitting on a big position in Countrywide Financial, which became a much smaller position because Muhlenkamp held on to it through July and August as the stock got cut in half, thanks to so many people defaulting on their mortgages. The risk here isn't that subprime mortgages will hurt you if you put your money in Muhlenkamp's fund. The risk is that he's lost his touch, and instead of making people money in bad markets, he might start losing you money in good ones. Then again, a lot of smart people got housing wrong. Is Muhlenkamp as good as the top guys on this list? Maybe not, but time will tell, and he's better than anyone except my top guys. If Muhlenkamp is offered on your 401(k), though, you've hit the jackpot because funds this good are rarely offered in 401(k) plans.

Honorable Mentions

These are funds that are worth investing in and that my methodology picked up as winners, but they aren't as good as the other funds on the list. If the other eleven fund managers were not around, these two would be at the top of the pile. Since there are better funds out there, and you've just read all about them, I would invest with them before I considered the honorable mentions. Still, these are two strong funds with strong managers and they deserve credit for their performance, just not as much credit as the other funds I've recommended.

1. SSgA Aggressive Equity Fund (SSAEX), run by Michael Arone. This is another fund that had a big 1999, up more than 120 percent, but suffered less than the market as a whole from 2000 to 2002. Arone tries to invest in stocks that are undervalued based on their growth, a process that I often lead viewers through during episodes of *Mad Money.* I doubt Arone uses the same method I employ, which is a simple rule of thumb, but his approach is basically sound. Arone had no wins in 2000, 2001, or 2002, but he did have smaller losses than the overall market in 2000 and 2002, when he was down 2.57 percent and 12.09 percent, respectively, compared to a 9.06 percent loss for the S&P 500 in 2000 and a 22.15 percent loss in 2002. Arone lost 19.63 percent in 2001, worse than the S&P's 12.02 percent decline. These returns are nothing to write home about, but a smaller-than-average loss coming off such a huge 1999 gets my attention. Arone was up 33.96 percent in 2003, more than 5 percentage points above the S&P 500's return, and he beat the S&P again by less than a point in 2004. Over the past two years, his fund has lagged the S&P 500 by 2 percentage points each year. I wouldn't invest in this mutual fund, but I do have confidence that Arone will start beating the indexes again. I just have a lot more confidence in the top five aggressive-growth funds I listed. If this fund is one of the offerings in your 401(k) plan, I'd take it over an index, but otherwise you've got five great aggressive-growth funds to choose from—why buy the one fund that's merely good?

2. Robeco Boston Partners Small Cap Value II (BPSCX), run by David Dabora. Dabora's figures for 2000 and 2001 just blew me away. I know you're sick of these small-cap funds, but they have been the winners. This is another small-cap value fund, but Dabora's a little different from the other value managers in that he was up 44.41 percent in 2000 and 47.49 percent in 2001. I was both shocked and awed when I first saw those numbers. You give your money to a manager so that he can produce results that are one-quarter that good during a down year. Dabora's 15.94 percent loss in 2002 is nothing next to his gains the two years before, both greater than 40 percent. Following a pattern that should be pretty familiar to you by now, he came back with a 52.90 percent win in 2003. His returns over the past three years were fine, but nothing special: 16.47 percent in 2004, 7.54 percent in 2005, and 15.66 percent in 2006. I will say that, at the end of July 2007, Dabora had way too much exposure to the financials, and especially to the mortgage issuers who had been self-evidently not worth owning for months, if not a year, before that point. If the guy loses money in 2007, he can blame his huge position in American Home Mortgage, a position that delivered a 96.65 percent loss in 2007 alone. His big position in IndyMac doesn't exactly inspire confidence either. Maybe IndyMac will eventually recover, but American Home Mortgage went bankrupt. It just seems like a big, obvious, avoidable mistake to have kept so much mortgage exposure on the table when Dabora did. That said, we need funds for all seasons, and from where I'm sitting in September 2007 it's possible Dabora could be right. The guy is still a great manager, and I'm man enough to admit that he could be right and I could be wrong. The only better funds out there are on this list. I'd invest with Dabora if his fund were offered in my 401(k), but I would rather own one of the top three value managers on this list before picking him.

You've got thirteen actively managed mutual funds representing growth, value, and aggressive growth. At least ten of these funds are absolutely worth investing in, and even if you prefer not to take my recommendations, you know how I put the lists together, and I believe my method works, so you can use it to pick your own funds. Maybe you'd rather invest in stocks than mutual funds, which would be the right move.

But let's say you're someone who doesn't have the time to go through these funds and research them. How can you still be a good mutual fund investor? I'll give you two options that are quick and easy to understand. They should make you all the money you're after. So here's how you can do well with mutual funds in as few words as possible.

First option: invest all of the money you intend for stocks in the Vanguard 500 Index Fund (VFINX). This is a great, low-cost index fund that will deliver returns essentially equal to what the market produces every year. You won't beat the market, but you won't get beaten either, and that's what happens to most mutual fund managers. For your bond exposure (10–20 percent in your 30s, 20–30 percent in your 40s, 30–40 percent in your 50s, 40–50 percent in your 60s, and 60–70 percent once you've retired), invest in a low-cost short-term bond index fund like the Vanguard Short-Term Bond Index (VBISX), or if you're wealthy, one of Vanguard's Admiral funds that invests in municipal bonds. You will have to stay on top of this bond option. One day it will pay to invest in longer-term bonds, but right now—and for the foreseeable future—the best gains are to be had in the shortest maturities because of the decision by the Federal Reserve to keep cash rates high to stifle inflation. When rates on longer-term bonds, meaning more than ten years, climb above 6 percent, or if short rates fall below 4 percent because of aggressive rate-cutting, you will have to readjust what's known as the "duration" of your bonds and go out longer-term. Right now, though, short rates are a gift and you want to take advantage of them until they go down or longer-term rates dramatically exceed them.

Second option: invest one-third of your money for stocks in Ken Heebner's CGM Focus Fund (CGMFX), another third in Charles Akre's FBR Small Cap Fund (FBRVX), and the last third in Edward Killen's Berwyn (BERWX). Invest in the same bond funds I just recommended to get your bond exposure. As long as you're invested in these funds, you should at the very least check once a month to make sure that the managers I named are still running the show; if they're gone, you have to sell. That's the least amount of homework you can get away with and still be a decent mutual fund investor.

Now you've got my list of great mutual fund managers, a fabulous list of my favorite long-term stocks, not to mention two new sets of rules for investing that directly apply to individual investors who manage their own money. You know why you should save, how to avoid going broke, how to set yourself up for retirement—you've got everything you need to ensure your long-term wealth, from big-picture general advice right down to the little details, such as which are the best funds and stocks to own. Now get ready to get rich, stay rich, and stay mad . . . for life!

INDEX